Second Language Acquisition
and the Critical Period Hypothesis

Second Language Acquisition Research: Theoretical and Methodological Issues
Susan Gass and Jacquelyn Schachter, Editors

Tarone/Gass/Cohen • Research Methodology
in Second-Language Acquisition

Schachter/Gass • Second Language Classroom
Research: Issues and Opportunities

Birdsong • Second Language Acquisition
and the Critical Period Hypothesis

Monographs on Research Methodology

Yule • Referential Communication Tasks

Markee • Conversation Analysis

Second Language Acquisition and the Critical Period Hypothesis

Edited by

David Birdsong
University of Texas

LAWRENCE ERLBAUM ASSOCIATES, PUBLISHERS
1999   Mahwah, New Jersey   London

The final camera copy for this work was prepared by the
editor, and therefore the publisher takes no responsibility for
consistency or correctness of typographical style. However,
this arrangement helps to make publication of this kind of
scholarship possible.

Lawrence Erlbaum Associates, Inc., Publishers
10 Industrial Avenue
Mahwah, NJ 07430

Cover design by Kathryn Houghtaling Lacey

Library of Congress Cataloging-in-Publication Data

Second language acquisition and the critical period hypothesis /
edited by David Birdsong.
     p.   cm. — (Second language acquisition research)
     Chiefly papers presented at a conference held Aug. 1996,
     Jyväskylä, Finland.
    Includes bibliographical references and index.
    ISBN 0-8058-3084-7 (alk. paper)
    1. Second language acquisition—Congresses. I. Series.
    P118.2.S428   1998
    401'.93—dc21

                        98-42609
                            CIP

Printed in the United States of America
10 9 8 7 6 5 4 3 2 1

CONTENTS

Credits   vii

Preface   ix

Chapter 1: Introduction: Whys and Why Nots of the Critical
            Period Hypothesis for Second Language Acquisition
            David Birdsong   1

Chapter 2: Functional Neural Subsystems Are Differentially
            Affected by Delays in Second Language Immersion: ERP
            and Behavioral Evidence in Bilinguals
            Christine M. Weber-Fox and Helen J. Neville   23

Chapter 3: Co-Evolution of Language Size and the Critical
            Period
            James R. Hurford and Simon Kirby   39

Chapter 4: Critical Periods and (Second) Language
            Acquisition: Divide et Impera
            Lynn Eubank and Kevin R. Gregg   65

Chapter 5: Age of Learning and Second Language Speech
            James E. Flege   101

Chapter 6: Ultimate Attainment in L2 Pronunciation:
            The Case of Very Advanced Late L2 Learners
            Theo Bongaerts   133

Chapter 7: Confounded Age: Linguistic and Cognitive Factors
            in Age Differences for Second Language Acquisition
            Ellen Bialystok and Kenji Hakuta   161

Author Index   183

Subject Index   189

CREDITS

Figures 2.1, 2.2, 2.3, and 2.4 are reprinted from Christine M. Weber-Fox and Helen J. Neville, "Maturational Constraints on Functional Specializations for Language Processing: ERP and Behavioral Evidence in Bilingual Speakers," *Journal of Cognitive Neuroscience, 8:3* (May, 1996), pp. 231-256. Copyright 1996 by the Massachusetts Institute of Technology. Reprinted with permission.

Tables 6.1 and 6.3 are adapted from Theo Bongaerts, Chantal van Summeren, Brigitte Planken, and Erik Schils, "Excellente tweede-taalleerders en uitspraakverwerving," *Gramma/TTT 4* (1995), pp. 87-102. Copyright by ICG Publications. Adapted with permission.

Table 6.2 is reprinted from Theo Bongaerts, Chantal van Summeren, Brigitte Planken, and Erik Schils, "Age and Ultimate Attainment in the Pronunciation of a Foreign Language," *Studies in Second Language Acquisition, 19:4*, pp. 447-465. Copyright 1997 by Cambridge University Press. Reprinted with permission.

Table 6.3 is adapted from Theo Bongaerts, Chantal van Summeren, Brigitte Planken, and Erik Schils, "Age and Ultimate Attainment in the Pronunciation of a Foreign Language," *Studies in Second Language Acquisition, 19:4*, pp. 447-465. Copyright 1997 by Cambridge University Press. Adapted with permission.

Note: Versions of Table 6.3 appear in both *Gramma/TTT* and *Studies in Second Language Acquisition*.

Tables 6.4, 6.5, and 6.6 are adapted from Marie-José Palmen, Theo Bongaerts, and Erik Schils, "L'authenticité de la prononciation dans l'acquisition d'une langue étrangère au-delà de la période critique: les apprenants néerlandais parvenus à un niveau très avancé du français," *Acquisition et Interaction en Langue Étrangère, 9* (1997), pp. 173-191. Adapted with permission.

PREFACE

In August 1996, a number of researchers converged on Jyväskylä, Finland, to participate in an Association Internationale de Linguistique Appliquée (AILA) symposium entitled "New Perspectives on the Critical Period for Second Language Acquisition." Under this banner, the participants took aim at the question of whether, or to what extent, a critical period limits the acquisition of a first language as well as a second language acquired postpubertally. Attendance at the symposium, as well as discussion, was robust. So, too, was the enthusiasm to use the presentations as a nucleus for the present volume.

As major players in this debate, the participants were well aware that positions on this issue run the gamut from outright rejection to empassioned acceptance. It is a question that has been approached by researchers working in linguistic theory, evolution theory, language processing, and neurophysiology, to name but a few of the relevant disciplines. The Critical Period Hypothesis for Second Language Acquisition (CPH–L2A) has spawned an abundance of data, ranging from grammaticality judgments to speech samples to Event-Related Brain Potentials. These data have lent themselves to interpretation in many ways: for example, as consistent with theories of access (or lack of access) to Universal Grammar; as suggesting post-maturational age effects and cross-linguisic (transfer) effects; and as evidence for the tremendous diversity of learner outcomes, ranging from little progress to nativelike mastery.

This diversity is represented in this volume. In addition, I have sought inquiry that cuts across several sub-disciplines of linguistics—phonetics, phonology, lexis, syntax, morphology—and that embraces modern sciences with such prefixes as *psycho-* and *neuro-* . I have aimed for an informative mixture of theory, evidence, and cautious argumentation. Finally, the contributions to the book are equally divided between the pro-CPH–L2A and the anti-CPH–L2A positions.

In these respects this book sets itself apart from other treatments of the CPH–L2A. By its breadth of inquiry, the volume should appeal to a wide range of readers. By its balance of competing views, the book should allow people to judge for themselves which arguments and what data are most compelling, thereby enabling an informed decision on the merits of the CPH–L2A.

I felt it was important to compile recent and largely unpublished research, and to expedite its publication. In this respect as well, the volume has inherent appeal to serious researchers and students of age-related linguistic development and the limits of bilingualism. Consequently, it is tempting to bill the collection of papers in this book as "state of the art." However, it would be presumptuous to maintain that, for this particular issue, there is a "state" of intellectual discourse. In this area of vigorous research and debate, the discourse is almost too fluid to pin down. This is not the first time the CPH–L2A has been visited, nor will it be the last.

There are dozens of individuals who have pushed the envelope of critical period inquiry. Were the world a perfect place, they would all be contributors to this volume. Reducing the number was not easy, and if there are conspicuous absences, it is the judgment of the editor alone that should be faulted. (At least it can be safely said that I didn't invite just my old buddies. Many of the people I met for the first time in Finland, and others I have yet to lay eyes on.)

ACKNOWLEDGMENTS

I am grateful to AILA for providing a forum for most of these papers. The session was organized under the auspices of the Scientific Commission for Second Language Acquisition, for which I was Chair during the period in which the symposium took place.

I wish to acknowledge the kind people who assisted with the preparation of the camera-ready copy, and who graciously put up with me during frustrating times: Judy Birdsong, Heather Butler, Sylvia Grove, and Christian Jennings.

My thanks extend to the staff at Lawrence Erlbaum Associates (LEA), for their consummate professionalism, their meticulousness, and for their patience as I barraged them with questions.

Friends Susan Gass and Jacquelyn Schachter, editors of the LEA series in which this work appears, have been supportive throughout the development of the project. Thank you both.

Finally, with great earnestness I applaud the contributors to the volume for their reasonableness and good cheer. These fine scholars are also fine human beings.

—David Birdsong

CHAPTER ONE

Introduction:
Whys and Why Nots
of the Critical Period Hypothesis
for Second Language Acquisition

David Birdsong
University of Texas

The facts of adult second language acquisition (L2A) contrast sharply with those of first language acquisition (L1A). Whereas the attainment of full linguistic competence is the birthright of all normal children, adults vary widely in their ultimate level of attainment, and linguistic competence comparable to that of natives is seldom attested. A reasonable explanation for the facts of L1A and L2A is given by the Critical Period Hypothesis (CPH). In its most succinct and theory-neutral formulation, the CPH states that there is a limited developmental period during which it is possible to acquire a language, be it L1 or L2, to normal, nativelike levels. Once this window of opportunity is passed, however, the ability to learn language declines. Consistent with the CPH are the morphological and syntactic deficits of Genie, who was largely deprived of linguistic input and interaction until age 13 (Curtiss, 1977), as well as the desultory linguistic achievements of most adult L2 learners.

With a focus primarily on L2A, the present volume explores reasons why humans might be subject to a critical period for language learning. It also examines the adequacy of the CPH as an explanatory construct, the "fit" of the hypothesis with the facts.

To both of these dimensions, the contributors offer cutting-edge thought and experimentation. In examining the possible causes of a

1

critical period for L2A, the researchers bring the CPH into line with specifics of recent linguistic theory (Eubank & Gregg, chap. 4), discern neurofunctional differences between early- and late-learned language (Weber-Fox & Neville, chap. 2), and suggest sources of limits to language learning that are accommodated in modern evolutionary thinking (Hurford & Kirby, chap. 3). In questioning the explanatory suitability of the CPH–L2A, contributors bring new empirical data and argumentation to bear on matters once thought to be settled, such as the heuristic utility of the CPH–L2A (Flege, chap. 5), the shape of the age function, in theory and in fact (Bialystok & Hakuta, chap. 7), and the possibility of nativelike attainment in L2 pronunciation (Bongaerts, chap. 6).

These two approaches—one that ponders the etiology of a critical period for L2A and the other that disputes the adequacy of the CPH–L2A—are representative of current intellectual discourse. In according equal time to each of the approaches, this volume aims at a balance of scholarship pro and contra the CPH in the L2A context.

As a prolegomenon to these chapters, it is instructive to examine a few of the more prevalent formulations of the CPH–L2A, looking in particular at the proposed mechanisms of age-related effects. The introduction will also situate this book within the current intellectual climate of questioning the received wisdom relating to the CPH–L2A.

THE WHYS:
VIEWS ON THE ONTOGENY
OF TIME-BOUNDED SUCCESS IN L2A

Earlier references to "the" CPH are somewhat misleading, for there is no single CPH.[1] Rather, there are varied formulations, each of which takes a different ontogenetic tack on the limits of language acquisition. It is customary, however, to refer to them collectively, because, manifestly, they share the common denominator of determinism. That is, they assume a nonnativelike end state for late language acquisition and seek explanations for this outcome in developmental factors that inevitably affect all members of the species.

In this volume, each of the chapters addresses at least one of several critical period hypotheses as they apply to adult L2A. As a preview of these varied formulations of the CPH—and as an introduction to other,

---

[1]Similarly, the present use of the term *critical period* is meant to encompass formulations of a weaker *sensitive period* as well. The latter is thought to be more gradual in offset, and to allow for more variations in end-state attainment, than the former (see Long, 1990). However, the present discussion applies equally to the strong and weak formulations, hence the use of a single label. For further distinctions between sensitive and critical periods, see Eubank and Gregg (chap. 4, this volume).

kindred proposals not mentioned in the chapters—this section offers sketches of some of the mechanisms that researchers have proposed as underlying age-related declines in language learning ability.

Loss of Neural Plasticity in the Brain

Because of progressive lateralization of cerebral functions and ongoing myelination in Broca's area and throughout the cortex, the neural substrate that is required for language learning is not fully available after the closure of the critical period. This formulation was originally proposed by Penfield and Roberts (1959), and later popularized by Lenneberg (1967), who postulated that the end of the critical period was marked by "termination of a state of organizational plasticity linked with lateralization of function" (p. 176). Variations on this line of thinking have been advanced for the L2A context (e.g. Long, 1990; Patkowski, 1980; Pulvermüller & Schumann, 1994; Scovel, 1988).

Lenneberg (1967) directed most of his argumentation to primary language acquisition. However, he made a brief foray into L2A and pointed to learners' progress as well as their shortcomings. Here, Lenneberg moved from brain-based to mind-based commentary, alluding to an appendix in his book—written by Chomsky—that outlines Universal Grammar (UG)-based formal similarities among natural languages. For adults learning an L2, Lenneberg (1967) invoked the presence of this mental "matrix for language skills" to square the facts of (partial) L2A success with closure of the critical period:

> Most individuals of average intelligence are able to learn a second language after the beginning of their second decade. ... A person *can* learn to communicate in a foreign language at the age of forty. This does not trouble our basic hypothesis on age limitations because we may assume that the cerebral organization for language learning as such has taken place during childhood, and since natural languages tend to resemble one another in many fundamental aspects (see Appendix [A]), the matrix for language skills is present. (p. 176)

For related thinking about the linkage of neurological development and the mental representation of UG, see Eubank and Gregg (chap. 4, this volume) and Jacobs (1988).

Loss of (Access to) the Language Learning Faculty

The closure of the critical period entails a loss of UG, a mental faculty consisting of innately specified constraints on the possible forms that natural language grammars may take. A weaker version of this approach suggests that UG continues to be mentally represented but for various reasons is no longer available or accessible to the language learner. It should be noted that, because the L1 grammar is an instantiation of UG (see previous section), one can plausibly account for at least some of the headway that learners do make in L2A.

With the offset of the critical period, there may also be a loss of innate learning strategies presumed specific to the learning of language. These include the Subset Principle, which guides the learner to posit the most conservative grammar consistent with the linguistic input. By hypothesis, these epistemological components are the sine qua non of language acquisition; their absence essentially guarantees failure to attain nativelike competence. Thus the Fundamental Difference Hypothesis (Bley-Vroman, 1989) attributes the divergent end states of early L1A and late L2A to loss of, or lack of access to, UG and associated learning principles.

Principled inquiry concerning the role of UG in both the initial and end states of adult L2A comes in many forms (for a recent selection, see Flynn, Martohardjono, & O'Neil, 1997). One prominent line of thinking holds that invariant principles of UG are not lost in adult L2A; rather, what is problematic is the acquisition of L2 parameters: "Parameter values become progressively resistant to resetting with age, following the critical period" (Towell& Hawkins, 1994, p. 126). Simplistically, the difficulty in resetting parameters resides in having to "unlearn," in the sense of relinquishing the representation of a parameter having a unique, L1-based setting, and establishing in its stead a biunique setting compatible with both the L1 and the L2 (for elaboration on parameter resetting, see Eubank and Gregg, chap. 4, this volume). In a later section, I summarize a contrasting approach to unlearning under the connectionist model of acquisition.

Maladaptive Gain of Processing Capacity with Maturation

As children develop, they are increasingly capable of processing linguistic input. However, Newport (1990, 1991) argued that cognitive *im*maturity, not cognitive maturity, is advantageous for language learning. Young children's short-term memory capacity allows them initially to extract only a few morphemes from the linguistic input. Working within these processing limits, children are more successful than adults, whose greater available memory allows for extracting more of the input, but who then are "faced with a more difficult problem of analyzing everything at once" (Newport, 1991, p. 126). The benefits of starting small have been demonstrated in simulations of the acquisition of English morphology (Goldowsky & Newport, 1993). Similarly, Elman's (1993) connectionist model starts with limited memory, then undergoes *maturational changes* (incremental increases in memory capacity). Training of networks under this condition succeeds in processing complex sentences. If the starting point is a fully formed adult-like memory, however, the complex sentences are not successfully processed by the network.

This "less is more" formulation of the CPH is apparently not confined to the domain of language acquisition: "The more limited abilities of children may provide an advantage *for tasks (like language learning)* which involve componential analysis" (Newport, 1990, p. 24; italics added). Nor is any loss of an innate language learning faculty implied: "the language acquisition capacity remains intact, but as children mature beyond the ages of four or five its function is impeded by the child's increasingly sophisticated cognitive abilities" (Meier, 1995, p. 613). In a similar vein of thought that specifically targets L2A, Felix's Competition Model (e.g., Felix, 1985) posits the coexistence of an intact UG and advanced domain-general cognition, and maintains that competition between the two systems results in victory for the latter. Mature domain-general cognition is thought to be ill-suited to the narrow, modularized task of acquiring language, hence the lack of success typically associated with adult L2A. The inappropriateness of certain mature cognitive mechanisms in the L2A context was explored by Birdsong (1994) and Bley-Vroman (1989).

Rosansky (1975) appealed to a Piagetian developmental model of cognition and argued that the emergence of Formal Operations during adolescence might forestall language learning. Although Rosansky's theoretical constructs differ from those of Newport, the reasoning of the two researchers is remarkably similar. For Rosansky (1975),

> initial language acquisition takes place when the child is highly centered [i.e., in stages prior to Formal Operations]. He is not only egocentric at this time, but when faced with a problem he can focus (and then only fleetingly) on one dimension at a time. This lack of flexibility and lack of decentration may well be a necessity for language acquisition. (p. 96)

Use It Then Lose It

After childhood, unneeded neural circuitry and the language learning faculty it underlies are "dismantled" because the relevant neural tissue incurs metabolic costs (Pinker, 1994). This reasoning, whereby early language learning is biologically favored over later learning, is rooted in modern evolutionary thinking. Early learning of language is preferred in order that we may reap the benefits of linguistic communication over a longer stretch of our lifetime. So whereas our use of language continues through adulthood, the language learning faculty has served its purpose early on. To retain it would be uneconomical.

The evolution of our species has taken account of this one-shot utility. As Pinker (1994) argued:

Language-acquisition circuitry is not needed once it has been used; it should be dismantled if keeping it around incurs any costs. And it probably does incur costs. Metabolically, the brain is a pig. It consumes a fifth of the body's oxygen and similarly large portions of its calories and phospholipids. Greedy neural tissue lying around beyond its point of usefulness is a good candidate for the recycling bin. (pp. 294–295)

Hurford (1991) similarly accommodated the "use it then lose it" version of the language learning faculty within an evolutionary model: "The end of the critical period at around puberty is . . . a point where the selection pressure in favour of facilitating factors ceases to operate, because of success at earlier lifestages. . . . The 'light' goes out for lack of pressure to keep it 'on'"(p. 193).

Pinker (1994) speculated that the critical period for language acquisition is evolutionarily rooted in the more general phenomenon of senescence. Natural selection asymmetrically favors young organisms over older ones, assigning to youth the emergence of the lion's share of genetic features, which deteriorate at differing rates with increasing age. Using the example of lightning striking and killing a 40-year-old, Pinker noted that if a bodily feature had been designed to emerge after the age of 40, it would have gone to waste:

Genes that strengthen young organisms at the expense of old organisms have the odds in their favor and will tend to accumulate over evolutionary timespans, whatever the bodily system, and the result is overall senescence. Thus language acquisition might be like other biological functions. The linguistic clumsiness of tourists and students might be the price we pay for the linguistic genius we displayed as babies, just as the decrepitude of age is the price we pay for the vigor of youth. (p. 296)

Use It or Lose It

On the mental muscle metaphor, the language learning faculty atrophies with lack of use over time. Paltry progress in postadolescent L2A is clearly compatible with this view. Further, deriving from "use or lose" the inference that if the language learning faculty is used it will not be lost, this "exercise hypothesis" can also accommodate anecdotal accounts of individuals who start L2 acquisition early and continue to acquire foreign languages successfully into adulthood.

The exercise hypothesis was elaborated in greatest detail by Bever (1981). Under Bever's view, for acquisition of a given linguistic structure to take place, the systems of speech production and speech perception should work in tandem. In the absence of ongoing language learning activity, however, the two systems become progressively independent (with perceptive abilities outstripping productive abilities), because the *psychogrammar*, which normally mediates production and reception, ceases to function. (Bever's psychogrammar may be likened to a combination of UG, plus an organizer of acquired linguistic knowledge, plus an equilibrator of production and reception capacities at the moment of acquisition of a given structure.) Under conditions of continual use, however, the psychogrammar does not cease to function, and production and perception do not dissociate:

> So long as one is continually learning a new language the systems of production and perception never become fully autonomous, and closed off from each other. That is, continuous acquisition can stave off the independence of the systems, and therefore delay the apparent critical period. (Bever, 1981, p. 194)

Whereas the use it or lose it formulation predicts that critical period effects can be skirted under conditions of continued language learning, the "use it then lose it" version would seem to imply inevitable loss of language learning ability at the offset of the critical period. The two conceptions also differ in terms of the postmaturational fate of language learning circuitry. For Pinker, natural selection eliminates the metabolically hungry but functionally obsolete language learning mechanism. For Bever (1981), the psychogrammar "does not disappear after its usefulness is past because it is so entrenched as a mental system"; rather, it hangs around, taking an enormous metabolic toll: "The psychogrammar is not a joy of adulthood, but a burden, an adventitious relic left over from a dozen years of language learning" (p. 188).

Learning Inhibits Learning

In connectionist networks, learning is a matter of progressively accumulating and strengthening input–output associations. The strength of an association is functionally a probabilistic weighting corresponding to the likelihood that a given output of the system is correct. One downside to this kind of learning is that it is difficult to undo: As Elman et al. (1996) noted, "across the course of learning . . . the weights within a network become committed to a particular configuration. . . . After this 'point of no return' the network can no longer return to its original state" (p. 389).

Consider the example of the word-final phonemic sequence /oral vowel + n/ in French, which is strongly correlated with feminine gender in nouns and adjectives. Under the connectionist model, an adult native French speaker develops a high weighting for the cooccurrence of this sequence with feminine gender. Once the weighting has become stable, it is difficult to perform the unlearning required for representational reorganization. So, if the French native encountered word-final /oral vowel + n/ in a foreign language, the learner's initial assumption would be that the gender of the word is feminine. This functional state would persist despite input to the system about the inadequacy of its output.

This scenario was summarized by Elman et al. (1996):

> All things being equal, the weights will be most malleable at early points in learning. As learning proceeds, the impact of any particular error declines. . . . If a network has learned the appropriate function, occasional outlier examples will not perturb it much. But by the same token, it may be increasingly difficult for a network to correct a wrong conclusion. Ossification sets in. The interesting thing about this phenomenon, from a developmental viewpoint, is that it suggests that *the ability to learn may change over time—not as a function of any explicit change in the mechanism, but rather as an intrinsic consequence of learning itself.* (p. 70)

For the context of language learning, Marchman (1993) produced critical period effects in her connectionist simulation. When a neural net becomes so "entrenched" with linguistic information that reorganization is too "costly," then it can be said that "it is *the act of language learning* itself that constrains the ability of the system to recruit new resources for solving linguistic problems" (p. 218).

Under this model, to attain success in L2A, the neural representation of a new language would in some sense have to supplant that of an earlier-learned language. That is, the idea that later language might be acquired alongside the old one is not explored. However, it is well known that the addition of an L2 does not imply subtraction of an L1, except to a modest extent in instances where continued use of the L1 is minimal (see Flege, chap. 5, this volume). This matter of ecological validity aside, such a model—or any other model that assumes inhibition of late learning by prior learning—is a reasonable point of departure for dealing with crosslinguistic (L1–L2) effects in syntax. (See MacWhinney's Competition Model (e.g., Liu, Bates & Li, 1992; MacWhinney, 1987), which examines the ways that L1 knowledge may influence L2 learners' representations of the relation between constituent position and semantic function in L2 sentences.) Something akin to inhibition may likewise underlie a learner's failure to develop new phonetic categories that properly distinguish L2 sounds from related L1 sounds, thus resulting in a foreign accent (see Flege, 1995; chap. 5, this volume). However, it would be inappropriate to apply an inhibition model straightforwardly to age effects in the L1: Despite having little or no language to unlearn, late learners of L1 such as Chelsea (Curtiss, 1989) or Genie (Curtiss, 1977) are unable to attain full linguistic competence.

Other Factors in Nonnativelike Outcomes

Any number of learner variables may contribute to nonnativelikeness at the end state of L2A. There is little doubt that exogenous factors, such as variations in the amount and type of target language input, play a role in determining the final product. Similarly, one cannot discount pressures of a psychosocial nature, especially learners' motivation to learn an L2 and their attitude toward assimilating within the foreign culture. Perhaps reflecting a conspiracy of several of these factors, the amount of use of the target language influences degree of foreign accent (Flege, Frieda, & Nozawa, 1997), as does phonetic training (Bongaerts, chap. 6, this volume). Thus, the CPH–L2A is not to be thought of as a unitary account of non-nativelike outcomes. For further discussion of the range of factors that may influence ultimate attainment in L2A, see Klein (1995), Bialystok & Hakuta (chap. 7, this volume), Flege (chap. 5, this volume), Birdsong (1998), and Bongaerts (chap. 6, this volume).

THE WHY NOTS:
REASONABLY DOUBTING THE CPH–L2A

On the face of it, the CPH–L2A is eminently plausible. We know that as humans mature, an earlier-is-better rule of thumb applies to any number of skills. Further, the case for the CPH–L2A is founded on a number of well-known studies, some of which we touched on earlier, others that are cited later. Moreover, until recently, there were few L2A success stories that would constitute counterevidence. Indeed, the case for the CPH–L2A is sufficiently solid that I am on record elsewhere as a staunch supporter (Birdsong, 1991).

The CPH–L2A would still have my support were it not for the unexpected findings of a study I carried out a few years ago (Birdsong, 1992).[2] Two distinct sets of results gave me pause. First, among the 20 native speakers of English who began learning French as adults, 15 fell within the range of native speaker performance on a challenging grammaticality judgment task, and several of these 15 participants deviated very little from native norms. This rate of nativelike attainment was unprecedented in the literature at the time. Second, I found that performance on the task was predicted by age of arrival (AOA) in France, even though the participants had moved to France as adults. Why should age effects continue to be found after the end of the presumed critical period?

Now that I am on the other side of the fence, it would be disingenuous of me to offer a neutral account of the CPH–L2A debate. Readers seeking the "pro" side will find it more than ably represented in this volume by Eubank and Gregg, Hurford and Kirby, and Weber-Fox and Neville. The following review is not meant to be exhaustive, because the book's "anti" chapters (those of Bialystok and Hakuta, Bongaerts, and Flege) cover the terrain thoroughly. Rather, I will

---

[2]I should point out that the study was not designed to test directly the CPH–L2A but to see if some areas of grammar might be less subject to age effects than others. Some of the more peripheral results turned out to be of enduring interest.

concentrate on two types of evidence I already alluded to—the nature of the age function and numbers of nativelike attainers—that have led me to reconsider my original position. In so doing, I hope to convey a sense of why the case is not closed on the CPH–L2A, and thus to justify the collection of papers in this volume.

The Age Function

In L2A research on ultimate attainment,[3] no single study has contributed more to the case for critical period effects than that of Johnson and Newport (1989). The Johnson and Newport participants were 46 Korean and Chinese learners of English, all of whom had lived in the United States for 5 years or more, but who varied in terms of their AOA in the United States. Participants were asked to provide grammaticality judgments of some 276 English sentences, roughly half of which were grammatical and the other half ungrammatical. The stimuli were presented on an audiotape, and participants provided binary judgments of acceptability by circling "yes" or "no" on an answer sheet. The stimuli exemplified basic surface contrasts in English, for example, regular verb morphology (*Every Friday our neighbor washes her car; *Every Friday our neighbor wash her car*), irregular noun morphology (*Two mice ran into the house this morning; *Two mouses ran into the house this morning*), and particle placement (*The horse jumped over the fence yesterday; *The horse jumped the fence over yesterday*).

Of the many findings in Johnson and Newport (1989), perhaps the most revealing is the age function, that is, the distribution of participants' scores on the instrument plotted against their AOA in the United States. For participants arriving in the United States prior to the presumed closure of an age-related window of opportunity, there was a linear decline in performance that began after AOA of approximately 7 years. However, after the window of opportunity closed, at AOA of about 17 years, the distribution of performance was essentially random ($r = -.16$). This outcome suggests that postmaturational AOA is not predictive of ultimate attainment; in other words, the L2 asymptote is determined not by a general age effect, but by one that operates within a defined developmental span. Consistent with critical period thinking, neurocognitive developmental factors are at work early on and cease when maturation is complete. Indeed, the asymmetry found by Johnson and Newport (1989), along with a similar finding by Patkowski (1980), may be straightforwardly

---

[3]"Ultimate" is not used here to suggest "nativelike." Ultimate attainment is to be understood as synonymous with the end state or asymptote of L2A, however close to or far from nativelike that state may be.

interpreted as evidence for a biologically based critical or sensitive period in L2A (e.g., Long, 1990; Pulvermüller & Schumann, 1994).

Understandably, the age function evidence in Johnson and Newport (1989) is a cornerstone in the CPH–L2A edifice. However, since that study, several researchers have found age effects among participants who began learning their L2 as adults. For example, Birdsong (1992), in a study of English-speaking learners of French (AOA varying from 11.5–28), found a –.51 correlation ($p = .02$) of AOA and performance on a grammaticality judgment task. Other researchers (see Bialystok & Hakuta, chap. 7, this volume) have shown age effects for both early and late AOA. In a variety of domains, including pronunciation, both late and early AOA effects have been found (Oyama, 1976; Flege, chap. 5, this volume). Contrary to the premises of the CPH–L2A, AOA is predictive of success, even when the AOA is later than the presumed end of maturational effects.

In the wake of these findings, the original Johnson and Newport (1989) results have been subjected to considerable scrutiny. For example, Bialystok and Hakuta (1994) reanalyzed the data from Johnson and Newport (1989) and found significant correlations of scores with age for both groups if the cutoff point was set at 20 years instead of 17. In addition, Birdsong and Molis (1998) conducted a replication of Johnson and Newport (1989), using the same materials, procedures, and tasks as the original. Our participants were 62 native speakers of Spanish. In contrast to Johnson and Newport (1989), we found a strong age effect among the 32 late arrivals (AOA ≥ 17 years). The correlation between age and performance on the grammaticality judgment task is significant ($r = -.69, p < .01$). The results of our study further suggest that earlier is better across the lifespan; for early and late arrivals together, the correlation ($r = -.77$) is likewise significant ($p < .01$). Consider, too, that the scores of the late arrivals are fairly closely clustered about the regression line; with an r^2 accounting for nearly half of the variance, the distribution is a far cry from the randomness found by Johnson and Newport.

Pulvermüller & Schumann (1994) maintained that "there is no clear evidence that after puberty the age of learning onset influences either mean or variance of grammaticality judgment scores" (p. 684). The present results constitute a direct and unambiguous challenge to this assertion. They should be sufficient, presumably, to prompt Pulvermüller and Schumann to revisit their neurobiological account of language acquisition: "If the decrease in grammatical proficiency with greater age in postpuberty starters could be confirmed, the present proposal would have to be modified" (p. 723).

Although these recent results are not consonant with the predictions of the CPH–L2A, they should not be interpreted as suggesting that maturational factors are not at play at all. Birdsong & Molis (1998) pointed out that there is an inevitable confound of AOA and development prior to the end of maturation, in the sense that, for early arrivals, age effects cannot be dissociated from maturational effects. It is not inconceivable that the attested straight-line age function in L2A over the lifespan is the product of different causal mechanisms along the way, that is, the result of developmental factors up to the end of maturation, and of nondevelopmental factors thereafter.[4]

Rate of Nativelike Attainment

Estimates of rate of success in adult L2A (defined in terms of attainment of nativelike competence) typically range from virtually nil (Bley-Vroman, 1989) to 5% (Selinker, 1972). Much has been made of the scarcity of nativelike attainers. Bley-Vroman (1989) spoke of "ineluctable failure" in L2A: if there are exceptional L2 learners, they are so rare as to be "pathological,' comparable to instances of failure in early L1A (p. 44). Bley-Vroman (1989)—along with Selinker (1972)—suggested that whatever successes there are "could perhaps be regarded as peripheral to the enterprise of second language acquisition theory" (p. 44).

To establish the adequacy of the CPH–L2A, however, the rate of success must be taken into account. For Long (1990), falsifiability of the CPH–L2A hinged on this type of evidence: "The easiest way to falsify [the CPH] would be to produce learners who have demonstrably attained native-like proficiency despite having begun exposure well after the closure of the hypothesized sensitive periods" (p. 274). Indeed, for Long, a single such learner would suffice to refute the CPH–L2A (p. 255).

At the time this criterion was suggested, there was little reason to suspect the CPH–L2A would be falsified. For example, Patkowski (1980) had found only 1 participant out of 34 late learners who performed in the native range. Johnson and Newport (1989) had found

---

[4]A few candidate variables were mentioned previously. Note too that neurophysiological factors after the completion of maturation are not to be overlooked in late AOA age effects. For example, myelination and dendritic pruning take place over the lifespan. Precisely what these processes might contribute to late L2A is still a mater of speculation, however. One direction of inquiry to consider is the possibility that different neural substrates are variably affected by senescence. Thus, for example, if the basal ganglia area that is responsible for the processing of regular morphology were less (or more) affected by aging than the temporal and parietal regions that subserve irregulars (see Ullman et al., 1997), we would expect to see a dissociation between regulars and irregulars in the ultimate attainment of late L2 learners (see Flege, Yeni-Komshian, & Liu, 1998; other dissociations are discussed by Weber-Fox & Neville, chap. 2, this volume, and Eubank & Gregg, chap. 4, this volume).

none. Moreover, not one of the adult learners in Coppieters's (1987) study had even come close to native performance in judgments of sentence acceptability in French. However, since 1990, several researchers have attested nativelikeness among their late-learning participants.

For example, Van Wuijtswinkel (1994) tested Dutch native speakers who had begun learning English after 12 years of age. Their task was to judge the grammaticality of a subset of the Johnson and Newport (1989) items, along with an assortment of other syntactic structures in English. Van Wuijtswinkel attested nativelike performance among 8 of 26 participants in one group of learners and 7 of 8 participants in another group. In a study of American Sign Language (ASL) as a second language, Mayberry (1993) found that late ASL–L2 learners (mean age of acquisition = 11) varied little from native ASL users on several tasks, including immediate recall of complex sentences and grammaticality judgments. White and Genesee (1996) studied the acquisition of English by French native speakers in Montreal. Some 16 of the 45 participants who appeared nativelike on various screening measures had had their first significant exposure to English after age 12. Participants were asked to make questions involving wh-extraction and to judge the grammaticality of 60 exemplars of various wh-movement structures such as "What did the newspaper report the minister had done?" and "*What did you hear the announcement that Ann had received?" The researchers found no significant differences between near-natives (including the 16 late learners) and native controls on any task.

As mentioned above, Birdsong (1992) looked at the acquisition of French by 20 native speakers of English who had been exposed to French postpubertally (range 11–28 years, M = 14.9), who had been residing in France for at least 3 years, and whose mean age of arrival was 28.5 years (range = 19–48). On scalar grammaticality judgments of seven French syntactic structures exemplifying parametric variation (e.g., *Diane a placé des fleurs dans sa chambre/*Diane a placé dans sa chambre des fleurs*—'Diane put flowers in her room'/'Diane put in her room flowers) and highly French-specific constraints (e.g. *Le très-connu Marcel Proust vient d'arriver/*Le connu romancier vient d'arriver*— 'The well-known Marcel Proust just arrived'/'The known novelist just arrived'), the performance of 6 of the 20 experimental participants (30%) was well within the range of performance of native controls.

Cranshaw (1997) investigated the acquisition of English tense–aspect features by 20 Francophone and 20 Sinophone participants, all of whom had begun studying English after age 12. Over a variety of production and judgment measures, and using stringent criteria for comparison, 3 (15%) of the Francophones were indistinguishable from native English controls, as was 1 (5%) of the Sinophones. Birdsong (1997) studied the acquisition of the distribution of the clitic *se* in

French intransitive constructions (e.g., *Les nuages se dissipent/*dissipent après l'orage*—'The clouds dissipate after the storm'; *Les doigts bleuissent/*se bleuissent de froid*—'One's fingers turn blue from the cold'). Participants were 20 English natives (average AOA = 23; average age of first exposure to French = 13; residence in France ≥ 5 years). The distribution of *se* is highly idiosyncratic; it was therefore felt that L2 acquisition to nativelike levels in this domain would be unlikely. As groups, natives and learners differed significantly. However, 4 (20%) of the non-natives scored above the native mean of approximately 95% accuracy. Finally, in the Birdsong and Molis (1998) replication of Johnson and Newport (1989), 3 of the 32 late-arriving subjects had scores that were above 95% accuracy, and 13 of these late arrivals performed at or above 92% accuracy.[5]

In the domains of phonetics and phonology, Bongaerts and his colleagues (see Bongaerts, chap. 6, this volume) showed in several experiments that native speakers of Dutch are able to attain a level of pronunciation in English and in French that is indistinguishable from that of native speakers, even though their study of the L2 began in late adolescence. Birdsong (1997) examined the acquisition of constraints on realization of liaison consonants in French, using the same participants from the *se* experiment. Although the group overall had an error rate of 22.5% (in contrast to the native controls, whose error rate was 0%), 4 of the nonnative participants, or some 20%, performed at 100% accuracy. Two of these participants were among the 4 who had performed at nativelike levels in the SE experiment.[6]

Note that, in bringing falsifying evidence to bear on the CPH–L2A, the rate of success should be based on the relevant population of learners. That is, to determine the proportion of nativelike attainers, we should look at only those learners with exogenous circumstances favoring language acquisition, not at any and all who have had some exposure to an L2 or who have tried to learn a foreign language. (I suspect that many long-held beliefs about the insignificant rate of success in L2A are based on the latter, much larger population.[7]) As an

---

[5]Other studies attesting nativelike attainment include Juffs and Harrington (1995), Ioup, Boustagui, El Tigi, and Moselle (1994), and White and Juffs (1997).

[6]Flege, Munro, and MacKay (1995) found that 6% of their late AOA participants performed at nativelike levels. However, no participant with AOA > 16 was found to have authentic pronunciation. Together, these findings suggest that nativelike pronunciation is possible but infrequent among late-arriving participants, and that age effects persist past the presumed end of maturation.

[7]To get an idea of how small the relevant population might be, let us construe "a fair chance of success" in terms of bringing L2 input into rough comparability with L1 input. It has been estimated that in the first five years of life a child has 9100 hours of exposure to L1 input; multiplying this figure by the average number of utterances that are directed to a child each hour (670), we arrive at a figure in excess of 6 million (see Birdsong, 1998). Were the relevant L2A population to be restricted to learners with such massive input, they would constitute a small

example, the success rate established in my work has been based on participants who have been immersed in the French language for a substantial length of time (minimum 3 years in the 1992 study, minimum 5 years in later studies). On the other side of the coin, when trying to determine the rate of success, we should not restrict the inquiry to "the cream of the crop," that is, to just those learners who have been screened for nativelikeness prior to experimentation. For this reason, my work has not been limited to a sample of exceptional learners. The success rate is based on participants meeting a residency requirement (and, in order to make valid comparisons with native controls, having an educational profile and chronological age similar to those of native-speaking participants).

How many nativelike learners would be required for falsification of the CPH–L2A is, of course, debatable. It is safe to say, however, that a strict Popperian criterion, where one exception suffices to reject the hypothesis (Long, 1990), is more than amply met. In studies of the relevant population, the attested rates of success mentioned earlier range from 5% to 25%. Assuming a normal distribution, a 15% success rate corresponds to all of the area from roughly 1 standard deviation above the mean and higher; as such, these participants cannot be regarded as mere outliers in the distribution. (By way of comparison, consider that approximately 10% of the world's population is left-handed. It would be folly to argue that left-handers are outliers in the human race.) Although for some observers a 10% or 15% success rate in L2A may not constitute adequate evidence for falsification of the CPH–L2A, it is nevertheless clear that nativelike learners cannot be dismissed as "peripheral."

THE PRESENT VOLUME

Having considered the intellectual backdrop to the present volume, let us now preview the contents of the collection individually.

Three chapters were selected to represent the pro side of the CPH–L2A debate. First, Weber-Fox and Neville examine bilinguals' Event-Related Brain Potentials (ERPs), which allow for measurement of electrical activity in various areas of the brain. A series of experiments reveals that late-learning bilinguals display slower linguistic processing than early-learning bilinguals, and that language-related neural systems of later learners are different in locus and function from those of early learners. Further, the processing of grammatical aspects of language (e.g., closed-class words and syntactic anomalies) is distinct

---

fraction of the universe of "second language learners." In all likelihood, the rate of nativelike attainment within such a population would surpass insignificance.

from the processing of semantic aspects (e.g., open-class words and semantic anomalies). The two processing subsystems are differentially affected by delays in the onset of language learning, suggesting the operation of different sensitive periods (see Seliger, 1978). Weber-Fox and Neville also review other applications of neural imaging techniques to bilingualism and L2A, underscoring the specific areas of linguistic competence in which differences between late and early bilinguals are to be found. These differences are viewed as being consistent with a Lenneberg-type conception of the CPH.

From an evolutionary perspective, Hurford and Kirby consider two components of restricted language learning capacity. First there is language size, the sum of all the complexities of a given language. Given our speed of acquisition, there is an upper limit on how much language can be acquired prior to puberty (biological selection favors attainment of maximal language size before the onset of sexual maturity). However, it is not the entrenchment of an acquired language that inhibits late learning (see the earlier discussion of Marchman, 1993). Instead, the attainment of maximal language size coincides with the decline of a second component, a facility for acquiring new linguistic knowledge. Like Elman and like Newport (see previous sections), Hurford and Kirby argue that this facility is optimized by starting small, in the sense of initially having a limited linguistic processing capacity. With development of increased processing capacity, this advantage is lost. For normal individuals, the upper limit of linguistic attainment is reached by the time the ability to learn language is lost. Thus, by virtue of the coincidence of these two developmental milestones, language size could be thought of as being predictive of the offset of the critical period, but it is clearly not its cause. In the L2A context, knowledge of the L1 can be recruited to the benefit of L2 attainment when the two languages are sufficiently similar. Success in L2A will nevertheless be limited, however, because the adult's linguistic processing resources are no longer well suited to the task.

Eubank and Gregg's chapter is broad in scope. First the authors seek to pin down the concept of plasticity as it relates to critical periods, detailing the interaction of input, neurophysiology, and neurochemistry in the processes of long-term potentiation and long-term depression. This section culminates in the outlines of distinct neurofunctional mechanisms whose decreased plasticity could be linked to the passage of a critical period for language learning. Eubank and Gregg then cite several critical periods in other animal species that could be compared in their domain specificity to humans' critical period for language acquisition. They go on to examine the evidence for critical periods in L1A, and contrast this with the case for the CPH in L2A. Casting the debate in terms of modern linguistic theory, Eubank and Gregg refine the notions of language, modularity, and access to UG, stressing the need for precision in use of these terms in discussing the CPH. A number of relevant L2A studies are reviewed and are found to offer only equivocal evidence for or against the role of UG in post-critical period L2A. However, Eubank and Gregg find the research of Weber-Fox and Neville promising, as it aims to identify precisely which aspects of language might be subject to a critical period. The authors conclude with speculations as to why (a) critical period(s) might exist.

On the anti side of the ledger, there are likewise three chapters. Flege is interested in the CPH as it pertains to L2 pronunciation. First, he shows that L2 pronunciation accuracy declines linearly with age (see Bialystok & Hakuta, chap. 7, this volume), and does not display a trademark discontinuity that Patkowski (1990) and others associate with the passing of a critical period. After reviewing the adequacy of several variants of the CPH, Flege proposes that nonnativelike accents do not result from a loss of ability to pronounce; rather, they are an indirect consequence of the state of development of the L1 phonetic–phonological system at the time L2 learning is begun. This conclusion is supported by the negative correlations of L1 pronunciation with L2 pronunciation, and of L1 use with L2 pronunciation. He goes on to adduce evidence that undermines Bever's (1981) formulation of the CPH, which depends crucially on the assumption of a loss of isomorphism between production and perception capacities in adults. For Flege, the difficulties associated with late learning of L2 pronunciation are not sufficiently captured by the CPH but are much more consistent with his Speech Learning Model. On this view, nonnativelike pronunciation results from learners' increasing difficulty in establishing new, distinct representations of L2 phonetic categories. This difficulty is exacerbated when a given target phonetic segment is perceived by the learner to be highly similar to a segment in the L1 repertoire.

Bongaerts likewise tackles the area of L2 pronunciation, which, of the various linguistic domains, has been identified as the most vulnerable to critical period effects (Long, 1990; Scovel, 1988). Reporting the results from three experiments, Bongaerts brings disconfirming evidence in the form of late learners who are able to attain nativelike accents. The first two studies involved Dutch native speakers learning English as adults. Native English controls and two groups of Dutch participants were asked to read aloud a set of English sentences containing phones both similar to and different from Dutch sounds. Their pronunciations were rated for nativelikeness by a panel of judges. Under a variety of different analyses and by stringent criteria for comparison, a significant proportion of late learners in both studies were judged to have nativelike English pronunciation. The third study tested Dutch natives' late acquisition of French. This target language was chosen because, unlike English and Dutch, it is not a Germanic language, and because it is less often encountered over the Dutch airwaves than English. Over a range of performances, and again using strict criteria for nativelikeness, 3 of 9 highly proficient late learners of French were judged to be indistinguishable from natives.

Bialystok and Hakuta grant that for L2A, earlier is better, but stake out the position that it is misguided to infer a causal relation between age and attainment. Rather, Bialystok and Hakuta liken age to an intervening variable in a design; were it to be controlled for experimentally or partialed out of a regression equation, then one would find linguistic factors and cognitive factors at play. The linguistic variable is exemplified in native-language transfer. If there is a change in the language acquisition mechanism over time, then what is transferred from the L1 to the L2 should also change: Early on, more abstract UG constraints should transfer, while later learning should be characterized by relatively more transfer of L1-specific surface features. A review of the relevant literature suggests that this is not the case. With respect to cognitive factors, Bialystok and Hakuta argue that literate versus nonliterate populations differ in ultimate attainment. This, along with the authors' demonstration of proficiency differences as a function of educational level, cannot be captured by a simple maturational account of L2A. Bialystok and Hakuta also argue that the declines in general cognitive abilities that come with aging, being gradual and linear, are a better fit with the L2A data—which include the authors' report of a large-scale survey of immigrants to the United States—than is a critical-period-type function which, arguably, should exhibit some form of discontinuity.

Each of these chapters, whether anti- or pro-CPH–L2A, illustrates the richness, depth, and breadth of critical period inquiry. Collectively, they testify to the unmistakable centrality of the CPH in L2A research.

REFERENCES

Bever, T. G. (1981). Normal acquisition processes explain the critical period for language learning. In K. C. Diller (Ed.), *Individual differences and universals in language learning aptitude* (pp. 176–198). Rowley, MA: Newbury House.

Bialystok, E., & Hakuta, K. (1994). *In other words: The science and psychology of second-language acquisition.* New York: Basic Books.

Birdsong, D. (1991). On the notion of "critical period" in UG/L2 theory: A response to Flynn & Manuel. In L. Eubank (Ed.), *Point-counterpoint: Universal Grammar in the second language* (pp. 147–165). Amsterdam: John Benjamins.

Birdsong, D. (1992). Ultimate attainment in second language acquisition. *Language, 68,* 706–755.

Birdsong, D. (1994). Decision making in second language acquisition. *Studies in Second Language Acquisition, 16,* 169–182.

Birdsong, D. (1997, November). *Intransitivity and SE in French: Aspects of late L2 learnability.* Paper presented at the Boston University Child Language Development Conference.

Birdsong, D. (1998). *The end state in second language acquisition.* Unpublished manuscript, University of Texas.

Birdsong, D., &, Molis, M. (1998). *Age and maturation in L2A: A replication of Johnson & Newport (1989).* Unpublished manuscript, University of Texas.

Bley-Vroman, R. (1989). What is the logical problem of foreign language learning? In S. Gass & J. Schachter (Eds.), *Linguistic perspectives on second language acquisition* (pp. 41–68). Cambridge: Cambridge University Press.

Coppieters, R. (1987). Competence differences between native and near-native speakers. *Language, 63,* 544–573.

Cranshaw, A. (1997). *A study of Anglophone native and near-native linguistic and metalinguistic performance.* Unpublished doctoral dissertation, Université de Montréal.

Curtiss, S. R. (1977). *Genie: A linguistic study of a modern day "wild child."* New York: Academic Press.

Curtiss, S. (1989). *The case of Chelsea: A new test case of the critical period for language acquisition.* Unpublished manuscript, University of California, Los Angeles.

Elman, J. L. (1993). Learning and development in neural networks: The importance of starting small. *Cognition, 48,* 71–99.

Elman, J. L., Bates, E. A., Johnson, M. H., Karmiloff-Smith, A., Parisi, D., & Plunkett, K. (1996). *Rethinking innateness: A connectionist perspective on development.* Cambridge, MA: MIT Press.

Felix, S. (1985). More evidence on competing cognitive systems. *Second Language Research, 1,* 47–72.

Flege, J. E. (1995). Second-language speech learning: Theory, findings, and problems. In W. Strange (Ed.), *Speech perception and linguistic experience: Theoretical and methodological issues* (pp. 233–273). Timonium, MD: York Press.

Flege, J. E., Frieda, A. M., & Nozawa, T. (1997). Amount of native-language (L1) use affects the pronunciation of an L2. *Journal of Phonetics, 25,* 169–186.

Flege, J. E., Munro, M. J., & MacKay, I. (1995). Factors affecting degree of perceived foreign accent in a second language. *Journal of the Acoustical Society of America, 97,* 3125–3134.

Flege, J. E.,Yeni-Komshian, G., & Liu, H. (1998). *Age constraints on Koreans' acquisition of English phonology and morphosyntax.* Unpublished manuscript, University of Alabama at Birmingham.

Flynn, S., Martohardjono, G., & O'Neil, W., Eds. (1997). *The generative study of second language acquisition.* Mahwah, NJ: Lawrence Erlbaum Associates.

Goldowsky, B. N., & Newport, E. L. (1993) Modeling the effects of processing limitations on the acquisition of morphology: The less is more hypothesis. In E. Clark (Ed.), *The proceedings of the 24th Annual Child Language Research Forum* (pp. 124–138). Stanford, CA: Center for the Study of Language and Information.

Hurford, J. R. (1991). The evolution of the critical period for language acquisition. *Cognition, 40,* 159–201.

Ioup, G., Boustagui, E., El Tigi, M., & Moselle, M. (1994). Reexamining the critical period hypothesis: A case study of successful adult SLA in a naturalistic environment. *Studies in Second Language Acquisition, 16,* 73–98.

Jacobs, B. (1988). Neurobiological differentiation of primary and secondary language acquisition. *Studies in Second Language Acquisition, 10,* 303–337.

Johnson, J. S., & Newport, E. L. (1989). Critical period effects in second language learning: The influence of maturational state on the acquisition of English as a second language. *Cognitive Psychology, 21,* 60–99.

Juffs, A., & Harrington, M. (1995). Parsing effects in second language sentence processing: Subject and object asymmetries in wh-extraction. *Studies in Second Language Acquisition, 17,* 483–516.

Klein, W. (1995). Language acquisition at different ages. In D. Magnusson (Ed.), *The lifespan development of individuals: Behavioral, neurobiological, and psychosocial perspectives. A synthesis* (pp. 244–264). Cambridge, England: Cambridge University Press.

Lenneberg, E. H. (1967). *Biological foundations of language.* New York: Wiley.

Liu, H., Bates, E., & Li, P. (1992). Sentence interpretation in bilingual speakers of English and Chinese. *Applied Psycholinguistics, 13,* 451–484.

Long, M. H. (1990). Maturational constraints on language development. *Studies in Second Language Acquisition, 12,* 251–285.

MacWhinney, B. (1987). Applying the Competition Model to bilingualism. *Applied Psycholinguistics, 8,* 415–431.

Marchman, V. A. (1993). Constraints on plasticity in a connectionist model of the English past tense. *Journal of Cognitive Neuroscience, 5,* 215–234.

Mayberry, R. (1993). First-language acquisition after childhood differs from second-language acquisition: The case of American Sign Language. *Journal of Speech and Hearing Research, 36,* 1258–1270.

Meier, R. P. (1995). Review of S. Pinker, The language instinct: How the mind creates language. *Language, 71,* 610–614

Newport, E. L. (1990). Maturational constraints on language learning. *Cognitive Science, 14,* 11–28.

Newport, E. L. (1991). Contrasting conceptions of the critical period for language. In S. Carey & R. Gelman (Eds.), *The epigenesis of mind* (pp. 111–130). Hillsdale, NJ: Lawrence Erlbaum Associates.

Oyama, S. (1976). A sensitive period for the acquisition of a nonnative phonological system. *Journal of Psycholinguistic Research, 5,* 261–285.

Patkowski, M. S. (1980). The sensitive period for the acquisition of syntax in a second language. *Language Learning, 30,* 449–472.

Patkowski, M. S. (1990). Age and accent in a second language: A reply to James Emil Flege. *Applied Linguistics, 11,* 73–89

Penfield, W., & Roberts, L. (1959). *Speech and brain mechanisms.* New York: Atheneum.

Pinker, S. (1994). *The language instinct: How the mind creates language.* New York: Morrow.

Pulvermüller, F., & Schumann, J. H. (1994). Neurobiological mechanisms of language acquisition. *Language Learning, 44,* 681–734.

Rosansky, E. (1975). The critical period for the acquisition of language: Some cognitive developmental considerations. *Working Papers on Bilingualism, 6,* 92–102.

Scovel, T. (1988). *A time to speak: A psycholinguistic inquiry into the critical period for human speech.* Rowley, MA: Newbury House.

Seliger, H. W. (1978). Implications of a multiple critical periods hypothesis for second language learning. In W. C. Ritchie (Ed.), *Second language research: Issues and implications* (pp. 11–19). New York: Academic Press.

Selinker, L. (1972). Interlanguage. *International Review of Applied Linguistics, 10,* 209–231.

Towell, R., & Hawkins, R. (1994). *Approaches to Second Language Acquisition.* Clevedon, England: Multilingual Matters.

Ullman, M. T., Corkin, S., Coppola, M., Hickok, G., Growdon, J. H., Koroshets, W. J., & Pinker, S. (1997). A neural dissociation within language: Evidence that the mental dictionary is part of declarative memory, and that grammatical rules are processed by the procedural system. *Journal of Cognitive Neuroscience, 9,* 266–276.

Van Wuijtswinkel, K. (1994). *Critical period effects on the acquisition of grammatical competence in a second language.* Unpublished BA thesis, Katholieke Universiteit, Nijmegen, Netherlands.

White, L., & Genesee, F. (1996). How native is near-native? The issue of ultimate attainment in adult second language acquisition. *Second Language Research, 12,* 238–265.

White, L., & Juffs, A. (1997). Constraints on wh-movement in two different contexts of non-native language acquisition: Competence and processing. In S. Flynn, G. Martohardhono, & W. O'Neil (Eds.), *The generative study of second language acquisition* (pp. 111–129). Mahwah, NJ: Lawrence Erlbaum Associates.

CHAPTER TWO

Functional Neural Subsystems
Are Differentially Affected
by Delays in Second Language Immersion:
ERP and Behavioral Evidence in Bilinguals

Christine M. Weber-Fox
Purdue University
Helen J. Neville
University of Oregon

AGE OF IMMERSION AND NEURAL SUBSYSTEMS IN L2A

Our aim has been to test the hypothesis that the age of immersion in a second language has differential effects on the neural subsystems involved in language processing. This hypothesis arises from consideration of studies of the development and organization of visual, auditory, and somatosensory systems. Within these systems, the nature of sensory input significantly affects the development of specific neurophysiological and behavioral processes (Freeman & Thibos, 1973; Kaas, 1991; Knudsen, 1988; Patkowski, 1980; Wiesel & Hubel, 1963, 1965). Morever, different functions within a system display distinct vulnerabilities to altered timing of input during development. For example, within the visual system, the timing of abnormal visual experience differentially affects the development of stereopsis, monocular spatial resolution, and spectral sensitivity (Harwerth, Smith, Duncan, Crawford & von Noorden, 1986). Although plasticity has been shown to characterize sensory and motor maps even in adult mammalian brains (Kaas, 1991; Kaas, Merzenich, & Killackey, 1983), many such experience-dependent changes occur only during specific critical or sensitive periods. A general principle that emerges from a variety of studies is that the impact of altered sensory experience for many functions diminishes with maturation.

Lenneberg (1967) hypothesized that maturational processes similar to those that govern sensory and motor development may also constrain capabilities for normal language acquisition. Results from a variety of behavioral studies indicated that for primary and secondary language learning, the age of immersion is the best predictive variable for the ultimate linguistic proficiency (Johnson & Newport, 1989; Mayberry & Eichen, 1991; Newport, 1988; Oyama, 1982). Further, particular aspects of language have been found to be more profoundly impacted by delays, for example, grammatical functions of language. Other aspects such as vocabulary are relatively unaffected by delays in language immersion. Recent evidence from a study utilizing functional magnetic resonance imaging (fMRI) raises the hypothesis that different cortical areas associated with first and second languages may be differentially affected by delays in language immersion (Kim, Relkin, Lee, & Hirsch, 1997). The fMRI findings indicated that, within anterior language areas, the cortical locations for some aspects of first and second language functions do not overlap in late learners of a second language. In contrast, the fMRI results for early second language learners indicated that their native and second language were represented in common cortical areas within these regions. The behavioral and fMRI findings indicate that different aspects of language function and neural representation show distinct effects attributable to variations in delays in second language immersion. We hypothesized that the relevant functional cerebral subsystems specialized for semantic and grammatical processing are differentially impacted by delays in second language immersion.

Utilizing a bilingual model, we investigated this hypothesis using a combined behavioral–electrophysiological approach. A large group of Chinese–English bilinguals was tested. These participants were divided into groups based on the age at which they were immersed in English: 1 to 3, 4 to 6, 7 to 10, 11 to 13, and greater than 16 years of age (Weber-Fox & Neville, 1994, 1996, 1998). All participants were immersed in English for at least 5 years. And, it should be noted that the years of experience with English were similar for the participants in the 11 to 13 and greater than 16 groups. Measures of self-rated proficiency and standardized tests of knowledge of English grammar were used to help determine linguistic knowledge for these groups of participants. Relevant results are displayed in Fig. 2.1 and Fig. 2.2.

Self-Rated Proficiency

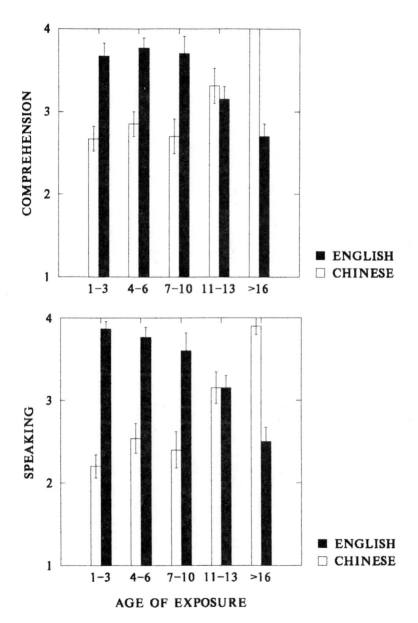

FIG. 2.1. Self-rated proficiency for comprehension and speaking in Chinese (white bars) and English (black bars). Scores are grouped according to age of exposure to English. Proficiency scale used: 1 = scarcely; 2 = sufficiently; 3 = well; 4 = perfectly. (From Weber-Fox & Neville, 1996).

Standardized Tests

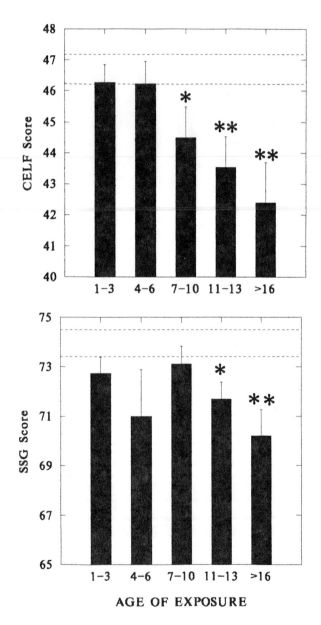

FIG. 2.2. Performance on standardized tests: Clinical Evaluation of Language Function (CELF–Word and Sentence Structure Subtest) and Saffran & Schwartz Grammaticality Judgment Test (SSG). Scores are grouped according to age of exposure to English. (From Weber-Fox & Neville, 1996).

Note: In Fig. 2.2, double dashed lines indicate the performance of monolinguals (mean scores +/− standard error). Scores of bilinguals which differed from those of monolinguals are asterisked (** $p < .01$; * $p < .05$).

Consistent with previous behavioral studies (Johnson & Newport, 1989; Newport, 1988), the findings shown in Fig. 2.1 and Fig. 2.2 indicated that the age of immersion in a second language is an important variable for predicting linguistic competence.

EFFECTS OF DELAYS ON PROCESSING SYNTACTIC VERSUS SEMANTIC ANOMALIES

The linguistic stimuli that allowed careful comparison between semantic and syntactic processing were previously developed for an ERP (Event-Related Brain Potential) study in English monolinguals (Neville, Nicol, Barss, Forster, & Garrett, 1991). The randomized sentence stimuli were presented one word at a time on a monitor (1 word per 500 msec). After each trial, participants were required to judge whether or not the sentence was "a good English sentence." Half of the 240 sentences included violations in semantic expectations (e.g., "The boys heard Joe's <u>orange</u> about Africa") or one of three syntactic rules: (1) phrase structure (e.g., "The boys heard Joe's <u>about</u> stories Africa"), (2) specificity constraint (e.g., "What did the boys hear Joe's <u>stories</u> about?"), or (3) subjacency constraint (e.g., "What were stories about <u>heard</u> by the boys?"). The remaining sentences served as semantically and syntactically appropriate controls. The underlined words in the anomalous sentence examples indicate the point of linguistic deviation and the ERP comparison points between the violation and their control sentences.

The effects of age of second language immersion on grammatical judgment accuracy in detecting syntactic and semantic anomalies in these stimuli sentences were investigated (Weber-Fox & Neville, 1996). As in previous studies, the relation between age of immersion and linguistic judgment accuracy was not uniform across different types of language constructs; namely, syntactic proficiency was more profoundly impacted than lexical (or semantic) judgment accuracy. Judgment accuracies for syntactic structures were reduced in bilinguals with delays of only 7 to 10 years. In contrast, judgment accuracy for semantic processing was decreased only for bilinguals with delays in second language immersion greater than 16 years. These findings are displayed graphically in Fig. 2.3 and Fig. 2.4.

Note: In Fig. 2.3 and Fig. 2.4, double dashed lines indicate the performance of monolinguals (mean scores +/− standard error). Scores of bilinguals which differed from those of monolinguals are asterisked (*** $p < .001$; ** $p < .01$; * $p < .05$).

Experimental Sentences

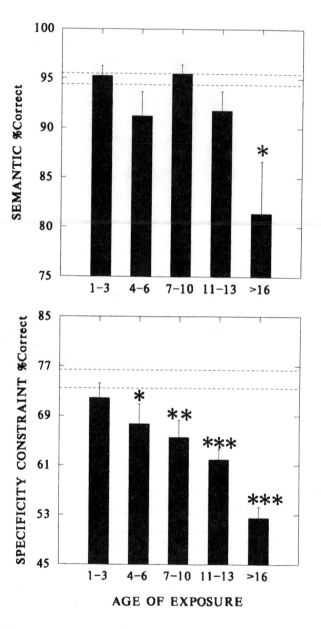

FIG. 2.3. Performance accuracy on judgments of experimental sentences: Semantic and Specificity Constraint. 100% is based on a possible 60 items correct (30 control and 30 violation sentences). Scores are grouped according to age of exposure to English. (From Weber-Fox & Neville, 1996).

Experimental Sentences

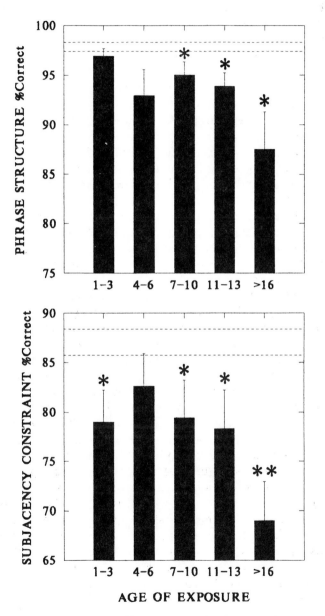

FIG. 2.4. Performance accuracy on judgments of experimental sentences: Phrase Structure and Subjacency Constraint. 100% is based on a possible 60 items correct (30 control and 30 violation sentences). Scores are grouped according to age of exposure to English. (From Weber-Fox & Neville, 1996).

Turning now to another source of evidence, electrophysiological findings in monolingual English speakers indicated that the ERPs elicited by semantic violations are distinct in timing and distribution from ERPs elicited by syntactic violations, and further, that different types of syntactic processing (e.g., phrase structure vs. specificity constraint) are associated with distinct neural subsystems (Neville et al., 1991).

Figure 2.5 displays averaged ERP waveforms over left and right parietal sites for monolinguals and each of the bilingual groups; Fig. 2.6 relates to anterior temporal sites. Traces in solid lines indicate responses to control words. Negativity is plotted upward. Dashed lines represent responses to violations: In Fig. 2.5, responses indicated by dashed lines were elicited by violations of semantic expectation; in Fig. 2.6, responses indicated by dashed lines were elicited by phrase structure violations.

As was the case with other evidence, ERPs showed differential vulnerabilities to delays in second language immersion. The amplitude and distribution of the N400 response to violations in semantic expectations were not affected by alterations in the timing of second language experience (Fig. 2.5). However, the latency of the N400 was longer (approximately 20 msec) for delays in immersion greater than 11 years, suggesting a slight slowing in processing. In contrast, ERP responses to each of the syntactic violations showed changes in amplitude and distribution, as well as actual presence of ERP components that were related to increased age of second language immersion. For example, for phrase structure violations, the distribution of the negativity increase between 300 and 500 msec poststimulus onset showed increased bilateral distribution with increased second language immersion. That is, with increasing delays of immersion in English, the asymmetry was diminished and increased negativity was observed over both the left and right hemispheres. ERP results for phrase structure violations are shown in Fig. 2.6.

The phrase structure violations also elicited a syntactic positive shift (SPS), as described by Osterhout and Holcomb (1992, 1996), in the latency range of 500 to 700 msec poststimulus onset. The SPS has been thought to index attempts to recover, or "patchup," syntactically anomalous sentences (Canseco et al., 1997). The SPS was observed in the ERPs of unilinguals (Neville et al., 1991) and the bilinguals who were immersed in their second language before the age of 11 (Weber-Fox & Neville, 1996). The mean amplitudes between 500 and 700 msec of the phrase structure difference ERPs (calculated by subtracting the waveforms for the control sentences from those elicited by violations in phrase structure) indicated that for bilinguals immersed in English after 11 years of age, there was no SPS within this latency range (Fig.

SEMANTIC ANOMALY

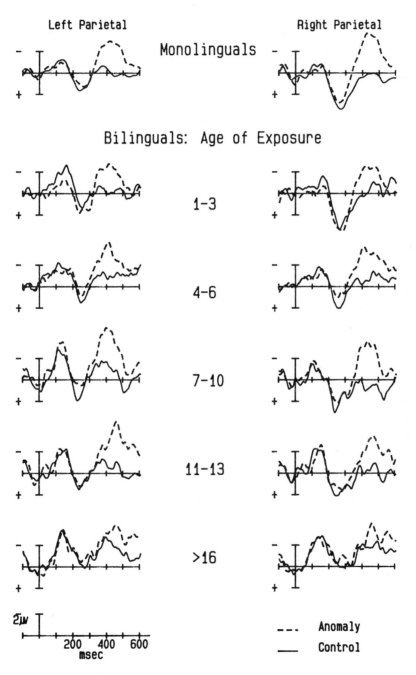

FIG. 2.5. Averaged ERP waveforms, violations of semantic expectation.

PHRASE STRUCTURE VIOLATION

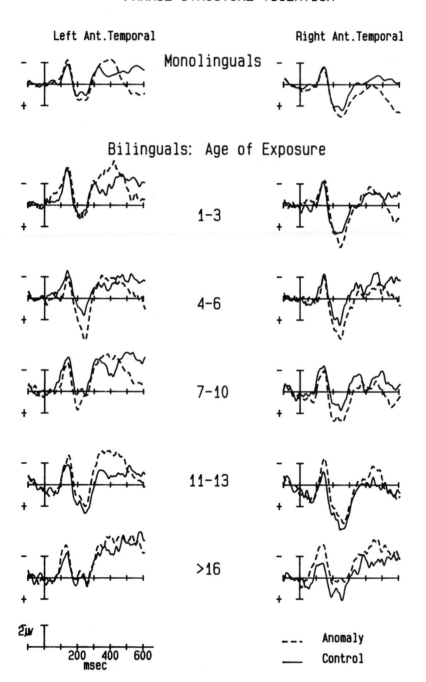

FIG. 2.6. Averaged ERP waveforms, violations of phrase structure expectation.

2.4). Analyses of a later latency window (700 to 900 msec) revealed that the 11 to 13 bilingual group did show an SPS in this later window; however, an SPS was still not evident in the ERPs of the bilingual group with the longest delays in second language learning. So, despite similar years of experience with English, the latest learning bilingual group members appeared to be much slower in their attempts to recover the sentence or perhaps utilized different strategies in interpreting the syntactic anomaly.

In summary, the N400 indices of semantic processing were relatively stable for each of the bilingual groups in terms of amplitude and distribution. However, a latency shift (approximately 20 msec) was noted for the bilingual groups who were immersed in English after 11 years of age, suggesting a slight slowing in processing. In contrast, our results suggested that for syntactic (grammatical) aspects of language, the actual presence and distribution of ERPs may be altered by delays in second language immersion. These results suggested that for processing syntactic anomalies, the ERPs of later learning bilinguals are associated with reduced specialization in the left hemisphere and include increased right hemisphere involvement, in some cases may reflect much slower processing, and overall may reveal differences in the strategies that later learners of English may utilize in the interpretation or recovery of violations of English syntax or grammar.

EFFECTS OF DELAYS ON PROCESSING
OPEN- VERSUS CLOSED-CLASS WORDS

In a second ERP experiment, the EEG was recorded and averaged separately for word types that occurred correctly in read sentences (Weber-Fox & Neville, 1994, 1998). The word types were open- and closed-class words. The open-class words—such as nouns, verbs, and adjectives—convey referential meaning. They are dependent on vocabulary knowledge and primarily related to the semantic content of a sentence. In contrast, the closed-class words—such as articles, conjunctions, and determiners—primarily provide structural or grammatical information in a sentence. Based on behavioral evidence and the ERP results reported earlier, we hypothesized that the neural subsystems postulated to mediate the processing of these two different word classes may be differentially affected by delays in second language immersion.

In normal-hearing adults, the ERP response to open-class words is characterized by a negative component that peaks at 350 msec post word onset (Neville, Mills, & Lawson, 1992). The distribution of this component is bilateral and is largest over posterior areas. In contrast, the ERPs elicited by closed-class words are characterized by a negative peak that occurs earlier (280 msec post word onset) and is lateralized over anterior temporal regions of the left hemisphere. Studies of deaf individuals and children have provided further evidence for the distinctness that characterizes the neural subsystems mediating the processing of open- and closed-class words (Neville, 1994; Neville, Coffey, Holcomb, & Tallal, 1993; Neville et al., 1992). These studies have shown further that the organization of neural subsystems associated with grammatical processing may be more vulnerable to alterations in early language experience, whereas the N350 elicited by open-class words is very similar in deaf and hearing adults. The N280 component is absent or small in deaf individuals who learn English late and imperfectly (Neville et al., 1992). Grammatical subsystems have been found to display a longer developmental time course in children compared with the ERPs for semantic processing (Neville, 1994). It has also been found that the neural subsystems associated with grammatical processing are more vulnerable in language developmental disorders (Neville et al., 1993).

We utilized the same linguistic stimuli employed in the study of monolingual speakers in pursuing the hypothesis that the neural subsystems associated with processing closed-class words (N280) and open-class words (N350) would be differentially affected by alterations in the timing of second language immersion (Weber-Fox & Neville, 1994, 1998). The bilinguals who participated in this second experiment were similar in characteristics to the groups described previously. These were adult Chinese–English bilinguals who were grouped according to the age at which they were immersed in their second language, English.

The ERP results in all groups of bilinguals supported the previous findings that the neural subsystems for processing open- and closed-class words are distinct in timing and distribution. The amplitudes, distributions, and latencies of the N350 elicited by open-class words were similar for all bilingual groups, regardless of age of immersion in their second language. The amplitudes and distributions of the N280 were also similar for all bilingual groups. All bilingual groups showed a similar left-anterior temporal negativity associated with processing closed-class words (Table 2.1). However, increases in delays of second language immersion of as little as 7 years were associated with increases in the peak latency of the N280 response, suggesting a slowing in the processing for these groups of bilinguals. For a detailed description of these findings, see Weber-Fox & Neville (1998).

These additional ERP findings for processing open- and closed-class words are consistent with the previous findings that grammatical or syntactic aspects of language processing appear to be more vulnerable to alterations in the timing of language experience compared to more semantic or lexical processing. These findings also indicate that even later learners of English display left-hemispheric specialization for at

TABLE 2.1
Closed-Class Words: Peak Amplitude
(Mean Microvolts and Standard Error)
in the 215 to 375 Msec Windows.

Group	Left Temporal Site	Right Temporal Site
Monolinguals	−1.803 (.47)	−1.054 (.32)
Bilinguals		
1–3	−1.544 (.54)	−.913 (.45)
4–6	−1.928 (.57)	−.986 (.71)
7–10	−1.120 (.53)	−.050 (.56)
11–13	−2.143 (.45)	−.925 (.61)
>16	−2.503 (.65)	−1.211 (.57)

Note: Measures are shown for the Event-Related Brain Potentials (ERPs) over the left and right temporal sites for monolinguals and each of the bilingual groups.

least some aspects of their second language, including the response to closed-class words. However, the results of the syntactic anomaly processing studies suggest that for some types of grammatical or syntactic processing, this left-hemispheric specialization may be reduced and increased right-hemisphere involvement may occur. Together, these findings suggest that later learners utilize altered neural systems and processing of English syntax.

Our ERP findings suggest a similar anterior left-hemisphere distribution for processing closed-class words for the bilingual groups (with a slight shift in latency noted). Because of the relatively poor spatial resolution of the ERP technique when employed with the number of electrodes in this study (16), it is not possible to determine whether the localization of the N280 within the left-anterior hemisphere differed among the groups. However, based on the recent fMRI and PET (Positron Emission Tomography) data (Kim et al., 1997; Perani et al., 1996), it could be hypothesized that for the later learner (>7 years), there may exist nonoverlapping cortical areas involved in the processing of closed-class word information in their two languages.

In conclusion, converging evidence from behavioral, electrophysiological, and fMRI studies suggests that specialized systems that mediate different aspects of language may be distinct in their susceptibilities to alterations in the timing of second language learning. Our findings are consistent with the hypothesis that the development of at least some neural subsystems for language processing is constrained by maturational changes, even in early childhood. Additionally, our results are compatible, at least in part, with aspects of Lenneberg's (1967) original hypothesis that puberty may mark a significant point in language learning capacity and neural reorganizational capabilities. The maturational constraints we observed were most profound for the bilinguals who learned their second language after puberty. These findings contribute to our understanding of the dynamics of the development of functional neural subsystems for language and carry implications for the design and timing of programs for language education and habilitation.

REFERENCES

Canseco, E., Love, T., Ahrens, K., Walenski, M., Swinney, D., & Neville, H. (1997). Processing of grammatical information in jabberwocky sentences: An ERP study. [Abstract]. *Cognitive Neuroscience Society, 4.*

Freeman, R. D., & Thibos, L. N. (1973). Electrophysiological evidence that abnormal early visual experience can modify the human brain. *Science, 180,* 876–878.

Harwerth, R., Smith, E. Crawford, M., & von Noorden, G. (1986). Multiple sensitive periods in the development of the primate visual system. *Science, 232,* 235–238.

Johnson, J. S., & Newport, E. L. (1989). Critical period effects in second language learning: The influence of maturational state on the acquisition of English as a second language. *Cognitive Psychology, 21,* 60–99.

Kaas, J. H. (1991). Plasticity of sensory and motor maps in adult mammals. *Annual Review of Neuroscience, 14,* 137–167.

Kaas, J. H., Merzenich, M. M., & Killackey, H. P. (1983). The reorganization of somatosensory cortex following peripheral nerve damage in adult and developing mammals. *Annual Review of Neuroscience, 6,* 325–356.

Kim, K. H. S., Relkin, N. R., Lee, K-M., & Hirsch, J. (1997). Distinct cortical areas associated with native and second languages. *Nature, 388* (10), 171–174.

Knudsen, E. (1988). Sensitive and critical periods in the development of sound localization. In S. S. Easter, Jr., K. F. Barald, & B. M. Carlson (Eds.), *From message to mind: Directions in developmental neurobiology* (pp. 303–318). Sunderland, MA: Sinauer Associates.

Lenneberg, E. H. (1967). *Biological foundations of language.* New York: Wiley.

Mayberry, R. I., & Eichen, E. B. (1991). The long-lasting advantage of learning sign language in childhood: Another look at the critical period in language acquisition. *Journal of Memory and Language, 30,* 486–512.

Neville, H. J. (1994), Developmental specificity in neurocognitive development in humans. In M. Gazaniga (Ed.), *The cognitive neurosciences,* (pp. 219–231). Cambridge, MA: MIT Press.

Neville, H. J., Coffey, S. A., Holcomb, P. J., & Tallal, P. (1993). The neurobiology of sensory and language processing in language impaired children. *Journal of Cognitive Neuroscience, 5,* 235–253.

Neville, H. J., Mills, D. L., & Lawson, D. S. (1992). Fractionating language: Different neural subsystems with different sensitive periods. *Cerebral Cortex, 2,* 244–258.

Neville, H. J., Nicol, J. L., Barss, A., Forster, K. I., & Garrett, M. F. (1991). Syntactically based sentence processing classes: Evidence from event-related brain potentials. *Journal of Cognitive Neuroscience, 3,* 151–165.

Newport, E. L. (1988). Constraints on learning and their role in language acquisition: Studies of the acquisition of American Sign Language. *Language Sciences, 10,* 147–172.

Osterhout, L., & Holcomb, P. J. (1992). Event-related brain potentials elicited by syntactic anomaly. *Journal of Memory and Language, 31,* 1–22.

Osterhout, L., & Holcomb, P. J. (1996). Event-related potentials and syntactic anomaly: Evidence of anomaly detection during the perception of continuous speech. *Language and Cognitive Processes, 8,* 413–438.

Oyama, S. (1982). The sensitive period and comprehension of speech. In S. D. Krashen, R. C. Scarcella, & M. H. Long (Eds.), *Child–adult differences in second language acquisition* (pp. 39–51) Rowley, MA: Newbury House.

Patkowski, M. S. (1980). The sensitive period for the acquisition of syntax in a second language. *Language Learning, 30,* 449–472.

Perani, D., Dehaene, S., Grassi, F., Cohen, L., Cappa, S. F., Dupoux, E., Fazio, F., & Mehler, J. (1996). Brain processing of native and foreign languages. *Cognitive Neuroscience and Neurophysiology, 7,* 2439–2444.

Weber-Fox, C. M., & Neville, H. J. (1994). Sensitive periods differentiate neural systems for grammatical and semantic processing: ERP evidence in bilingual speakers. [Abstract]. *Cognitive Neuroscience Society, 18,* 89.

Weber-Fox, C. M. & Neville, H. J. (1996). Maturational constraints on functional specializations for language processing: ERP and behavioral evidence in bilingual speakers. *Journal of Cognitive Neuroscience, 8,* 231–256.

Weber-Fox, C. M. & Neville, H. J. (1998). Neural subsystems for open and closed class words differentially impacted by delays in second-language immersion: ERP evidence in bilingual speakers. Unpublished manuscript, Purdue University.

Wiesel, T., & Hubel, D. (1963). Effects of visual deprivation on morphology and physiology of cells in the cat's lateral geniculate body. *Journal of Neurophysiology, 26,* 978–993.

Wiesel, T., & Hubel, D. (1965). Comparison of the effects of unilateral and bilateral eye closure on cortical unit responses in kittens. *Journal of Neurophysiology, 28,* 1029–1040.

CHAPTER THREE

Co-Evolution of Language Size
and the Critical Period

James R. Hurford
Simon Kirby
University of Edinburgh

INTRODUCTION: GENE–LANGUAGE CO-EVOLUTION

Species evolve, very slowly, through selection of genes that give rise to phenotypes well adapted[1] to their environments. The cultures, including the languages, of human communities evolve much faster, maintaining at least a minimum level of adaptedness to the external, noncultural environment. In the phylogenetic evolution of species, the transmission of information across generations is via copying of molecules, and innovation is by mutation and sexual recombination. In cultural evolution, the transmission of information across generations is by learning, and innovation is by sporadic invention or borrowing from other cultures. This much is the foundational bedrock of evolutionary theory.

But things get more complicated; there can be gene–culture co-evolution.[2] Prior to the rise of culture, the physical environment is the only force shaping biological evolution from outside the organism, and cultures themselves are clearly constrained by the evolved biological characteristics of their members. But cultures become part of the external environment and influence the course of biological evolution. For example, altruistic cultures with developed medical knowledge reduce the cost to the individual of carrying genes disposing to certain

---

[1]Not every property of an organism is adaptive, of course; spandrels do exist.

[2]Although not uncontroversial, the idea of gene–culture co-evolution has been developed in a variety of models, including Lumsden and Wilson (1981) and Boyd and Richerson (1985); Dawkins and Krebs (1984) proposed a co-evolutionary mechanism at the root of the evolution of signaling systems, and Deacon (1992) discussed human brain–language co-evolution in detail.

pathologies (e.g., diabetes); and such genes become more widespread in the populations maintaining such cultures. Assortative mating can affect biological evolution, and particular cultures may influence the factors that are sorted for in mating. (For a careful discussion of the effects of cultural evolution on natural selection, see Cavalli-Sforza & Bodmer, 1971, pp. 774–804.)

This chapter examines mechanisms involved in the co-evolution of a biological trait—the critical period for language acquisition—and a property of human cultures—the size of their languages. A gene–culture interaction is shown that can be described as a kind of symbiosis, but perhaps more aptly as an "arms race." In this introduction, we sketch the basic mechanics of the interaction in very broad terms; the rest of the chapter explains and justifies the details. The implications of our model for second language acquisition are given toward the end of the chapter.

Put simply, the speed at which an individual can learn the language of the community, plus a critical period in which it can be learned (both biologically given), together determine the maximum size of the language the individual can command as an adult. As this is true for all individuals, a limit on the size of the language as it exists in the community, and the typical agespan in which it can be learned, are determined by these biological factors. With no biological mutation and no cultural innovation (e.g., invention or borrowing of novel expressions or even of new constructions), the interaction of biology and culture remains static. But mutation and cultural innovation can give the interaction an interesting dynamic.

Assume a biologically uniform population using a language of a fixed size. Say also that, in this hypothetical situation, the biology and the language are "in harmony," in the sense that all individuals learn at a speed that enables them to learn the community language by the time their critical period elapses. Taking a simple view of "size" (see following discussion), the language fits neatly into the time biologically allotted for its acquisition. In this situation, there is no possibility of any lasting cultural innovation, as nobody would have any spare time within their critical period to acquire anything in addition to the existing language.

Now a biological mutant arises, who can acquire language faster, thus arriving at mastery of the community language some time before puberty. If there is an innovation now (perhaps by the mutant itself), there is at least one individual who can acquire it. If the mutant's relevant faster-language-acquisition genes spread through the community, more people will be able to acquire innovations, and the size of the community's language can expand. But the (now faster) innate learning speed and the critical period still put a limit on the possible size of the community's language.

In what follows, computational simulations of these biocultural mechanisms are described in detail. The key propositions established (which are therefore not built in as assumptions) are the following:

1. There is an evolutionary mechanism locating the age of the end of the critical period at around puberty.

2. The size of the language of a community adjusts itself to coincide with the maximum that can be acquired within the critical period, given the speed at which children can acquire it.

It goes without arguing here that there is a critical period for language acquisition and that it coincides roughly with puberty. Although the critical period for language acquisition in humans varies across individuals, and the mean age of steepest decline in language acquisition capacity is no doubt not exactly at the mean age of puberty (see Long, 1990), we nevertheless believe that the approximate correlation is close enough to warrant exploring possible explanatory mechanisms. This is analogous to noting that the typical cycle of menstruation coincides strikingly with phases of the moon, although in individual women the menstrual cycle may vary and the average period is no doubt not exactly one lunar month (Knight, 1991). In such cases, it it worth seeing whether a proposed explanatory mechanism can withstand criticism.

We give some discussion later of what might count as the size of a language.

PREVIOUS WORK:
CONCLUSIONS AND UNRESOLVED ISSUES

Hurford (1991)

In an earlier article (Hurford, 1991), a mechanism was shown whereby the critical period evolves to fit in the period of life before puberty. Assuming that possession of language confers fitness, it is evolutionarily advantageous to acquire one's whole language before the onset of one's reproductive years. In simulations described in that work, however, the maximum amount of language that could be learned was a postulated value, externally imposed, and not subject to change.

A space of possible genomes was defined, providing for a range of "language acquisition profiles," including many deliberately implausible ones. A given language acquisition profile would specify how much of the whole language (whose size was fixed) the organism could acquire at each stage of its life. Thus, in principle, an organism could be born with an innate disposition to arrange its life history in such a way that language acquisition took place near the end of life. Of course, the space of possibilities also allowed for genomes specifying a concentration of language acquisition capacity near the beginning of life.

A simulated population was set up, endowed with random innate language acquisition profiles, in a simulated environment where the language to be acquired was initially set at zero. Modeling the creative acquisition of language in the absence of (good) exemplars, individuals were able to acquire at least some language, even in an environment with the initial zero level of language, but they could never acquire more language at a given stage in life than was permitted by their innate language acquisition profiles. In this way, through a run of the simulation, the language size could grow, but an artificial ceiling of 10 (notional units) was set; no organism could acquire more than 10 "units" of language.

Selective breeding was organized, in such a way that possession of more language conferred reproductive advantage. The populations always evolved to contain only individuals whose language acquisition capacity was concentrated in the period before puberty. In retrospect, this makes obvious sense, as it pays to have all of any reproductively advantageous trait ready for use on time for the period in life when reproduction is possible (i.e., post puberty). The absence of any language acquisition capacity in post puberty lifestages in the evolved populations was explained, not as an adaptation, but as due to evolutionary mutation pressure. Whereas there is selective pressure to maintain language acquisition capacity in early life, there is no such pressure in later life, because it can be assumed that language has already been acquired by then.[3]

But there was a biasing factor in the arithmetic of the notional numbers used to define language size and the language acquisition profiles. The maximum size of a possible language (the ceiling value mentioned earlier) was set within the limits of what it was possible to acquire within the lifestages before puberty. In principle, a language could be so big that it takes a whole lifetime to learn it, and this possibility was excluded in the simulations of Hurford (1991). If the maximum notional language size had been permitted to vary above the limit of what could be acquired before puberty, then it is still likely that a critical period would have emerged, but a much longer one, culminating, for example, around middle age.

Couched in the terminology of innate language acquisition profiles, the study in Hurford (1991) might have been identified with a particularly nativist view of language acquisition. In fact, however,

---

[3]As Christiansen (1994) crisply noted, "Hurford (1991) also finds the critical period to be a spandrel" (p. 147).

nothing was argued in that study about domain specificity; the same evolutionary mechanism could equally apply to the acquisition of any advantageous skill. That study also said nothing about any maturational factors that might also be involved in language acquisition. This a matter taken up in Elman's article.

Elman (1993)

Elman's approach was not evolutionary, but ontogenetic. He showed, with elegant experiments with the training schedules of neural nets, that an organism whose syntax acquisition resources "start small" can successfully acquire a language with the human-like characteristics of nested long-distance dependencies. A network without the maturational starting small strategy could not be trained to acquire such a language. The starting-small strategy involves concentrating at first only on very short stretches of input and gradually expanding the window of attention to longer and longer stretches. The network learns basic facts about the input language, such as Noun–Verb classification, before it even sees (and risks being confused by) evidence for more complex aspects of linguistic organization, such as long-distance dependencies.

The key to successful learning, in Elman's (1993) study, is the maturational schedule whereby the window of attention (which he called *working memory*) gradually expands. The implication is that this is what happens in children and that the schedule of expansion is nicely timed to allow just the right amount of time at each stage for the acquisition of enough language to provide a firm foundation for the next stage in learning. Elman tried various schedules and found one that worked, given the predefined learning task. Interestingly, it needed a longer period at the first "narrow window" stage than at later stages. Elman's explanation for the existence of a critical period for language acquisition relied on the maturational schedule being built into development. If, as in the tragic case of Genie, a child is given no language input in early life, the maturational schedule expanding the size of the relevant attention span carries on regardless. A person who is only exposed to language abnormally late will not have the advantage of starting small, and will not be able to learn the language.

It might be thought that the two explanations of the critical period just presented (Hurford, 1991, and Elman, 1993) were incompatible rivals, but they are not. Hurford gave an evolutionary mechanism by which (with certain assumptions about language size) the critical period ends near a specific life history event (puberty), but mentioned no psycholinguistic mechanisms relating to the learning process or to the structure of the language being learned. Elman's study, on the other hand, made specific and interesting proposals about the relation of the learning process to linguistic structure but did not deal at all with the life history timing of the maturational schedule that he invoked and proposed no evolutionary mechanism. The two accounts are complementary. It is suggested in Hurford (1998) that the two accounts could in fact be combined; evolutionary processes giving rise to the kind of maturational schedule that Elman (1993) described could be sought, and one could attempt to show how such a schedule becomes calibrated to relate to crucial life history events, such as puberty. This is what the next study does.

Kirby and Hurford (1997)

This study assumes the relation between incremental learning of language and the steady expansion of a resource, such as Elman's (1993) working memory. That it, is is assumed that for each stage of language learning to be successful, the previous stage must have been successfully completed, and the resource drawn on by the learning mechanism, the working memory, must be expanded one notch to the right size for the next stage to begin. Kirby and Hurford (1997) examined the evolutionary processes by which this expansion of resource could be programmed into development; it used computer simulations of evolution.

The simulations defined a population with life history characteristics of birth, puberty, and death; reproduction was only possible after puberty, and the probability of thus passing on one's genes was related to the amount of language the prospective parent had acquired. In the simulations, evolution was given two different ways of expressing the expansion of working memory: as a function of chronological age or as a function of exposure to input (or as some mixture of these two). The structure of the simulated genome allowed in principle for the construction of various phenotypes. In one possible phenotype, the maturation of language-relevant working memory was tied to chronological age; in another possible phenotype, the expansion of working memory was triggered by language input; and various mixed possibilities were also allowed. One such (hypothetical) mixed strategy, for example, would be an individual whose working memory expansion was triggered by chronological age early in life, but by exposure to language later in life.

What emerged from these simulations was a mixed genome, in which expansion of working memory is triggered by exposure to language early in life and by chronological age later in life. In other words, with such a genome, some slight delay in exposure to language would not be disastrous; the expansion of working memory could wait around for a while, during childhood, and it would be possible for a child starting to learn language somewhat late to catch up. Too great a delay would be disastrous, as sooner or later, the age-determined expansion of working memory would kick in and take working memory to a size where the possibility of starting small had disappeared. The evolved genomes in this study all encoded a switch from input-sensitive expansion of the resource to age-related expansion. In some conditions, this switch even happened to coincide with puberty.

The switch from input sensitivity to age-related growth did not coincide with puberty in all the simulations. Instead, it coincided with a time in life history that was a construct of various parameters chosen for the running of the simulations. In all these simulations, as with the earlier study (Hurford, 1991), an arbitrarily chosen size for language was fixed. Also fixed was a measure of "input quality," simulating a degree of unreliability in the environment. This variable could be set, for example, at 50%, expressing the fact that a learner had only a 50% chance of actually getting any language input at a particular lifestage. The actual number of lifestages taken to acquire the full language was a function of language size and input quality. Naturally, individuals exposed to more language, or exposed to the same amount of language less reliably, learned it more slowly. For example, to learn a language of notional size 10 at 50% input quality would take 20 lifestages; to learn a language of notional size 9 at input quality 75% would take 12 (= 9 divided by 0.75) lifestages. Systematic variation of these parameters, independent of the age set for puberty, showed that the critical period emerged at the age of typical acquisition of full language and not necessarily always at puberty.

A clear graphic way of depicting a critical period effect is with a graph of final attainment against length of deprivation. Figure 3.1 is one such graph. This figure shows the results of four different runs of the simulations. In these runs, the language size was set at 7 units and the input quality was set at 0.5 (50%). With this language size and this input quality, the expectation is that with normal exposure, one will acquire one's whole language by the end of the 14th lifestage. The four curves give the predicted results of simulated Genie-experiments on individuals with the genome that evolved in the main (nondeprived-environment) simulations. They show that with deprivation of language input up to the end of the 14th lifestage, the expected attainment is close to zero. What is important to note for our purposes here is that these four runs were conducted with puberty set at very different lifestages, 5, 10, 15, and 20; Figure 3.1 shows no effect of puberty on the expected end of the critical period.

In Kirby and Hurford's (1997) study, the lifestage at which normal language acquisition is complete is a construct derivative of language size; in the simulations, language size is simply given, and the critical

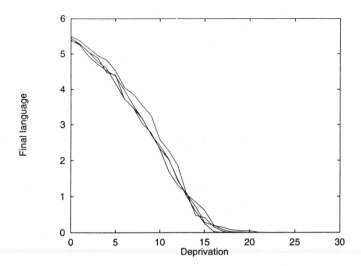

FIG. 3.1. How language competence declines with age of initial exposure to a
language.

period evolves to coincide with this construct. This is an example of
the Baldwin Effect (Baldwin, 1896; Hinton & Nowlan, 1987), by which
the presence of learning can in fact guide phylogenetic evolution. In an
environment stable over millennia, some constant aspect of the learning
process becomes innate. In this case, the constant aspect of the learning
process that gets biologized is its timing in relation to life history.

HOW IS THE SIZE OF A LANGUAGE FIXED?

What comes out of these previous studies is that the evolutionary
emergence of a critical period can be modeled, but so far all models
suffer from two related defects, namely:

1. No strongly convincing mechanism is shown linking the critical
    period to puberty without building in a fixed ("God-given," as it
    were) quantity for language size. Hurford (1991) did show that,
    given a certain assumption about language size, the critical
    period evolves to fit within puberty. But on the other hand,
    Kirby and Hurford (1997) showed that if this fixed quantity is

varied, then the critical period can be systematically "made" to evolve at lifestages other than puberty.

2. No suggestions are made at all regarding how the size of a language can become fixed, or evolve.

Languages exist in communities. The language acquired by children of one generation is the language that they, in their turn, transmit to the children of the next generation. Transmission is not always perfect, of course, as languages evolve over the course of history. The approach we take here is that the size of a language is also an aspect that is held in the community and is subject to the slight changes with each generation that accumulate to constitute the history of the language. As with other features of a language, its size has to pass through the filter of language acquirers in each generation. If (hypothetically) a language were too big for the innate language acquisition device to cope with, its size would not be preserved into the next generation, just as a (hypothetical) language containing an impossibly complex construction would not be faithfully transmitted to the next generation. Indeed, the size of a language can be thought of as the total of all its complexities.

Linguists usually believe that no language is, overall, any more complex than any other. Admittedly, no metric exists to test this common assumption, but it is one that we accept here. But although languages may not vary in their overall complexity (read "size"), it is well known that languages vary in the complexity of their subsystems. Some languages, for example, have no numeral system at all but may have complex kinship naming systems; a language may have a very complex case system but a relatively simple aspect system; or a rich lexical tone system with simple phonotactics; or complex constraints on word order but no case system; and so on. We claim that a language in which all the most complex subsystems were put together would be unviable, for a combination of psychological and social reasons. Imagine a language with rich Arabic template-type derivational morphology; a set of noun suffixes as detailed as those of Finnish; vowel harmony as in Turkish; a lexical tone system as rich as that of Cantonese; consonantal phonotactics as permissive as Russian; as many vowel distinctions as British English; the click phoneme inventory of a Khoisan language, such as Nama; pharyngeals, uvulars, velars, palatals, palato-alveolars, alveolo-palatals, alveolars, dentals, labiodentals, and bilabials; three degrees of voicing; a combined aspect–mood system as complex as that of Navaho; both head marking and dependent marking; a rich system of deixis as in Inuit; singular, dual, paucal, and plural number; as many noun classes as a Bantu language; four varieties of past tense; definite and indefinite conjugations as in Hungarian; mixed ergativity; switch reference; . . .

That would be an impossibly large language; the reasons for its impossibility would be a combination of the social and the psychological. It would put a heavy burden on the acquirer, and the communicative load of much of its complexity would be relatively low, as messages would be massively redundant.

The sense in which, we claim, the size of a language is "held in the community" does not rely on an ontological category such as (Durkheimian) social fact. The size of a language can be taken to be (depending on one's purpose) the average, or the maximum, of the language competences stored in the heads of individuals in the community and expressed by them in behavior. In a similar way, one could talk about the average loudness, or the average pitch, or the average speed in syllables per second, of the voices of individuals in a crowd. The set of language competences acquired by the individuals in one generation determines their linguistic output, which is the basis of the language acquisition by the next generation.

In the next section, we describe the implementation of a model in which language size is not imposed by the programmer but is determined by the (simulated) biological factors involved in language acquisition and the (simulated) social–historical factors involved in the constant cycle of acquisition and retransmission of language to the next generation. In this model, language size is constantly adjusted during the history of a community. Given a particular innate speed of language acquisition and a socially presented language of a particular size, there is a typical age for complete language acquisition. Previous results, summarized earlier (Kirby & Hurford, 1997), showed that the biologically given critical period for language acquisition tracks the age of complete language acquisition. The outcome is that the end of the critical period approximates to the age of puberty.

NEW SIMULATIONS

The explanatory scheme for this work is given in Fig. 3.2. In this diagram:

- The heavily outlined boxes represent genetically encoded properties of human language acquirers;

- The lightly outlined boxes represent social processes or constructs, which occur or exist in the social communities of language users.

- The heavy arrows represent phylogenetic evolutionary processes, determined by natural selection.

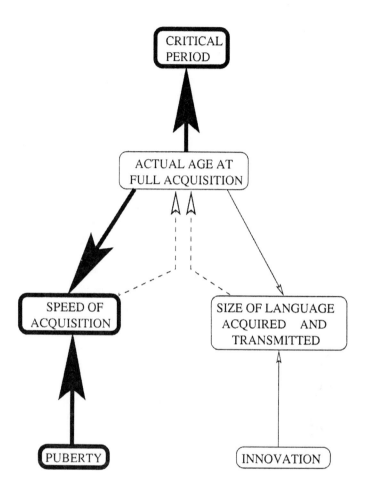

FIG. 3.2. Co-evolution mechanism for speed of acquisition and language size.

- The light arrows represent social processes, operating within the social communities of language users.

- The dashed arrows represent a logical definitional relation.[4]

---

[4]One should not get too carried away by "box and arrow" diagrams; they are expository schemes intended to clarify the issues involved. There are alternative ways of schematizing any domain with boxes and arrows. We hope our way illuminates the problem area.

Two of the boxes in Fig. 3.2 have no arrows entering them. These two, puberty and innovation, are taken as given in this study and are not explained. But a few words about each are in order.

Puberty is the biological lifestage after which an organism is capable of reproduction. We assume that the age of puberty evolved long ago in our prehominid ancestors, well before language entered the picture. A given age of puberty is the biological foundation on which our explanations rest.

Innovation is a social force (operating within biological constraints, of course) by which individuals may sporadically introduce new social constructs into their communities. In the linguistic domain, a tiny example of innovation would be the coining of a new word; a more substantial innovation would be the "invention" of a new grammatical construction. We assume that innovation is possible, but rare. Without innovation by individuals there could be no mechanism by which the social constructs we know as languages could have arisen. An innovation, although originating with an individual, needs to be adopted by the community as a whole. It is not necessary for our argument that innovations adopted by the community be functional, but it seems natural to assume that they are. We also assume that the effect of an innovation is to increase the size of a language, that is, in effect, to place a greater burden on subsequent acquirers of the community's historically evolving language.

The remaining four boxes in Fig. 3.2 all have arrows entering them. The arrows entering a box all, in some sense, explain its contents. We deal with each explanandum box, or factor, in turn, in separate subsections. The first two factors discussed, age at acquisition and the critical period, can be dealt with quite briefly. Our main focus is on the mechanisms explaining the other two factors, speed of acquisition and size of language.

Actual Age at Acquisition

By definition, the variables *size of language acquired* and speed of *acquisition* give the *actual age at full acquisition*, at any stage in history. This is not an empirical claim, but merely a tautology; just as in a physical situation Time = Distance/Speed, so here Acquisition Age = Size/Speed. This is the most elementary part of our story, with which there can be no argument, with the one obvious reservation that if Size/Speed is greater than Age at Death, then Acquisition Age = Age at Death.

Our model shows the co-evolution of the two variables, size of language and speed of acquisition. The factor mediating their co-evolution is their joint outcome, age at acquisition. They co-evolve in such a way as to keep age at acquisition close to puberty, as shown. The dotted arrows in Fig. 3.2 show this relation, whereby speed of acquisition and size of language simply define the age by which language is acquired.

Critical Period

The connection between age at acquisition and the critical period is a result argued for in detail in Kirby and Hurford (1997). We summarized the work leading to this result in a previous section and we simply assume it here. The heavy arrow leading into the Critical Period box in Fig. 3.2 represents this correlation between age at acquisition and the critical period. To accept this correlation is not to build in a solution to our problem. On the contrary, it is precisely this correlation that seems to be our problem, as Kirby and Hurford (1997) showed that the critical period can be made to vary independently of puberty, given various settings of language size and the average rate at which it is acquired.

Speed of Acquisition

The heavy arrows into the Speed of Acquisition box in Fig. 3.2 show an evolutionary effect of puberty and actual age of language acquisition. There is phylogenetic evolutionary pressure to adapt speed of acquisition so that actual completion of full acquisition, for a language of a given size, occurs by puberty. This gives an evolved lower bound on speed of acquisition. We now describe simulations modeling this effect.

For a simulated population, facts including the following were defined:

- Size of population: 50 individuals

- Age of death: 40 lifestages

- Age of puberty: variously 6.5, 12.5, and 18.5 lifestages

- Initial language maximum size: various, from 10 to 1000 units

- Initial speed of acquisition: various, from 0 to 5 units per lifestage

Fifty is a large enough population size for this kind of simulation; larger numbers would not change the outcome. The scale of lifestages by which death and puberty are defined was chosen to be reminiscent of years. Puberty, an immutable genetic property of individuals, was set at various ages, so that an effect of the age of acquisition relating to puberty could be demonstrated. The puberty numbers are the halfway points between the last lifestage at which an individual could not reproduce and the first lifestage at which he or she could. The initial language maximum size was simply an arbitrary number used to get the simulations started. The maximum language size changed constantly during the course of the simulations, determined by the greatest size of language acquired by any adult in the population, at any given cycle in the simulation. The speed of acquisition was a genetically encoded property of each individual, inherited from a parent, and subject to sporadic mutation in newborns after initialization of the simulation; this property was represented as a single number.

The simulations went through cycles, outlined briefly as follows (some details will be elaborated later):

1. Individuals at lifestage 40 die.

2. A subset (usually 25%) of the adult population (i.e., those past puberty) are selected as prospective parents for the next generation. This selection is made on the basis of how much language the individuals have acquired at the time.

3. Parents are selected at random from this elite subset and breed sexually, producing enough new individuals to keep the population constant. At this point, there is a small chance of a random mutation, so that speed of acquisition in the genes of a newborn may differ from that of the parents.

4. Language acquisition: Any individual whose language is not yet at the maximum established by the community acquires as much language as his genetically given speed of acquisition will allow in one lifestage, up to the limit of the community maximum.

5. All individuals advance one lifestage.

To show how language size is affected during the simulation, we give an example with some specific numbers. Take a case where the initial (arbitrary) language size is set at 1000 units and the individuals are genetically endowed with an acquisition speed of 5 units per lifestage. An individual newborn at the beginning of a run has 40 lifestages ahead, during each of which just 5 units of language can be acquired. This individual will live for 40 lifestages, acquiring language throughout life (in this artificial initial situation). At the end of this individual's life, she will have acquired a language of size 200 (5 x 40), and 200 now becomes the maximum language size in the community. No subsequent individual can acquire any more than 200 units of language.

Alternatively, take the case where the initial (arbitrary) language maximum size is set relatively low, say at 10 units, with the same initial innate speed of acquisition in all individuals, 5 units per lifestage. In this case, all individuals will acquire the full language by the second lifestage. In this version of the simulation, the maximum language size will remain fixed at 10 for the rest of the run.

This fixing of the maximum community language size happens rapidly, of course, always within the first 40 cycles of a run; it is still something of an artifact, being either the initial arbitrary language size or the product of the initial genetically given speed of acquisition and age at death, which ever is the lesser. In the simulations described in this subsection, language size gets rapidly fixed in this manner in the very first cycles of a run and does not change further during a long run. In the next subsection, we show how the introduction of an "innovation" factor allows language size to change constantly during a simulation. But now we focus on how the speed of acquisition may change to affect age at acquisition.

As the simulation progresses, mutants arise whose innate speed of acquisition is either faster or slower than that of the rest of the population. Assuming the community maximum language size is still such that it takes nonmutant individuals a whole lifetime to acquire it, a mutant slower acquirer will get to the end of life without acquiring the whole language. At any stage in life, such a mutant slow acquirer will possess less language than his lifestage cohorts and will be relatively disadvantaged in the competition for selection for parenthood. (If, most improbably, such a slow-acquirer mutant gene were to wholly invade the population, then the community maximum language size would, of course, drop to the size acquirable within a lifetime by such a population of slow learners.) By contrast, a mutant fast acquirer will acquire the whole community language before the last lifestage and throughout life be at a relative advantage in the competition to be a parent. Such faster mutant genes are likely to spread through the population. But, as there is (so far) no mechanism for increasing the size of the community's language, the mean age at which the whole language is acquired will be reduced.

The competition to be a parent takes place among those who have passed puberty. In that adult population, individuals who have relatively more language will be at an advantage. Thus, there is selection pressure in favor of genes which will speed up language acquisition to acquire the whole language before puberty. Speed of acquisition adapts to be at least fast enough to get the job done before puberty. There is nothing to prevent speed of acquisition from becoming (by mutation) even faster, so that language acquisition could be complete well before puberty, but there is no pressure on prepuberty individuals to learn any faster than they need in order to be finished in time for their entry into the mating competition.

These effects, which occurred in our simulations, are shown in Figs. 3.3 to 3.5.

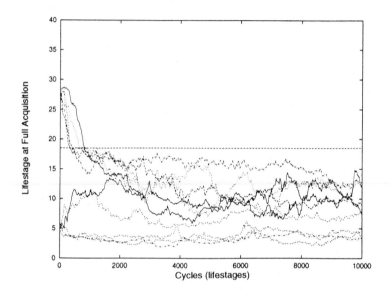

FIG. 3.3. Age at acquisition settles and walks randomly below puberty (18.5).

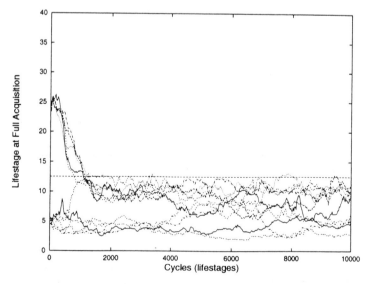

FIG. 3.4. Age at acquisition settles and walks randomly below puberty (12.5).

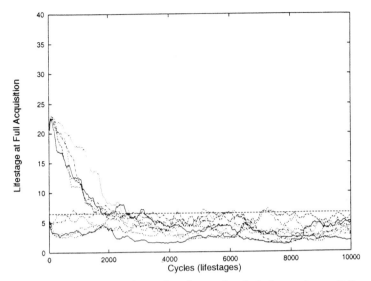

FIG. 3.5. Age at acquisition settles and walks randomly below puberty (6.5).

Each of these figures shows the population's average lifestage at complete language acquisition, as it evolved through 10,000 cycles of a simulation. Each figure shows 10 separate runs, 5 runs with an initial high language size and 5 runs with an initial low language size. Each figure shows runs with puberty set at a different level (18.5, 12.5, 6.5). In all cases, it can be seen that where language size started high, the average lifestage at full language acquisition was well above puberty but quickly dropped, by selection pressure on speed of acquisition, to below puberty. Once the average lifestage of full language acquisition was below puberty (or if it had started below puberty), it simply wandered randomly (due to the effects of random mutations), there being no pressure on prepuberty individuals to acquire language any faster.

So far, then, we have half of the story. We showed (a model of) speed of language acquisition evolving in such a way that the average age of acquisition is below puberty. And we showed how language size can be stored in the community, acquired, and retransmitted by successive generations. So far the only demonstrated effect on language size is the relatively trivial constraint that it cannot be greater than any individual can learn within a lifetime. But we have shown how this upper bound on language size plays a role in the co-evolutionary process whereby language size and speed of learning are together adjusted so that language is learned by puberty. We have not yet shown what prevents the average age of language acquisition from wandering well below the age of puberty, as it does in many of the runs shown in Figures 3.3 to 3.5. We will fill these gaps in the next subsection.

Size of Language Acquired and Transmitted

We postulate that innovative potential, fueled by social and communicative considerations, provides pressure to increase the size of language acquired. In a second version of our simulations, we added this factor of innovation. All other conditions remained as before, but now an individual who had acquired the full language of the community was permitted, at very rare intervals, to add to the language by a small increment. In this way, the language of the community actually expanded.

We now have two factors at work: a biological factor of mutation affecting speed of acquisition, and a social factor of innovation periodically increasing the size of the language to be acquired. Fast learner mutants are advantaged, up until the point where language is acquired by puberty, as we have seen. Consider a population with a uniform evolved speed of acquisition such that the community language is acquired just by puberty. Now, if the language size increases, the age of language acquisition for all individuals will increase to an age above puberty. A new mutant, with an even faster speed of language acquisition, will now have an advantage, and this mutation will tend to spread through the population.

In our simulations, we made innovation a constant force, exerting constant upward pressure on language size. Thus, for a population with an evolved speed of acquisition such that all individuals acquire the language well before puberty, this upward pressure on language size will tend to make the age at acquisition rise (because there is more to acquire). So long as the age at acquisition stays below puberty, biological selection pressure will not react to this, by speeding up acquisition, as only adults are involved in the selection process. Biological selection pressure to speed up language acquisition only bites where the language size has increased to such a size that it cannot be completely acquired by puberty.

The results of these simulations are shown in Figures 3.6 to 3.8, again with puberty set at various ages—18.5, 12.5, and 6.5. As before, these figures plot average age at acquisition against time (in cycles of the simulation). These graphs each show the results of five separate runs. In these runs, the initial language size was set low, so that initially, age at full acquisition was well below puberty.

There is a clear tendency for age of acquisition initially to rise, due to the slow but constant force of innovation, which enlarges the target language of acquirers. During this initial phase, the genetically given

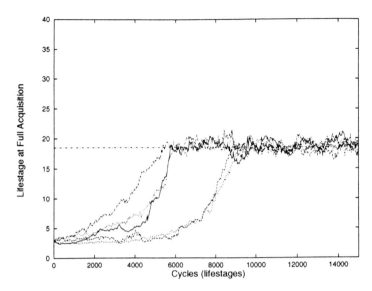

FIG. 3.6. Language size expands and age of acquisition settles at puberty (18.5).

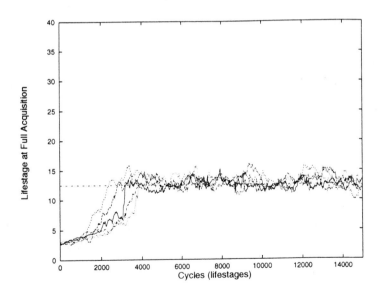

FIG. 3.7. Language size expands and age of acquisition settles at puberty (12.5).

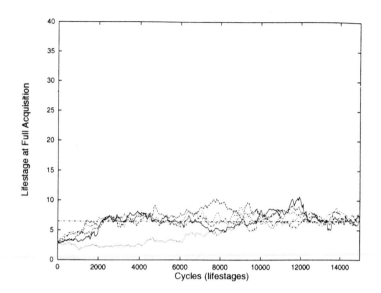

FIG. 3.8. Language size expands and age of acquisition settles at puberty (6.5).

speed of acquisition is under no selection pressure. When the language size reaches the point where Size/Speed = Puberty, biological selection begins to bite, and an "arms race" between language size and speed of acquisition begins, keeping age of acquisition near the age of puberty.

Figures 3.6 to 3.8 should be compared with the previous Figs. 3.3 to 3.5. The random walk below puberty in the earlier figures is replaced in the later figures by a balancing act in which counterposed forces (biological speed of acquisition and social innovation) keep age of full language acquisition near puberty.

A final figure, Fig. 3.9, plots speed, language size, and acquisition age on a log scale, taking results from a single run. The x axis of this graph gives time (in cycles of the simulation). The y axis actually represents several different kinds of quantities, measured in different units. The numbers on the y axis (0.1, 1, 10, 100) express age, in lifestages; the straight line at 12.5 expresses the age of puberty on this scale; the curve for acquisition age, which rises to about 12.5 and then flattens out, is also drawn to this numerical scale. Innovation increases language size exponentially, as shown by the straight diagonal line sloping upward from 10; this line expresses the size of the language in notional units (not lifestages). The lower curve plots speed of acquisition in terms of units per lifestage.

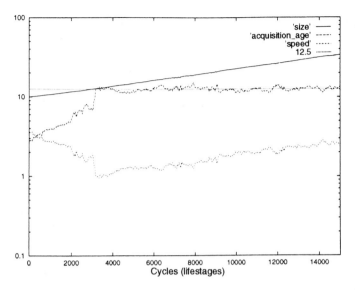

FIG. 3.9. Size increases: When age of acquisition hits puberty, speed also increases (log scale).

The significant point to note in Fig. 3.9 is the relation between the curves for speed and age at acquisition. The curve for speed starts in this case by wandering downward; simultaneously, the curve for age at acquisition moves upward, due both to the (intentionally) slowly increasing language size and the (so far, randomly) decreasing speed of acquisition. At exactly the point where the curve for age at acquisition moves above the puberty line at 12.5 lifestages (at around 3,200 cycles), the curve for speed of acquisition responds by turning upward, and from then on it follows an upward course essentially parallel to the curve of language size. Of these two parallel curves—size and speed—one is straight (on this log scale) and the other is wiggly. This is because in this simulation, innovation proceeded with a very regular beat and always in the same upward direction; the biological mutations for speed were also introduced at completely regular intervals, but the direction of mutation (acceleration or deceleration) was chosen randomly, and the progress of any particular mutant gene through the population was affected by the random processes involved in the simulated sexual reproduction. Somewhat different treatments could have been adopted, but there is no reason to suppose that the outcome would have been significantly different.

There is a coincidence in Fig. 3.9 that is <u>not</u> significant. The fact that the acquisition-age and speed curves change direction at more or less exactly the time when the size curve crosses the puberty line is not at all significant. Size and puberty are measured differently: size in units, puberty in lifestages. This is an accident of the scaling of the size numbers. In similar diagrams from other runs, this coincidence does not occur.

To summarize this section and express our central point, (a) language size evolves socially, by innovation; (b) speed of acquisition evolves biologically by natural selection; and (c) the two evolutionary processes coordinate in such a way that

$$\frac{Size}{Speed} \approx Puberty.$$

The implications for second language acquisition of the models developed in Kirby and Hurford (1997) and in the present chapter can be summarized as follows. The effect of applying language-acquisition resources to a first language, early in life, is to build up a store of knowledge about the language acquired. The knowledge of a first language might now be considered an additional resource, which can be deployed in the acquisition of a second language. It is, however, theoretically clarifying to distinguish between two different kinds of "resource," that is, between the facility for processing data and turning it into (more) knowledge, on the one hand, and actual knowledge of language, on the other. The model of Kirby and Hurford (1997) showed the likely evolution of a certain kind of genetic control over the processing facility subserving language acquisition. This form of control dictates that exposure to language early in life alters the parameters of this facility, making it progressively more adapted to acquisition of the higher reaches of linguistic knowledge, but probably, following Elman's and Newport's ideas on "starting small" and "less is more," less well adapted to the demands of beginning a new language. It is an open, and empirical, question to what extent the acquired knowledge of a first language can substitute for the lost processing facility. To the extent that a second language is similar to the first language acquired, the amount of knowledge to be gained by the second language acquirer is diminished. The adult second language acquirer has less to learn, but has impoverished processing resources with which to learn.

The main consequence of the model developed in this chapter for second language acquisition, as for first language acquisition, concerns the life-history timing of the switch away from the early facility with language input. It shows how a co-evolutionary process can be expected to define the age at which one becomes an adult language learner to coincide closely with the age at which one becomes reproductively adult. Onset of sexual maturity is not logically connected with language acquisition capacity; this chapter has shown the possibility of an evolutionary connection.

IN CONCLUSION

It might be thought that the issues discussed here are something of a specialism. The notions of language size and speed of acquisition are barely discussed in such general terms as they are here. Although we have been utterly unspecific about the details of exactly what structures children acquire, and at what stages in development, our model deals with the fundamental dimensions of human language. The introductory literature on both generative grammar and language acquisition always stresses the impressive richness (complexity, size) of the competence acquired and the impressive speed of acquisition. Naturally, speed and size are never quantified—just asserted to be impressive, as indeed they are. This raw speed and size are what language acquisition is fundamentally all about; they are what makes the subject so important. Detailed studies of language acquisition never engage in discussion of raw speed and size, just as practicing terrestrial mapmakers do not preface their maps with discussion of the fundamental dimensions North–South and East–West. The geographic dimensions are given by the nature of the earth's rotation controlled by a balance of physical forces. We proposed that the linguistic dimensions of size and speed evolved to maintain a balance between natural selection for greater advantage by breeding age and social construction of systems with greater representational power.

The model we presented is clearly idealized in a number of ways, as are all such models. We aimed to capture the mechanism central to language evolution. This model differs from a common early type of model of language evolution (e.g., Hurford, 1991, 1998). Early models treated the evolution of the language capacity as a biological phenomenon essentially unaffected by any changes in the cultural environment created by the community of language users. Clearly, such interactions of the biological and social have to be treated with caution. For one thing, it is essential to try to ascertain whether the rates at which the biological and social processes happen can be coordinated in the ways suggested. At present, our notion of language size is so simple, and our knowledge of the genetic contribution to speed of learning so incomplete, that this study remains highly speculative.

Venturing to speculate even further, our kind of model of gene–language co-evolution might conceivably hold some potential for explaining the spectacularly fast increase in brain size between the australopithecines and ourselves. The essential idea would be that by some potential for culturo-linguistic innovation, a new, nonphysical type of environment (rudimentary languages) arose, susceptible to change at a much faster rate than the physical environment, which had previously been paramount in steering the course of evolution. No correlation between brain size and language size is likely to be straightforward, but it would be surprising if there were no correlation at all.

Culture in the modern era is evolving at a much faster rate than at any previous stage. The 20th century, in particular, has seen dramatic changes in the human (largely human made) environment. Even if the rates of biological and social evolution were ever coordinated in the way our model proposes, it is quite possible that they have become uncoordinated in the modern era. If we include acquisition of the conventions of written language as part of language acquisition, modern language acquisition takes longer than the time to puberty (see Miller & Weinert, 1998). This may be an instance of cultural evolution racing along so fast that it is now impossible for biological evolution to adapt.

Our model depicts a self-feeding spiral of language size responding to increases in speed of acquisition and speed of acquisition in turn responding to increased language size. Where will it end? It cannot go on for ever. At some stage, considerations external to the closed system of our model will exert an influence. Language acquisition cannot be speeded up indefinitely; there must be some cost. Languages will not expand indefinitely in size; there must be some principle of diminishing returns for increased size. It is possible that the evolution of human language in the modern age has reached the point where such external factors of cost and benefit, which we have not modeled, have come into play.

ACKNOWLEDGMENTS

This work was supported by two fellowships at the Collegium Budapest Institute for Advanced Study, and by Economic and Social Research Council research grant R000326551. We thank our colleagues at the Collegium Budapest, Eörs Szathmary and Axel Kowald for their helpful input.

REFERENCES

Baldwin, J. M. (1896). A new factor in evolution. *American Naturalist, 30,* 441–451.
Boyd, R., & Richerson, P. J. (1985). *Culture and the evolutionary process.* Chicago: University of Chicago Press.
Cavalli-Sforza, L. L., & Bodmer, W. F. (1971). *The genetics of human populations.* San Francisco: Freeman.

Christiansen, M. H. (1994). *Infinite languages, finite minds: Connectionism, learning and linguistic structure.* Doctoral dissertation, University of Edinburgh, Scotland.

Dawkins, R., & Krebs, J. R. (1984). Animal signals: Mind-reading and manipulation. In J.R. Krebs & N.B. Davies (Eds.), *Behavioral ecology: An evolutionary approach* (2nd ed., pp. 380–402). Oxford, England: Blackwell.

Deacon, T. W. (1992). Brain-language coevolution. In J.A. Hawkins & M. Gell-Mann (Eds.), *The evolution of human languages* (Proceedings Vol. XI, Santa Fe Institute Studies in the Sciences of Complexity, pp. 49–83). Redwood City, CA: Addison-Wesley.

Elman, J. L. (1993). Learning and development in neural networks: The importance of starting small. *Cognition, 48,* 71–99.

Hinton, G., & Nowlan, S. (1987). How learning can guide evolution. *Complex Systems, 1,* 495–502.

Hurford, J. R. (1991). The evolution of the critical period for language acquisition. *Cognition, 40,* 159–201.

Hurford, J. R. (1998). Functional innateness: Explaining the critical period for language acquisition. *Proceedings of the UWM Linguistics Symposium on Functionalism and Formalism.* Amsterdam: Benjamins.

Kirby, S., & Hurford, J. R. (1997). The evolution of incremental learning: Language, development and critical periods. Manuscript submitted for publication. Available as University of Edinburgh Occasional Paper in Linguistics EOPL-97-2, http://www.ling.ed.ac.uk/~eopl.

Knight, C. (1991). *Blood relations: Menstruation and the origins of culture.* New Haven, CT: Yale University Press.

Long, M. (1990). Maturational constraints on language development. *Studies in Second Language Acquisition, 12,* 251–285.

Lumsden, C. J., & Wilson, E. O. (1981). *Genes, mind, and culture: The coevolutionary process.* Cambridge, MA: Harvard University Press.

Miller, J., & Weinert, R. (1998). *Spontaneous spoken language.* Oxford, England: Oxford University Press.

CHAPTER FOUR

Critical Periods
and (Second) Language Acquisition:
Divide et Impera

Lynn Eubank
University of North Texas
Kevin R. Gregg
St. Andrew's University, Osaka

PRELIMINARIES

Does the critical period (CP) phenomenon have an effect on the acquisition by adults of second language (L2) competence? We believe it does; but we also believe that most discussions of the phenomenon in hte L2 literature are far too imprecise to be of much value. The imprecision begins at the most fundamental level, with basic presuppositions about language itself. Thus, we begin our discussion by laying some groundwork.

The Modularity of Mind—The Modularity of Language

To start with, we assume a modular view of the mind–brain in general and of linguistic competence in particular. That is, we assume that there are various, relatively autonomous, mental faculties—memory, face recognition, visual perception, and so forth—and that these may also be broken down further into (perhaps less mutually autonomous) subfaculties—short-term memory, episodic memory, and so forth. Similarly, we assume that linguistic competence (i.e., knowledge) is relatively autonomous from other forms of competence on the one hand and includes various relatively autonomous competences on the other. The fact that in normal life, for normal people, these competences work together to form an apparently seamless, unitary *knowledge of language* should not blind one to the possibility—for us, the strong likelihood—that in fact *language* is a folk-psychological cover term, a house with many mansions, and perhaps a few outbuildings as well.

It is thus for us highly likely that only some subcomponents of language are subsumed to any significant degree by domain-specific hardwiring[1] laid down prenatally as an effect of genetic specialization. One might imagine, for instance, that (parts of) what is sometimes called *pragmatic competence* are not so subsumed. Gricean principles, for instance, may be exponents of genetic hardwiring, but not specifically of linguistic hardwiring. In other areas of pragmatic competence, one would expect a good deal of variation both between and within speech communities, in response to heterogeneous stimuli from the environment. This is different from what one finds with those subcomponents that are subsumed to a significant degree by predisposition: Here, responses to heterogeneous environmental stimuli vary between speech communities but not within. More generally, our assumption here is that the native speaker's implicit knowledge of (morpho)phonology and (morpho)syntax—what we refer to henceforth as the native speaker's competence—is the result of an intricate interplay between domain-specific, hardwired machinery and stimuli from the periphery. By periphery, we mean both the extrasomal world and those parts of the body other than the relevant specifically linguistic mechanisms in the brain.[2]

Our position, then, is that in fact *Language* is not a natural kind or category, but an epiphenomenon, and hence not a proper subject for scientific investigation.[3] It should of course follow from this point of view that we have a very simple answer to our question: Of course there is no critical period for language acquisition, because there is no such thing as Language for there to be a critical period for. Nor is this intended facetiously; we wish to stress that discussions of the CP

---

[1]With some reluctance, we are using the term *hardwired* as a convenient way of characterizing brain functions that are fairly narrowly determined genetically, as opposed to those that are much more dependent on, hence liable to variation according to, the environment. We realize, of course, that there is often more plasticity, at least early in development, than the term *hardwired* suggests; see Neville (1995) for some examples from human perception.

[2]We stress here that the term *periphery* includes both intrasomal and extrasomal stimuli; the stimulus could be some hormone produced elsewhere in the body, some signal from neurons elsewhere in the brain, or input originating outside the body, such as linguistic input.

[3]We recognize that this is not a universally accepted position, but we are not convinced by the sorts of holistic arguments offered in the language acquisition literature (see, e.g., Eubank & Gregg, 1995, for a critique of one antimodular position). For an interesting argument—one that does not imperil our position here—for *Language* as naming a coherent ontological object, see Hurford (1987, pp. 15–35).

conducted at the level of Language are inherently unfruitful. But we entertain the proposition that there may be one or more critical periods for one or more elements of what is folk-psychologically called *Language*: That, for example, there may be a CP for syntax or for phonology, or that different CPs may affect different theory-defined areas of, for example, syntax at different times. (We return to the question of linguistic modularity when we look at claims for a CP in native language acquisition.)

What Is a Critical Period?

Our other variable is the term *critical period* itself. The general literature on second language acquisition (L2A), such as Larsen-Freeman and Long (1991) or Ellis (1994), is not too helpful here, usually just saying something about relative ease or difficulty of language learning before or after some point, usually the beginning of puberty, perhaps as a result of loss of brain *plasticity*, itself perhaps a consequence of *lateralization*, and so forth. We need to be rather more precise as to what sort of phenomena might be relevant to the concept of CP.

First of all, of course we are talking about a physiological phenomenon that implicates some aspect of the central nervous system (CNS) during the course of development. More specifically, CPs for us involve an interaction between some innately given part of the CNS and input from the periphery. For example, although the development of visual cognition in primates involves brain mechanisms laid down during the prenatal genesis of the neural architecture (Rakic, 1991) as well as exposure to optic stimuli, that exposure must take place within a rather narrow slice of time, a critical period (see, e.g., Marler, 1991). For us this connection between innate structure and peripheral stimulus is a necessary, albeit not sufficient, condition on CPs: CPs appear only where development of the mature state depends on a significant contribution of both the relevant neural architecture and peripheral exposure.[4]

Further, for us CPs involve so-called *canalized* behaviors, behaviors that, according to Brauth, Hall, and Dooling (1991) are critical for species identification and survival. Waddington (1975) defined canalization as "the capacity to produce a particular definite end-result in spite of a certain variability both in the initial situation from which development starts and in the conditions met with during its course" (p. 99). A CP

---

[4]Note that we are merely stipulating here, in order to narrow the range of phenomena to be considered. As is widely recognized, virtually any developmental process requires at least some minimal peripheral input. Still, it seems eminently worthwhile to exclude such processes as the onset of sexual drive, the development of sphincter control, the loss and replacement of teeth, and so on, from the set of CP phenomena; if the exclusion is, strictly speaking, arbitrary, it is an arbitrariness we can live with.

would thus be the period during which such entrenchment of the developmental path is carried out, and during which it is susceptible to alteration by sufficiently powerful peripheral influences. Andriew (1996) proposed an interesting extension of Waddington's (1975) concept, wherein degree of canalization is the criterion for degree of innateness: "[T]he degree to which a biological trait is innate for a genotype is the degree to which a developmental pathway for individuals possessing an instance of that genotype is canalized" (p. #S25). The relevance to language acquisition of this conception of canalization and innateness becomes evident later.

Finally, a distinction is often made between critical periods and sensitive periods: between a comparatively well-defined *window of opportunity* on the one hand, and a progressive inefficiency of the organism, or a gradually declining effectiveness of the peripheral input, on the other; the former would be a CP *sensu stricto*. As Hurford (1991) said, this is like the distinction between a mountain and a hill; and it is of about as much usefulness, given the extreme difficulty in drawing the line between the two phenomena in practice. Later, we introduce a different distinction, although we may find its usefulness limited too, at least for discussions of the acquisition of competence.[5]

Our question then is this: In the acquisition of L2 competence (morphophonological and morphosyntactic knowledge) by an adult, are there effects that can be attributed to the existence, in the developing human, of a critical period or periods?

NEUROLOGICAL PROCESSES INVOLVING CPS

Having clarified our approach to the question of CP effects in L2A, we ask the more fundamental question: What is the neurobiological basis for the CP phenomenon? Here we find not only that the bulk of relevant information comes, unsurprisingly, from nonhuman species, but also that this information is by no means complete. But what is known is, we

---

[5]There have been other attempts to differentiate the two terms as well. Fox (1970), for example, used *critical period* to refer to periods during which peripheral exposure is needed for normal development; a *sensitive period*, on the other hand, would be a period during which the organism is particularly vulnerable to harmful stimuli, as in the case of the period during which mice are particularly susceptible to noise-induced cochlear damage (e.g., Henry 1983). By contrast, Moltz (1973) and Krashen (1975) distinguished a critical period from a sensitive or optimal period on the basis of potential recovery effects: The organism presumably retains enough plasticity after a sensitive period to allow recovery, but critical periods allow no such subsequent recovery. As Colombo (1982) pointed out, however, uses like these are unfortunate because of the difficulty in practice of determining the difference between vulnerability and need or between therapeutic manipulations of behavior and basic physiological change. More on this latter point follows.

believe, enough to allow us to make some progress in evaluating the CP question with regard to L2 competence.

A CP is often characterized as a period of (relative) plasticity, during which there is a possibility of change in the relevant domain. The term *plasticity* can be a bit misleading, however, or at least unenlighteningly metaphorical; the brain, after all, is not a muscle that gets stiffer with age. For us, plasticity means the ability of neurons to make new connections, and varied connections depending on the stimulus. In this sense, plastic is opposed to *hardwired*: Hardwired connections are connections that are made in accordance with genetically determined instructions, largely or totally without reference to the periphery. Learning, including of course the learning of some particular language, is a function of cortical plasticity in this sense: the ability of cortical neurons in the relevant cognitive area to form new connections based on peripheral stimuli.

However, connections once made are not necessarily permanent, and indeed one fundamental aspect of growth and development in the organism is the severing of connections (Thompson, 1993). To maintain a connection it is necessary that the connected neurons fire simultaneously; as the slogan has it, "Neurons wire together if they fire together" (Singer, 1995). Thus, one aspect of a CP in a given domain would be the possibility of forming new connections relevant to that domain and maintaining them, with the loss of such a possibility after the end of the CP.

The neural mechanisms underlying the CP phenomenon remain somewhat elusive, but the available laboratory evidence suggests the twin processes of long-term potentiation (LTP) and long-term depression (LTD)—the former an activity-dependent change resulting in increased synaptic efficiency and the latter an activity-dependent change resulting in decreased efficiency. Identified in a number of brain regions, LTP—apparently the more studied of the two—appears to be modulated especially by the presence of receptor molecules known as N-methyl-D-aspartate (NMDA), which are located in dendritic membrane near sites of interneural communication (see e.g., Collingridge & Watkins, 1994; Haas & Buzsaki, 1988). Ignoring many (potentially important) details, the general picture seems to be that particular arrays of neurally transmitted stimuli, if present in sufficient quantity, cause NMDA receptors to become active, and the receptors in turn, allow calcium to flow through the neural membrane to result, ultimately, in increased synaptic efficiency. Crucially, when the function of NMDA is blocked, the relevant neurons respond to stimulation, but LTP does not develop. More generally, CP-relevant brain regions require a coordination of particular qualities and quantities of peripheral activity (stimuli) with subneural components that include the NMDA mechanism to result in a sustained response pattern like LTP–LTD. Just as important, it appears that NMDA is involved in neural development in response to new

information, but not in the subsequent expression or retrieval of that
information (Morris & Davis, 1994).

We are too sketchy, no doubt, on the details of neural mechanisms;
but the fact is that it is not yet even known whether LTP–LTD occurs at
all in natural (nonlaboratory) settings during learning, or how such
laboratory-induced changes in neural function or morphology affect
behavior. Indeed, although a role for NMDA has been isolated in cases
of filial imprinting (for discussion, see Morris & Davis, 1994), it is
nonetheless not yet evident that LTP participates in acquisitional
processes that go beyond standard cases of long-term memory storage.

Still, the current state of understanding does allow for a number of
limited and tentative conclusions, some more speculative than others. At
the most speculative, it is tempting to imagine, following Kalil (1989),
that the absence or presence, respectively, of NMDA-like mechanisms
might divide the (nonhardwired parts of the) brain into regions in which
plasticity is temporally limited and in which long-term stability of neural
response is evolutionarily desirable, and other regions in which plasticity
is essentially unlimited and in which neural adaptations to
environmental stimuli are desirable in the long term. In this respect, we
find it suggestive that in the somatosensory cortex of rats, the critical
period for reorganization of the barrel cells in response to haptic
stimulation from the vibrissae is essentially coterminous with the period
when LTP can be induced in those cells (Crair & Malenka, 1995). As
exciting as this scenario may be, however, it is still far too early to have
anything like complete confidence in it.

Several other conclusions seem less speculative. First and most
broadly, one expects the CP phenomenon only where a confluence of
neural architecture and random exposure to peripheral stimuli of the
relevant general type (e.g., visual stimuli) conspire to form the mature
state. Second, the mature state, so developed, remains stable in response
to stimuli; this stable state might be linked to NMDA-induced LTP or
some related process. Finally, if crucial developmental components—
especially either stimulation from the periphery or possibly an NMDA-
type mechanism—are missing or blocked during the crucial time
window (CP), then the usual stable state will never develop. In the case
of missing peripheral stimulation, one would find neural regions that are
unorganized and unspecific, an architecture in which the relevant
dendritic pathways for neural intercommunication remain significantly
redundant.

NONLINGUISTIC CRITICAL PERIODS: SOME EXAMPLES

It is important to keep in mind that CPs are not something unusual in the
animal world and definitely not something restricted to humans. As
noted earlier, our knowledge of CPs, like our knowledge of the

biochemistry of the brain, largely comes from the study of nonhuman species, where CPs seem to be ubiquitous.[6] Perhaps the most precise neurobiological information on the phenomenon comes from studies of the development of visual cognition among mammals with forward-facing eyes, especially among felines. Mature vision in cats develops in significant ways postnatally. In particular, it has been known for some time now that the feline visual cortex is only partially organized into ocular dominance columns at the time of birth and that the complete development of these columns depends on exposure to visual stimuli that are first received by the ganglion cells in the retina and pass via the geniculate nuclei to the visual cortex. Hubel and Wiesel (1965) showed that when stimuli are prevented from reaching the visual cortex (e.g., by suturing the eyes closed; see Kalil, 1989, for a summary of research employing more refined techniques), mature-state dominance columns do not form. Moreover, this research also demonstrated that such stimuli must reach the visual cortex within a CP extending to approximately 3 months after birth. Stimuli entering the cortex after the CP do not produce the development of the mature state.[7]

Other CPs include those for haptic perception in mice (Glazewski, Chen, Silva, & Fox, 1996) and for mating song in the African frog *Xenopus laevis* (Kelley, 1992). Investigations of haptic perception in mice are of relevance to the L2A–CP question for several reasons: For one thing, they reveal the plasticity of the immature CNS: Snipping off all but one of the vibrissae in a young mouse leads to a distinctly different pattern of neural connections between the remaining vibrissa and the relevant cortical area than would obtain in normal conditions. For another, it has been shown that the CP for haptic perception is actually (at least) two critical periods, varying according to cortical layer. It is always risky to generalize from mice to men, but at the very least this kind of highly

---

[6]For example, in his review of the CP phenomenon, Bornstein (1989) included CP effects for sensorimotor connectivity in *aplysia*, cocoon preference in ants, susceptibility to noise-induced cochlear damage in mice, aggression in mice, imprinting in ducks, orientation to maternal call in duck embryos, sensitivity to maternal androgen levels in lamb embryos, cortical cell specificity in felines, (visual) orientation selectivity in felines, sociability in canines, territoriality in canines, emotionality and normal social behavior in rhesus monkeys, imprinting in zebra finches, courting behavior in zebra finches (male only), imprinting in Japanese quail, responsiveness to young of species among ungulates, primary socialization in foxes, object contact in rats, taste sensitivity to sodium in rats, socialization in rats, "rough play" in rats (male only), object attraction in chicks, reactivity to stimulation in gerbils, masculinization–feminization in turtles, egg laying and recognition in orioles, species-normal song development in song birds, and imprinting in gulls.

[7]It is perhaps of interest to note, with Neville (1995), that visual processes in the retina itself are also subject to a CP, one of much shorter duration than the one that affects processing in the neocortex.

particularized CP phenomenon may give us pause before talking about *a* critical period for linguistic competence, *tout court*.

The mating call of the African frog illustrates two other important parameters of CP phenomena: the degree and duration of susceptibility to stimuli, and the duration of the period during which lack of stimulus can be compensated for without loss. Kelley (1992) and others made an interesting distinction between sensitive periods and critical periods, one that has the virtue of being immune to Hurford's (1991) charge of vagueness: A sensitive period is one during which peripheral stimuli can have a permanent instructive effect on the organism; a critical period is the period during which the negative effect of the absence of stimuli can still be overcome by the restoration or provision of the stimulus. As Kelley (1992) pointed out, this definition allows for the possibility that the CP can continue past the end of the sensitive period. Kelley found that adolescent, but not adult, female frogs could acquire the male vocalization pattern if implanted with male gonads. Gonadectomized males—who hence were deprived of the testicular androgen necessary for male vocalization—were able to vocalize appropriately when injected with androgen, up to a fairly late stage of development. Thus, Kelley concluded that the "critical period for androgen rescue of male courtship song remains open into adulthood" (p. 184).[8] We return to this distinction at the end of the chapter; in the meantime, we continue to use *CP* in its more widely accepted sense, while ignoring the term *sensitive period* as unhelpful.

Given the abundance and variety of CPs in various nonhuman animals, it would be surprising if there were none in humans; and indeed, there is evidence available, both for linguistic competence and for other domains. In his review, Bornstein (1989) included for humans the replication of adipose cells and sudden infant death syndrome. Perhaps the most clear-cut example among humans, however, is for vision, where a critical period extends from birth to around age 6, after which provision of previously delayed visual stimuli will be of no avail. For humans with congenital opacities of the cornea, lens transplant procedures have been developed that restore the physical media of the eye. However, if the relevant operation is performed when the patient is a juvenile or adult, visual function will not be recovered (Artola & Singer, 1994; Thompson, 1993). Compared to the neurobiological information available on other animals (felines, primates, etc.), this kind of evidence is less compelling because physiologically less detailed. Still, the parallel between such cases and those of other mammals is so

---

[8]The situation is actually more complex; whereas the castrated young frogs could acquire the male trill rate, they were less completely successful in achieving normal amplitude modulation. It would seem that there is modularity even in frogs.

striking that the idea of a CP becomes quite appealing, especially in the absence of any other plausible explanation for the differential success rate of lens transplants.

CRITICAL PERIODS AND FIRST LANGUAGE ACQUISITION

What of linguistic competence? This is, of course, the very kind of capacity for which one might expect a CP: It is clearly strongly canalized, and the development of the mature state clearly depends on a significant contribution from both peripheral stimuli and hardwired neural architecture.[9] Even so, none of the examples we looked at so far compares to the difficulty in isolating a specifically linguistic CP for humans. Not only are there obvious ethical considerations precluding the sort of experimental manipulation allowed with nonhuman participants, there is also the extreme complexity of the relevant collection of phenomena, that is, language. Further, development of crucial components of linguistic competence involves brain mechanisms that themselves may have little to do with linguistic matters as such. Thus, for instance, children acquiring a spoken language must have functioning auditory systems, and those acquiring a signed language must have functioning visual systems. Given that there may be CP effects in such perceptual systems—and the evidence reviewed previously suggests as much for vision at least—we must face the possibility that what appears to be a CP phenomenon for linguistic competence is merely an epiphenomenal consequence of a nonlinguistic perceptual CP.

Finally, we must repeat that *language*, or even *linguistic competence*, is too gross a categorization of the phenomena of interest; modularity requires appealing to a far finer, more detailed analysis of linguistic competence. Happily, brain science and linguistic theory seem to be moving toward a consensus, albeit still a very broad one, on this point: On the one hand, neurolinguistic research such as the studies by Neville and her associates (e.g., Neville, Nicol, Barss, Forster, & Garrett, 1991; Shao & Neville, 1996) suggests a locational differentiation in brain processing among types of grammatical anomalies as categorized by

---

[9]Some analysts of the CP phenomenon have attempted to set forth other criteria by which CP effects can be recognized and categorized (e.g., Bornstein, 1989; Colombo, 1982). Bornstein's (1989) criteria, among the most extensive that we have found, included five "structural" characteristics (developmental dating, onset, offset, duration, and asymptote), three characteristics involving mechanisms (experience, system, and pathway), and four involving consequences (outcome, manner, outcome conditions, and duration). We do not provide discussion of the match-up between assumed CP effects in linguistic competence and, for example, Bornstein's criteria. Suffice it to say that we find no evidence whatever that the findings reviewed subsequently fall outside the CP-defining parameters described by these authors.

recent linguistic theory, whereas research into Specific Language Impairment reveals highly specific deficits in certain individuals (see e.g., Clahsen, 1989; Gopnik, 1990; Rice, 1991; Van der Lely, 1996; Van der Lely & Ullman, 1996), again categorizable within a specific linguistic theory; and on the other hand, linguistic theorizing like that in Webelhuth (1995) suggests that linguistic competence would, of theoretical necessity, decompose into separate components. To the extent that such differentiation among subcomponents of language can be theoretically and empirically justified, one cannot exclude the possibility that there may be multiple CPs for linguistic competence, perhaps with different timings, or that some components (modules) of linguistic competence may be subject to CPs whereas others are not.

Whereas ethical constraints preclude invasive forms of experimentation on human participants, there are "natural experiments" (fortunately rare) that reveal a good deal about linguistic development under conditions of degraded or absent stimuli. The best-known case of course is that of Genie (Curtiss, 1977, 1988), who from the age of 1;6 to the age of 13 was totally deprived of language input. Of relevance here is the differential nature of her language learning during the years in which she was institutionalized after rescue: She made significant progress in some respects of language, and absolutely none in others. Her vocabulary grew dramatically, for instance, as did her communicative powers; whereas on the other hand, her intonation remained bizarre and she never was able to produce an embedded sentence or a grammatical Wh-question. Given the extended period of sadistic abuse and deprivation to which Genie was subjected, it would not be surprising if she had failed across the board to learn English; but there is no reason to predict that she would be unable to grasp the concept of structure dependence while still being able to learn new nouns and verbs. Genie's syntactic deficits, in other words, seem more plausibly attributable to lack of input itself during a critical period, rather than to the viciousness with which that input was withheld.

There are also cases of linguistic deprivation in the absence of abuse; namely, those cases of congenitally deaf children of hearing parents where sign language input is not provided, or is provided only after some years. An extreme case, bearing comparison with Genie's, is that of Chelsea (see, e.g., Curtiss, 1988, 1989), who was misdiagnosed as retarded or emotionally disturbed in early childhood, and who was found only to be deaf when she was reevaluated at the age of 31. Unlike Genie's utterances, which at least sometimes seemed to have the structural complexity of a normal 2-year-old's (e.g., *Another house have dog*), Chelsea's utterances appeared to have almost no structure at all (e.g., *Breakfast eating girl*). Noting the differences between Genie's development and Chelsea's, Gleitman and Newport (1995) speculated that the CP may have a middle, "marginal" time during which partial development is possible—what some researchers would refer to as a sensitive period. Hence, they suggested, whereas Genie's acquisition took place during the marginal period (i.e., 0–1;6, and 13+), Chelsea missed the entire CP. As with most sensitive–critical distinctions, this one seems unsatisfyingly vague.[10] More important, it obscures a more intriguing possibility, namely, that there are multiple CPs for linguistic competence, with different time courses. It is possible, in other words, that whereas Genie only missed a CP that affects the projection of functional categories (such as Tense and Agreement), Chelsea missed both this CP and one that affects more basic syntactic relations like X-bar theory. This is, of course, not much more than a speculation at this point, and a post hoc one at that. But it has the advantage of being related to a precise characterization of linguistic competence for which there is powerful independent theoretical evidence. It has the further advantage of being, in principle at least, empirically testable. We return to this speculation subsequently.

Chelsea is an example—albeit an extreme one—of a comparatively frequent case of linguistic deprivation: namely, the case of congenitally deaf children of hearing parents. Although few of these children have to wait as long as Chelsea did to get linguistic input, there is a good deal of variation in the age at which sign language stimuli are initially made regularly available. This allows for the possibility of establishing the boundaries of a CP by comparing terminal competence with age at initial exposure. A well-known study is that of Newport (1990), who examined three groups of learners of American Sign Language (ASL); the first group had been exposed to ASL from early childhood, the second from between ages 4 and 6, and the third only after the age of 12. The differences among the three groups were interesting: Those exposed since early childhood showed native-like ASL performance, as expected; the middle group showed generally high levels of performance, with only subtle defects; but the late learners' performance was significantly deficient, with problems similar in kind to those of Genie (e.g., problems with functional morphology). These findings fit in neatly with findings from cases of extraordinary deprivation such as Genie and Chelsea; and like them, they appear consistent with the idea that a CP affects the development of competence in the native language.

---

[10]An interpretation that is not entirely out of line with the marginal period suggested by Gleitman and Newport (1995) involves the apparent capacity to modify CP effects. Hence, Bornstein (1989) noted that CP effects may potentially be reduced, extended, or even reinstated or eliminated altogether by various means, including depletion or infusion of the relevant neurotransmitters, isolation, stress, genital stimulation, and dark rearing. Of particular relevance here would obviously be the extreme deprivation of Genie's prediscovery environment, which may well have caused a change in her CP. Still, this explanation remains as imprecise as that of Gleitman and Newport (1995).

Newport's (1990) conclusions are not universally accepted, of course, but they find support in a study reported by Neville (1995), who also examined congenitally deaf adult signers whose first exposure to a spoken language (English) occurred later in life. In contrast to Newport, Neville and her colleagues employed event-related potentials (ERPs), a means of measuring electrical activity in different brain regions. In adults with normal early exposure to linguistic stimulation, one finds different types of activity in response to different classes of words: Open-class words (nouns, verbs, adjectives) elicit a negative potential of 350 msec (N350) that is most pronounced over the posterior regions of both hemispheres, but grammatical function words (articles, conjunctions, auxiliary elements) elicit an N280 reponse that is localized to anterior temporal regions of the left hemisphere. Significantly, this N280 response obtains only with the early-exposure participants, even though there was no difference across participants for open-class words. Neville's (1995) findings, like Newport's (1990), are consistent with the idea that a CP affects the development of native-like linguistic competence, or at least of some aspects of that competence. Once again we see an apparently modular distinction within the realm of language.

Given the complexity of linguistic phenomena and the ethical considerations limiting experimental research on human participants, it should not be surprising that we cannot offer more concrete physiological evidence demonstrating the existence of CPs in the acquisition of linguistic competence. We should stress that these difficulties are in no way peculiar to this kind of research: On the one hand, virtually any form of investigation using human participants is fraught with ethical dangers—for instance, researchers, in the United States at least, have to convince academic watchdogs that there is no danger in "teaching" children nonsense words in acquisition experiments. On the other hand, it is naive to imagine that there is some way to directly observe *any* natural phenomenon of scientific interest; whether in psychology or geology, we must be indirect, making inferences from what we can observe to the phenomena, which we cannot observe (Bogen & Woodward, 1988). If somehow we could look directly at the brain, our guess is that we would see, only in the case of late-exposure participants, comparatively unorganized and overly redundant neural interconnection, as a result of the failure of environmental stimuli—linguistic input—to select for certain connections over others. We are not able to conduct such direct observation—it is not clear that we ever will be—but we do have relatively useful, noninvasive techniques such as ERP that can give us highly suggestive information.

Not, we hasten to add, that we should necessarily assume that ERP data are privileged over less high-tech methods. It is only common sense, of course, to prefer more sensitive instruments to less. But it is important to remember that there is no point in gathering any kind of data—high tech or low tech, behavioral or physiological—without having some idea of what we are looking for. We get an idea of what to look for not from brain science but from linguistic theory. The open- versus closed-class distinction used by Newport (1990) and by Neville (1995) is a fairly rough one, but a theoretical one nonetheless; we recast the distinction next in somewhat more specific theoretical terms.

CRITICAL PERIODS AND L2A

The difficulties encountered in trying to ascertain whether there are CPs for native language (L1) competence are magnified when dealing with adult L2 acquisition. Perhaps the most general difficulty is simply to conceptualize the problem appropriately.[11] One could simply sweep the whole thing under the rug: One could point out, as has often enough been done in such discussions, that normal adults did not miss the critical period for their L1 and that they do not respond to L2 input as Genie or Chelsea did to L1 input, and one could conclude that hence for normal adults, the question is misguided. Alternatively, noting that with few exceptions adult learners fail, often miserably, to become indistinguishable from members of the ambient L2 speech community, one could argue that there *must* be a CP that affects L2 competence. In other words, (a) obviously there is no CP effect for adult L2A and (b) obviously there is.

We think there is a way to resolve this seeming contradiction, a way suggested by some of the neurobiological considerations touched on earlier. First of all, once a CP has elapsed, certain possibilities are excluded that were available during the passage of the CP; certain plasticities disappear. Granting that there is a CP (or several CPs) for L1 acquisition, the question is whether the stable, mature state of linguistic competence can be altered by new linguistic stimuli and if so, how much. The question is crucial because of the vast difference in neural architecture in the two cases: Where a CP has been missed outright, as we assume to be the case with Chelsea, the relevant neural architecture is presumably unorganized and unspecific, and the relevant dendritic pathways for neural intercommunication remain significantly redundant or simply unavailable; but in the case of exposure to secondary stimuli after the CP has been successfully traversed—the case, for instance, of

---

[11]A conceptualization of the phenomenon that we reject out of hand is that the specifically linguistic machinery of the mind–brain underlies a CP that affects only L2 acquisition, that is, one that stands independent of NL acquisition. In fact, the various means by which evolution has been thought to result in CP effects across species (see, e.g., Bornstein, 1989; Hurford, 1991) all would appear to militate against a CP that is specific only to the development of L2 competence.

adult L2 acquisition—the neural architecture is already developed. We would thus predict that secondary linguistic development would entail changes in the neural architecture of an adult learner on a far more limited scale than the kind of fundamental change that characterizes the difference between the child's preexposure state and the mature state.

The neurobiological evidence alluded to earlier suggests that post-CP brain regions have attained a remarkable level of stable responsivity—a lack of plasticity, in other words—and we speculated that this steady state might perhaps be related to processes like LTP–LTD. In vision, for instance, studies indicate that the visual cortex does not develop if not exposed to visual stimuli that originate in the retina and pass through the lateral geniculate nucleus to the neocortex. However, more recent work on the adult (i.e., post-CP) visual cortex of felines and primates (Gilbert & Wiesel, 1992; Pettet & Gilbert, 1992) demonstrates that cortical activity in an already developed area can, in fact, change in response to changes in sensory input. Gilbert and Wiesel (1992) eliminated visual input by lesioning the retina and then measured changes in the receptive field. Interestingly, after the passage of a few months, the areas of the neocortex that were initially silenced by the lesions had become active; these areas began responding to stimuli that originally only activated cortical cells in surrounding regions (cf. Zohary, Celebrini, Britten, & Newsome, 1994).

Findings such as these do not demonstrate that CP effects are either void or wholly reversible; the changes observed were changes in mature-state neural receptivity, not changes of the magnitude that one observes in the metamorphosis from preexposure state to mature state. These findings do, however, suggest that in a brain region known in advance to be affected by a CP, post-CP changes are, in fact, possible to a limited degree. In other words, there is a certain level of neurobiological support for the idea that the mature state of a neural region is not totally incapable of alteration by altered peripheral exposure. To the extent that it is possible to extend such findings to the case of linguistic competence, one could conclude that a mature-state change from competence in one language to competence in another language is not ruled out on a priori neurobiological grounds.

Putting together the compelling evidence for powerful CP effects in L1 acquisition on the one hand, with, on the other, the evidence discussed here for limited plasticity in some post-CP regions, and with the existence of countless cases of moderate, limited L2 learning ability by adults, we are led to the conclusion that evidence for a CP affecting L2 knowledge will not be on a par with evidence for a CP affecting L1 knowledge. Where pathological cases like Genie or Chelsea show a gross difference in behavioral reflexes from those of normal native speakers—a difference reflecting CP effects—with normal adult L2 learners, the relevant neural architecture is already highly organized, so that the effects of any new peripheral stimuli (i.e., input in a different language) should be more like the relatively minor changes of the sort found by Gilbert and Wiesel (1992). We would expect, in other words, neither native-like mastery of the L2—the learner is, after all, past the CP—nor the near-total incompetence in the L2 that Genie or Chelsea manifested in their first. With adult L2 acquisition, one is required to look for behavioral reflexes that may be relatively minor in scope, hence demanding refined examination.

An essential source of the requisite refinement, we must point out, is linguistic theory, which for us means generative linguistic theory. Although there has been important work done outside this framework on the relation between age and ultimate L2 attainment (e.g., Long, 1990, 1993),[12] this research lacks the descriptive apparatus to distinguish with sufficient precision between an L1 and an L2, hence to provide an explanatorily adequate account of a learner's respective competences. The L2 studies we consider here all share the crucial assumption that the innate, domain-specific neurobiological architecture essential for L1 acquisition is nothing other than what linguistic theory calls Universal Grammar (UG; see, e.g., Chomsky 1995; Cook & Newson, 1996). Based on this assumption, these studies addressed the question of whether the adult L2 learner's grammar is constrained by UG—whether, as it is often (unaptly and misleadingly) expressed, the adult still has *access* to UG. Although not that many studies explicitly speak in terms of CPs, the debate can be recast in CP terms with little distortion: The logic—which we reexamine—has often been that if there is a CP for L1, then L2 grammars should fall outside of the range of grammars permitted by UG, whereas if there is no CP, then these grammars should be UG constrained.[13]

A number of studies have been conducted to date, but the results do not uniformly support any single conclusion. For example, Clahsen and Muysken (1986) and Schachter (e.g., 1989) argued that adult L2 learners' grammars do not fall within the range of those permitted by UG; compatible with this view is that of Johnson and Newport (1989), who

<hr>

[12]One of the concerns addressed in earlier discussions of maturational effects (i.e., CP effects) on L2 development is the "cut-off" point beyond which learners would not be able to attain a final state comparable to that of native speakers. In this regard, it is revealing to note that whereas CP onsets are generally quite abrupt, CP offsets, in nonhuman species and in other CPs affecting humans, are typically gradual. The onset of the CP affecting the development of binocular vision in humans, for instance, appears over a period of about 1 month, whereas the offset extends over some 5 years. Likewise, the onset of the imprinting CP in the zebra finch takes only a very short time in early life, but its offset endures well into the finch's adolescence. See Bornstein (1989) and Colombo (1982) for further discussion of the lengths of onsets and offsets.

[13]Flynn (see, e.g., Epstein, Flynn, & Martohardjono, 1996; Flynn & Manuel, 1991) has been one of the more explicit theorists in committing herself to the position that access to UG entails the absence of a CP for NL acquisition.

argued that the maturational state of adult L2 learners precludes full development in the L2 (see also, e.g., Johnson & Newport, 1991; Johnson, Shenkman, Newport, & Medin, 1996). In contrast, Schwartz and Sprouse (1994, 1996), among others, maintained that L2 grammars are fully UG constrained. A kind of intermediate position, developed in recent work on ultimate attainment by White and Genesee (1996), is that UG is in principle accessible to the adult L2 learner and thus that there is no CP that affects L2 acquisition. White and Genesee did recognize clear-cut age effects in their findings, but did not attempt to explain them.

Perhaps due to its recency, the White and Genesee (1996) study has not been examined independently; we return to a more detailed discussion of it shortly. However, both the full-access and the no-access positions have been challenged. In the case of Clahsen and Muysken (1986), there is the well-known reply of duPlessis, Solin, Travis, and White (1987), who reinterpreted the Clahsen and Muysken (1986) data and concluded that UG is indeed accessible to the L2 learner. The recent findings of Vainikka and Young-Scholten (1994, 1996) might also be interpreted to mean that Schachter's participants had not yet acquired the syntactic projections (IC, CP) that her conclusion crucially relied on. Likewise, Martohardjono and Gair (1993) suggested that at least some of Schachter's participants might have had syntactic representations that would completely undermine her conclusions about UG access. Regarding the Johnson & Newport (1989) study, Kellerman (1995) argued that it is undermined by a number of methodological as well as conceptual flaws. (We might add that Johnson et al., 1996, based its conclusions on a limited and superficial collection of morphosyntactic phenomena, whose relation to UG the authors did not discuss.) Finally, examining Schwartz and Sprouse's (1994, 1996) analysis, Eubank (1995) and Meisel (1996) argued that it is not strongly supported by the very data they presented to make their case.

It is hardly surprising that such extreme views on access to UG should come under fire; after all, even though adults are generally not particularly successful L2 learners, they are also not total failures (Felix, 1995, made a similar point). We already noted that there is a vast architectural difference between post-CP L1 acquisition and post-CP L2 acquisition; this difference alone suggests that an effect as plainly gross as no access or full access is not particularly plausible in the latter case. In fact, we think the access debate has been largely misconceived. Not only are the two extreme positions—total access, zero access—self-evidently incompatible with the evidence; any account that simply stakes out a position in between the two—pretty accessible, not too accessible—is going to be too simpleminded to be of any explanatory value.[14]

---

[14]For an instructive, albeit perhaps comparatively egregious, recent example, see Epstein, Flynn, and Martohardjono (1996). Epstein et al. are typical of many

As noted earlier, however, White and Genesee (1996) requires a more detailed treatment (in part because it is much more recent). White and Genesee set out to locate (primarily) Francophone learners of English whose overall proficiency in the L2 is as close to that of native speakers as possible. In this sense, the study is strongly reminiscent of the well-known work of Coppieters (1987) and Birdsong (1992), although White and Genesee employed not the more impressionistic means of selecting participants of, say, Coppieters (1987), but specific criteria-based means to establish levels of near-nativeness. Having located such a sample, White and Genesee (1996) then examined these participants for UG effects—the Empty Category Principle (ECP) and Subjacency—in their L2, using two measures: a grammaticality judgment task presented on a computer that also measured reaction times (length of time until judgment), and a standard question-formation task requiring participants to front Wh-words, including out of strong islands (where the resulting Wh-question would be ungrammatical in both English and French). Crucially, White and Genesee avoided the potentially confounding problem of parametric differences between English and reflectFrench (the L1 of the majority of the participants) by examining UG effects for which the two languages exhibit largely similar reflexes. The results from their near-native L2 group, especially on the grammaticality judgment task, indicate no statistically significant difference from the English native-speaker control group, as well as no effect for age. Although White and Genesee acknowledged age effects and apparent grammatical disturbances among their less proficient participants, the findings from the near-native group prompted them to conclude that there is no age-related decline in access to UG and no CP that affects L2 competence.

On the face of it, the White and Genesee (1996) study might be taken to provide just the kind of evidence to suggest the discrete change in neural architecture that we predicted previously to result from secondary linguistic exposure. In other words, even if there is a CP affecting L1 acquisition, the neural architecture that develops after primary linguistic exposure may be such that secondary linguistic exposure can bring about whatever changes are necessary. On the other hand, it is also possible that White and Genesee's choice of tasks, along with their selection of only L2 participants with near-native proficiency, resulted in findings that are not entirely revealing. In fact, what we suggest later is that this particular combination could easily result in findings that provide misleading clues to the CP question for L2A.

L2A researchers in conducting their access discussion within a simplistic, Goldilocks-like framework of *total*, *partial*, or *zero*. For detailed criticism of Epstein et al., see the commentaries that follow the Epstein et al. article by, inter alia, Bley-Vroman, Eubank, Gregg, Schwartz, and White.

To understand this view, recall the work cited earlier on the modifiability of CP effects across the species, especially the apparent recovery from these effects. In his overview, Colombo (1982) suggested that recovery effects that appear after therapeutic intervention are irrelevant to the question of whether a particular CP obtains in principle, because the therapy may just mask underlying physiological CP events. More interestingly, Colombo pointed out that CP effects appear more robustly in studies of physiology than in studies of behavior. Among the studies of the CP affecting orientation selectivity in felines, for instance, a number of studies suggest that manipulative therapy can bring about (at least partial) recovery, but no studies indicate that such therapy has any effect on the underlying neural substrate affected by the CP. Colombo's own suggestion was that the organism may be trained to employ secondary neural mechanisms not affected by the CP to solve at least simple orientation tasks.

With Colombo's (1982) points in mind, we now return to White and Genesee (1996). First, it is noteworthy that White and Genesee examined participants whose metalinguistic awareness was undoubtedly very high; that is, participants who had the wherewithal to extract information from exposure, whether primary linguistic data (input) or otherwise. Second and relatedly, it is also noteworthy that White and Genesee examined UG effects with stimulus sentences that did not obviously require learners to draw grammatical conclusions that outstrip their exposure (or some combination of exposure and L1 knowledge); in other words, they did not, strictly speaking, examine underdetermination effects, in that their participants' knowledge of English may well derive from the L1 grammar and not from UG.

Putting these two points together, it is possible that the responses given by the near-native participants reflect not access to UG itself in L2 grammar construction, but rather L1 knowledge combined with advanced metalinguistic skills. What adds a level of plausibility to this alternative account is the nature of the White and Genesee measurement instruments: They are, of course, behavioral measurements, not physiological measurements.   As Colombo pointed out, behavioral measurements, such as White and Genesee's, may well miss the relevant effect in the neural substrate; physiological measurement should not. (Later, we find in an L2 study exactly the kind of physiology–behavior split that Colombo found in the feline research.)   Thus whereas we do not dispute White and Genesee's results, neither do we draw White and Genesee's conclusion from those results. They interpreted their results as evidence against the existence of a CP for UG-related linguistic competence; in the absence of physiological evidence, however, we can conclude only that *if* there is a CP for linguistic competence, it can be overcome in some cases.

We have suggested, then, that the access studies, including White and Genesee (1996), may not have been entirely fruitful because their underlying expectations—UG, no UG—are not well supported by considerations of the way that the CP phenomenon would apply to L2 competence. A more profitable way of approaching the problem, and one that may be more in line with our framing of the question, can be seen in some of the studies that examine whether parameter (re)setting is possible in L2 acquisition. It is parameters and their various settings, after all, that make for the crucial differences between natural languages; acquisition of the appropriate parametric values for the target language is essential for successful acquisition of the language. On the other hand, the success or failure in acquiring a given setting for a given parameter should result in comparatively limited behavioral reflexes on the part of the learner: precisely the subtle sort of behavioral reflexes we suggested earlier would be the evidence to expect in post-CP acquisition.

Studies of L2 parameter (re)setting appear, at first glance, to provide the same sort of equivocal findings that plague the access literature. For example, a number of such studies (e.g., Eubank, 1992; Tomaselli & Schwartz, 1990; Vainikka & Young-Scholten, 1994, 1996; but see Mueller, 1996) have shown that adult L2 learners can successfully reset parameters that determine basic relations like OV versus VO. For parameters such as the one posited to determine verb raising (see, e.g., White, 1990–1991), a similar conclusion initially seemed plausible, but further analysis has revealed significant difficulties. In particular, the data suggest a level of syntactic optionality that is allowed neither by the native language nor by the target language (White, 1992, p. 285)— indeed, in some cases a level that may not be allowed by UG in general (Eubank, 1995).

What to make of such apparently conflicting findings? As always, of course, there are short-term solutions possible: For instance, one could argue that evidence against accessibility of UG is artifactual, based on inadequate analysis, perhaps involving problems with learnability from positive data. Or one could argue against evidence for apparent success in parameter resetting by appealing to simple learning mechanisms that are not specifically linguistic, or at least not specifically UG related. There is certainly nothing illegitimate about such kinds of argumentation; indeed, they are often justifiable and in specific cases even compelling. Still, we would like to be able to transcend this level of argumentation and try a different conceptualization of the problem.

To start with, consider what we see as a fundamental problem with the "no access" position: This position in effect assumes that UG is simply a language acquisition device (LAD), indeed the LAD of earlier transformational grammar. As such, it can effectively be jettisoned once the specific grammar (of English, Swahili, whatever) has been constructed in the learner's mind or brain.[15] A no access position must conceive of UG in this way; otherwise it will be unable to explain how we can continue to use our L1 once UG has faded from the scene.

This view of UG as simply a machine for grammar building is a perfectly plausible one, but unfortunately it is not the view of UG that has been held by generative linguists for the last 15 years or so. Since the introduction of the so-called Government and Binding (GB) theory (Chomsky, 1981) and continuing within the Minimalist program (Chomsky, 1995), language-specific rules have been viewed as mere epiphenomenal exponents of more abstract principles and parameters. A learner of English does not acquire a specific rule of passivization (or Wh-movement or whatever); rather, input leads to setting of the relevant parameter, and specific phenomena such as passivization simply fall out as the logical consequence of that parameter setting. What this means is that, although it is (in principle) possible to write an English grammar in terms of principles and parameters, just as it is possible to write a list of rules of the sort that constitute traditional reference grammars, such a grammar would have no more psychological reality than would a traditional reference grammar. There is no "English grammar" in the head of a native speaker of English; there is, rather, a set of principles and a set of parameters with particular values that have been set as a result of exposure to certain kinds of input (and of course there is a lexicon with masses of idiosyncratic morphosyntactic and phonological information). In other words, a native speaker literally embodies UG in one of its possible versions. If this is the case, then there is no way we could jettison UG and still function linguistically: In order to interpret the reference of *himself* in *John wants Bill to introduce himself*, the hearer cannot use a rule of English grammar but rather must use (*inter alia*) Binding Theory and the Governing Category Parameter, as set for English.

Thus, it seems to us that a no access position is in effect a "no UG" position, at least insofar as one accepts the current conception of UG. It would be a consistent position, of course, either to subscribe to a theory of UG-as-LAD-only or to reject the idea of UG itself as, say, false or epiphenomenal. We do not subscribe to either position, however, and do not discuss them here. (See Eubank & Gregg, 1995, and Gregg, 1996, for critical discussion of some proposed alternatives to UG-based L2A theories.) But having argued for a CP in L1 acquisition (and given the problem of general failure to acquire an L2), we clearly cannot accept a

---

[15]Bever (1981) gave an argument to this effect; Bley-Vroman (1990) committed himself to much the same line. Bley-Vroman noted, however, that the idea would not work in terms of the (then new) GB theory: The principles of Binding Theory, for example, would be necessary for everyday processing.

"full access" position either. Current UG theory, however, may give us a way to accept UG as operating in the acquisition and use of an L2, while explaining the limitations on that acquisition.

Starting with Borer (1984) and continuing through present-day work (e.g., Chomsky, 1995), a common understanding has been that the locus of cross-linguistic variation (parameters) is not in the syntax per se but rather in the lexicon. Consider the case of verb raising, a parametric difference that manifests itself, for instance, in the following sort of distinctions in grammaticality between English and French:

(1) a.   John often drinks coffee.
    b.   *John drinks often coffee.
(2) a.   *Jean souvent boit du café.
    b.   Jean boit souvent du café.

What one finds in contrasts like those in (1) and (2) is that the (finite) main verb appears to be separated from the object by an adverb in French (-like languages), but must remain adjacent to the object in English (-like languages). Omitting considerable detail, the essential explanation for the difference between (1) and (2) involves verb movement in a representation like the one shown in (3):

(3)

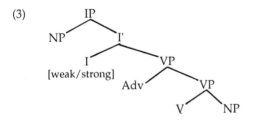

In (3), an abstract feature representing tense–agreement morphology originates in the lexicon and is situated in syntax under I. In French, this feature carries the value [strong], whereas in English the feature carries the value [weak]. The movement of the verb from its underlying position in VP shown in (3) up to I is sensitive to the value of the lexical feature under I: If the value is [weak], then verb raising is not permitted, and so the verb remains in the VP adjacent to its object. If, however, the value of the lexical feature is [strong], then the verb must raise from its underlying position in VP past the adverb up to I, hence causing the verb to be separated from its object.[16]

---

[16]This account is simplified for expository purposes. In analyses like that of, say, Pollock (1989), what allows verb raising to occur and what makes verb raising obligatory are different affairs. The idea that parametric variation is located in the lexicon is, however, a constant throughout.

Interestingly, this more recent understanding of parameterization drives a wedge between UG as such and the lexical information, such as features of verbal inflection, that results in the appearance of cross-linguistic variation. In other words, parametric values are, at a certain level, separate from UG. Indeed, under this view, the child's initial state is simply the principles and parameters of UG, but without any of the information provided in the lexicon. The child's task during acquisition would thus involve primarily determining the values of various lexical features that are reported in the syntax.

More interestingly, this view allows one to conceive of the possibility of specifically linguistic pathological deficits that do not involve UG per se, but do involve parametric values. Imagine a grammar lacking only the appropriate lexical values. In such a case, most grammatical functions would operate in the usual way: Verbs would project as verb phrases, nouns as noun phrases, and so forth, and verbs would still require certain subjects and complements, and so forth. But we would expect to find failure in terms of head movement (e.g., verb movement) and, perhaps, XP movement (e.g., NPs or Wh-phrases) as well. To use our example, if the [weak] or [strong] value of verbal inflection in the language failed to report under INFL, then the syntax would simply not be constrained to either obligatory movement or obligatory nonmovement. Now, so far as we know, optional verb raising does not occur in natural languages; verb movement is either required ([strong] value of inflection, as in French) or prohibited ([weak] value of inflection, as in English). Thus, our hypothetical pathological grammar would be exceptional among natural languages; but crucially, *it would not be a violation of UG*. In other words, Subjacency would still be available to the L2 learner, as would the ECP and other UG principles. The learner's internal L2 grammar would not be a "rogue" grammar in the sense of Finer (1991), in glaring contradistinction to, say, Chelsea's or Genie's "grammar".

The idea of lexical parameters, as distinguished from the syntactic parameters of Principles and Parameters theory, clearly requires further elaboration, and in particular, a more differentiated account of the lexicon itself, and of course work in this direction is proceeding (see, e.g., Webelhuth, 1992, for an ambitious attempt). What is important for the present discussion, however, is that our hypothetical speaker who lacks the capacity to represent the syntactically relevant lexical information turns out to be real: components of such lexical information appear to be susceptible to damage or loss in certain cases of L1 pathology. For example, Gopnik (e.g., 1990) argued that the values of lexical features that have syntactic consequences in nominal phrases are missing in certain cases of Specific Language Impairment ([SLI]; see also Rice, Wexler, & Cleave, 1995). Importantly, the syntactic representations of these speakers are UG constrained, but an array of the superficial

4. CRITICAL PERIODS AND LANGUAGE ACQUISITION

grammatical constructions generated by their grammars may be of a type not attested in natural languages.

It may be possible to apply this deficit model to adult L2 learners. Given that crucial grammatical information is located in a highly differentiated lexicon, and positing that certain components of this information are susceptible to loss in (exceptional) native speakers, one could easily conceive of a CP that would affect the adult learner's ability to represent syntactically important aspects of the lexicon. Indeed, Beck (1996)—following a general conception presented in Beck (1997)— offered exactly this kind of account to explain her experimental data, which indicate a dissociation between lexical knowledge (verbal inflection) and the syntactic effects (verb raising) that such knowledge would otherwise be expected to cause (see Eubank & Grace, 1996, for similar findings).

More interestingly, Beck's (1996) data and her analysis of them provide a way to try to deal with the equivocal findings referred to earlier on parameter (re)setting in L2A. As we noted, a number of studies indicate an ability to readjust basic relations like OV versus VO, but that certain problems subsequently appeared when parameters involving movement were examined. In the terms of the standard access debate this is a contradiction: There should be either an ability to reset parameters or no such ability, yet the findings suggested something in between. Within Beck's framework, however, a lexically based failure in verb raising does not necessarily imply failure in other areas, for example, basic relations like OV versus VO, which may involve somewhat different parameters. In other words, the framework employing lexical parameters predicts a priori that failure (or success) in one area of competence does not necessarily entail failure (or success) in another, thereby providing at least a means of avoiding the impasse created by the syntactic parameters of Principles and Parameters theory. Verb raising is a particularly telling example of what this impasse could otherwise be like: Francophone speakers of L2 English persist in making errors like (1b), even after they have reached very high proficiency levels, and even though it is exceedingly easy to formulate a pedagogical rule to block such errors. (Similarly, the otherwise intelligent participants in Van der Lely & Ullman, 1996, appeared to have a good deal of difficulty with simple past-tense forms like *looked*, leading these researchers to conclude that these children may not be able to make a simple generalization to form the past of regular verbs.)

Where does this leave us in regard to the CP phenomenon? We argued earlier that behavioral reflexes indicating a CP effect on the development of secondary competence would be relatively minor in scope: The gross physiological difference alone between the initial state of L1 development and the "initial state" of adult L2 development strongly suggests as much. This comparatively narrow range of expected variation between normal adult L2 competence and normal adult L1 competence—in stark contrast to the wide, qualitative differences between normal adult L1 competence and pathological adult L1 competence—will thus require a commensurably fine-grained analysis of the data. As we also pointed out, one of the most crucial sources of refinement comes from linguistic theory.

Still, it would be revealing if one could point to a physiological effect for L2 development. After all, we pointed out previously, with Colombo (1982), that the behavioral manifestations of a presumed CP may mask underlying physiological disturbances. In fact, just such findings were reported by Weber-Fox and Neville (1996; also chap. 2, this volume). In this study, Weber-Fox and Neville performed what amounts to a replication of Neville (1995) as discussed earlier, except that in this case the participants were L2 learners. What makes this study particularly interesting in the light of our discussion of White and Genesee (1996) is that Weber-Fox and Neville (1996) employed both a behavioral measure (acceptability judgments) and a physiological measure (ERPs from scalp recordings). In general, the findings mirror the findings of the earlier study: An effect for age of acquisition appeared for syntactic anomalies (i.e., violations of UG) but not for semantic–pragmatic anomalies. Just as interesting, however, is that they also found a mild discrepancy between participants' behavioral responses to some linguistic stimuli and the ERP data: (This subset of) the behavioral results do not strongly support an L1–L2 difference, but the physiological data do support such a difference. Again, this is fully consistent with Colombo's (1982) observations on the effects of post-CP therapy seen in studies of behavioral manifestations versus the physiological effects of CPs. The Weber-Fox and Neville (1996) findings thus suggest that our reservations about White and Genesee's (1996) findings are well founded.

In summary, our review of research on L2 competence suggests that studies of the access question may have produced anomalous findings precisely because of their general (and often unstated) conceptualization of how a CP might affect L2 competence. Our fundamental conceptual point here is that when comparing L1 competence with L2 competence, one would, a priori, not expect to find the gross differences that one expects to find in comparing normal L1 competence with the pathological competence of those who have missed the assumed CP outright (Genie, Chelsea, late ASL learners). In addition, our reading of L2A research that has based itself on linguistic theory leads us to conclude that whereas "proficiency" can vary widely across adult learners, there seems to be a theoretically characterizable natural class of linguistic phenomena that are affected by a CP or CPs for L1 acquisition: namely, parameters.

Interestingly, current linguistic theory identifies functional categories as the locus for parameters. This is especially interesting for the CP question because of the ERP research referred to previously: There seems to be reliable evidence of physiological differences in the processing of functional categories according to whether the stimulus is L1 data or L2 data. That is to say, we seem to have the suggestive beginnings of physiological evidence, not merely of a closed-class–open-class distinction, but further of an age-related difference in whether this distinction operates. If, that is, linguistic theory is correct in telling us that parametric variation is expressed via the functional categories, and if the ERP data are telling us that the adult brain does not deal with new linguistic stimuli differentially according to whether those stimuli express lexical categories or functional categories, then it just may be that we have a convergence of linguistic and neurological evidence that adult L2 learners, however proficient they may be in other areas of language, share an inability to represent parametric values drawn from the lexicon.[17]

SPECULATIONS IN LIEU OF A CONCLUSION

One of the hallmarks of the human mind is a seemingly inexhaustible capacity to learn, a capacity that evidently is limited only by our mortality.[18] This argues for a continued cortical plasticity (cf. Singer, 1995; Zohary et al., 1994); yet as we have seen, there seem to be fairly well-defined linguistic phenomena where plasticity is lost after a CP. If in fact we are correct in thinking that there is a CP for the ability to determine parametric values, but not for all language-related knowledge across the board, one may reasonably ask the following questions: Why should there be such loss of plasticity in the first place? Why should parameters be the locus of CP effects? We are not prepared to offer anything like definitive answers to these questions, but we would like to suggest some possible steps toward an explanation.

First of all, we should recognize that plasticity is a two-edged sword: It allows the organism to learn, but it also makes learning necessary.

---

[17]This is, of course, not to say that we necessarily expect L1 parametric values to play an all-encompassing role in L2 development. Indeed, whereas Schwartz and Sprouse (e.g., 1996) argued for such a view, the data presented by Vainikka and Young-Scholten (e.g., 1996) and Eubank (e.g., 1996) suggest rather different conclusions.

[18]Not that the aged brain is as spry as the younger brain, of course; declines in language-related abilities have been documented in a number of areas (see, e.g., Cohen, 1981; Zelinski & Hyde, 1996). Anderson and Rutledge (1996) found a negative correlation between age and number of dendrites; interestingly, there is a hemispheric asymmetry, with dendrites becoming fewer and shorter in the putative language cortex in the left hemisphere than in its right hemisphere analogue.

There are many things it would be profitable not to have to learn over and over; it is certainly an advantage to any organism not to have to redevelop, say, visual cognition on a daily basis. In this sense we would want either no plasticity from the word go—mature visual capacity at birth—or we would want a limited amount of plasticity, on the assumption that the necessary stimuli will almost definitely be available in time. We certainly would *not* want the brain to be endlessly susceptible to, and endlessly dependent on, instructional effects from visual input. In Kelley's (1992) terms, we would want a short or nonexistent *sensitive* period—we would want the stimuli to do their instructional work and have done with it; and we would want a permanent *critical* period—we would like to hedge our bets and be able to use input to make up for some lost opportunity during the sensitive period, such as defective corneas.

Similarly, it might be nice if the neurons that in normal humans get committed to the visual system and the neurons that get committed to the aural system could switch allegiances if called, as Neville (1995) showed they could to some extent in the early months or years of life. In the absence of aural input—say, because of a congenital cochleal defect unrelated to the CNS—neurons normally committed to aural cognition become connected to the visual system, with the result that congenitally deaf people have peripheral vision superior to that of normals; a useful talent when using sign language, as it turns out. If one suddenly went deaf, it would surely be nice if one could recruit the now useless "hearing" neurons to the "seeing" business. But of course one cannot; once fixed, the aural connections are useless for nonaural functions.

By the same token, it would be nice if we could speak foreign languages like a native, but we cannot. Perhaps one reason we cannot is that there is a CP, or there are CPs—again, in Kelley's (1992) terms, sensitive periods—for certain aspects of language, and that once this period is past, linguistic input ceases to have an instructional effect with regard to those aspects. Why should this be? Well, imagine the results if visual and aural cognition were permanently plastic; that is, if neurons normally committed to the visual system were permanently susceptible to aural stimuli, and vice versa. The result, of course, would be perceptual chaos (cf. Baron-Cohen, 1996, for an account of some rare cases of synaesthesia, or cross-modal mixing of perceptual input). The immature CNS has a comparatively short time during which relevant stimuli can be received that will commit the relevant neurons to their normal duties. In the normal situation, those stimuli will be received and the duties fixed; otherwise, there will be (limited) reassignment of duties. But what we do not find, either in the normal case or the stimulus-deprived case, is neural systems that can "switch-hit", processing visual stimuli one day and aural stimuli another.

Now, the difference between competence in English and competence in French is not of the same order as the difference between visual cognition and aural cognition, but the effects of plasticity may nonetheless be, to an interesting extent at least, similar. On the one hand, of course, for many aspects of language there is nothing analogous to the cross-modal plasticity we see in the congenitally deaf, for example: There is no reason to expect, for example, the learning of French vocabulary to be possible only when the learning of English vocabulary is not, or to be enhanced by lack of English input in early childhood. On the other hand, parametric variation seems to be an either–or sort of affair: Languages are either plus or minus prodrop, either head initial or head final, have either strong or weak inflection, and so forth but, not both at the same time or one today and the other tomorrow. We note that for L1 acquisition, whereas, for example, lexical acquisition continues at a rapid pace well into adolescence (Pinker, 1995) and remains possible throughout life, and whereas various subtleties of the language may not be fully grasped until age 10 or so (see, e.g., Chomsky, 1969), parameters seem to be set at a very early age. To take but one example, cross-linguistic data on the appeerence of null subjects in child language suggest strongly that the so-called pro-drop or null subject parameter is set at a very early age, perhaps prior to the two-word stage (see, e.g,. Bloom 1990; Valian, 1991; Wexler, 1996).

One possibility, then, is this: Certain aspects of linguistic competence—structure dependence, for example—are, although not strictly speaking hardwired, universally fixed for any member of the species on the provision of some minimal amount of linguistic stimuli. Certain other aspects are determined variably (within narrow limits) by the interaction of variable input and neocortex. These variable linguistic aspects include syntactic and phonological parameters as specified in (a perfected) linguistic theory. The relevant input in both cases must be provided within a critical (= Kelley's sensitive) period, which may even vary for various parameters. During this period, the human brain is capable of adjusting to varying input, as witness bilingual children (although we recognize the need for a caveat or two here). The CP for (these aspects of) linguistic competence does not extend beyond the sensitive period; by the time the sensitive period is over, it is too late, as Genie and Chelsea indicate.

There are, however, other aspects of linguistic competence besides principles and parameters, such as the lexicon and rules related to it, which may not be subject to a sensitive period. Genie was able to learn new words, for instance, including fairly complex ones, although she couldn't put them into, say, a well-formed Wh-question. With these aspects of linguistic competence, we would expect to see fairly weak age effects, aside from the general decline in powers one attributes to senescence. Thus, in cases of significant adult failure to acquire these aspects of L2 competence, we would expect to find causes unrelated to a biological CP: limited input, insufficient motivation, and so forth.

There are yet other aspects of linguistic competence about which it is hard to say anything at this point: There are a number of phenomena that certainly seem to raise the question of the poverty of the stimulus on the one hand, but for which there are no UG proposals (yet) on the table. Consider the so-called paths that Ross (e.g., 1995) recently examined; or some of Whorf's (1941) covert categories, such as when you can affix the negative *un-* to an adjective; or the Time Sequence Constraint on Japanese conditionals.[19] There definitely seem to be distinct native–nonnative differences with respect to these phenomena, but in the absence of a linguistic-theoretical way of dealing with them, we hesitate to say anything at all about CPs.

Returning to our earlier speculation about the function of CPs, it would surely seem unlikely for there to be any advantage to the organism in losing the ability to learn, say, new words in adult life; although there certainly would be a disadvantage in having to learn new semantic principles on which to classify them or new morphological rules to subject them to. Thus, we would not expect a CP to arise for this aspect of language. On the other hand, such basic structural relations as head position or active–passive differences can be of use in producing and comprehending sentences only if they are reliable; if there is a prodrop parameter, for instance, it would not do for English native speakers to be continually thrown into doubt about its value every time they heard an imperative sentence or a token of Bushspeak. It may be the case that a sensitive period for L1 acquisition is what enables us to make up our mind, as it were, about certain aspects of our language in the absence of overpowering inductive evidence, and in the face of seeming counterevidence. It may be the case, to put it overly bluntly, that the price we pay for successful L1 acquisition is the inability to acquire an L2.

Why there should be the possibility in human language for both "plus" and "minus" values for a prodrop parameter in the first place is a question we have no answer for; there is certainly no reason to assume that the limited variation built into UG is the result of selectional pressure based on adaptive advantage for those multiple values. But such multiple values are a fact, and given that fact, we might want to call a halt to the multiplicity—to the plasticity—as soon as possible, by having the parameters set within a critical period.

---

[19]Briefly, in a Japanese conditional sentence, the event indicated by the verb in the apodosis must take place at a later time than that indicated by the verb in the protasis. Hence, whereas sentences like the equivalent of *If I go to Chicago I'll meet my friend* are allowed, sentences like *If I go to Chicago I'll go by plane* are not.

ACKNOWLEDGMENTS

We are grateful to Roger Hawkins, James Hurford, Eric Kellerman, Michael Long, Lydia White, and Helmut Zobl for helpful comments. Thanks also to Justine Cullinan of the New York Academy of Sciences for tracking down some bibliographic information. Earlier versions of this chapter were given by Gregg at a symposium on CPs and L2A organized by David Birdsong at the Association Internationale de Linguistique Appliquée (AILA) conference in Jyväskylä, Finland, August 1996; at the University of Durham, February 1997; and at Thames Valley University, March 1997. We thank David, Bonnie Schwartz (Durham), and Peter Skehan (Thames Valley) for providing these opportunities to test our ideas.

REFERENCES

Anderson, B., & Rutledge, V. (1996). Age and hemisphere effects on dendritic structure. *Brain, 119,* 1983–1990.

Andriew, A. (1996). Innateness and canalization. *Philosophy of Science, 63,* (Suppl., *Proceedings of the PSA, 1996*), S19–S27.

Artola, A., & Singer, W. (1994). NMDA receptors and developmental plasticity in visual neocortex. In G. L. Collingridge & J. C. Watkins (Eds.), *The NMDA receptor* (2nd ed., pp. 313-339). Oxford, England: Oxford University Press.

Baron-Cohen, S. (1996, June). Is there a normal phase of synaesthesia in development? *Psyche: An Interdisciplinary Journal of Research on Consciousness 2* (27).

Beck, M.-L. (1996). The status of verb-raising among English-speaking learners of German. In E. Kellerman, B. Weltens, & T. Bongaerts (Eds.), *EuroSLA 6: A selection of papers* (pp. 23–33). Amsterdam: Nederlandse Vereniging voor Toegepaste Taalwetenschap.

Beck, M.-L. (1997). Regular verbs, past tense and frequency: Tracking down a potential source of native NS/NNS speaker competence differences. *Second Language Research, 13,* 95–115.

Bever, T. G. (1981). Normal acquisition processes explain the critical period for language learning. In K. Diller (Ed.), *Individual differences and universals in language learning aptitude* (pp. 176–198). Rowley, MA: Newbury House.

Birdsong, D. (1992). Ultimate attainment in second language acquisition. *Language, 68,* 705–755.

Bley-Vroman, R. (1990). The logical problem of foreign language learning. *Linguistic Analysis, 20,* 3–49.

Bloom, P. (1990). Subjectless sentences in child language. *Linguistic Inquiry, 21,* 491–504.

Bogen, J., & Woodward, J. (1988). Saving the phenomena. *Philosophical Review, 97,* 303–52.

Borer, H. (1984). *Parametric syntax.* Dordrecht, Netherlands: Foris.

Bornstein, M. H. (1989). Sensitive periods in development: Structural characteristics and causal interpretations. *Psychological Bulletin, 105,* 179–197.

Brauth, S. E., Hall, W. S., & Dooling, R. J. (Eds.). (1991). *Plasticity of development.* Cambridge, MA: MIT Press.

Chomsky, C. (1969). *The acquisition of syntax in children from 5 to 10.* Cambridge, MA: MIT Press.

Chomsky, N. (1981). *Lectures on government and binding.* Dordrecht, Netherlands: Foris.

Chomsky, N. (1995). *The minimalist program.* Cambridge, MA: MIT Press.

Clahsen, H. (1989). The grammatical characterization of developmental dysphasia. *Linguistics, 27,* 897–920.

Clahsen, H., & Muysken, P. (1986). The availability of universal grammar to child and adult learners: A study of the acquisition of German word order by adult and child learners. *Second Language Research, 2,* 93–119.

Cohen, G. (1981). Inferential reasoning in old age. *Cognition, 9,* 59–72.

Collingridge, G. L., & Watkins, J. C. (Eds.). (1994). *The NMDA receptor* (2nd ed.). Oxford: Oxford University Press.

Colombo, J. (1982). The critical period concept: Research, methodology, and theoretical concerns. *Psychological Bulletin, 91,* 260–275.

Cook, V. J., & Newson, M. (1996). *Chomsky's universal grammar: An introduction* (2nd ed.). London: Blackwell.

Coppieters, R. (1987). Competence differences between natives and near-native speakers. *Language, 63,* 544–573.

Crair, M. C., & Malenka, R. C. (1995). A critical period for long-term potentiation at thalamocortical synapses. *Nature, 375,* 325–328.

Curtiss, S. (1977). *Genie: A psycholinguistic study of a modern-day "wild child."* New York: Academic Press.

Curtiss, S. (1988). Abnormal language acquisition and the modularity of language. In F. J. Newmeyer (Ed.), *Linguistics: The Cambridge Survey,* Vol. II (pp. 96–116). Cambridge, England: Cambridge University Press.

Curtiss, S. (1989). *The case of Chelsea: A new test case of the critical period for language acquisition.* Unpublished manuscript, University of California, Los Angeles.

duPlessis, J., Solin, D., Travis, L., & White, L. (1987). UG or not UG, that is the question: A reply to Clahsen and Muysken. *Second Language Research, 3,* 56–75.

Ellis, R. (1994). *The study of second language acquisition.* Oxford, England: Oxford University Press.

Epstein, S., Flynn, S., & Martohardjono, G. (1996). Second language acquisition: Theoretical and experimental issues in contemporary research. *Behavioral and Brain Sciences,19*, 677–758.

Eubank, L. (1992). Verb movement, agreement and tense in L2 acquisition. In J. Meisel (Ed.), *The acquisition of verb placement: Functional categories and V2 phenomena in language development* (pp. 225–244). Dordrecht, Netherlands: Kluwer.

Eubank, L. (1995, August). *Some views on the L2 initial state.* Paper presented at the 1995 Language Acquisition Research Symposium, Utrecht.

Eubank, L. (1996). Negation in early German-English interlanguage: More valueless features in the L2 initial state. *Second Language Research, 12*, 73–106.

Eubank, L., & Grace, S. (1996). Where's the mature language? Where's the native language? In A. Stringfellow, D. Cahana-Amitay, E. Hughes, & A. Zukowski (Eds.), *Proceedings of the 20th annual Boston University Conference on Language Development* (pp. 189–200). Somerville, MA: Cascadilla Press.

Eubank, L., & Gregg, K. R. (1995). "Et in amygdala ego"?: UG, (S)LA, and neurobiology. *Studies in Second Language Acquisition, 17*, 35–57.

Felix, S. (1995). Universal grammar in L2 acquisition. In L. Eubank, L. Selinker, & M. Sharwood Smith (Eds.), *The current state of interlanguage* (pp. 139–151). Amsterdam: John Benjamins.

Finer, D. L. (1991). Binding parameters in second language acquisition. In L. Eubank (Ed.), *Point/counterpoint: Universal grammar in the second language* (pp. 351–374). Amsterdam: John Benjamins.

Flynn, S., & Manuel, S. (1991). Age-dependent effects in language acquisition: An evaluation of 'critical period' hypotheses. In L. Eubank (Ed.), *Point/counterpoint: Universal grammar in the second language* (pp. 117–145). Amsterdam: John Benjamins.

Fox, M. W. (1970). Overview and critique of stages and periods in canine development. *Developmental Psychobiology, 4*, 37–54.

Gilbert, C. D., & Wiesel, T. N. (1992). Receptive field dynamics in adult primary visual cortex. *Nature, 256*, 150–152.

Glazewski, S., Chen, C.-M., Silva, A., & Fox, K. (1996). Requirement for a-CaMKII in experience-dependent plasticity of the barrel cortex. *Science, 272*, 421–423.

Gleitman, L., & Newport, E. (1995). The invention of language by children: Environmental and biological influences on the acquisition of language. In L. Gleitman & M. Liberman (Eds.), *Language: An invitation to cognitive science* (2nd ed., Vol. 1, pp. 1–24). Cambridge, MA: MIT Press.

Gopnik, M. (1990). Feature blindness: A case study. *Language Acquisition, 2*, 139–164.

Gould, J., & Marler, P. (1991). Learning by instinct. In W. S.-Y. Wang (Ed.), *The emergence of language: Development and evolution* (pp. 8–103). New York: Freeman.

Gregg, K. R. (1996). The logical and developmental problems of second language acquisition. In W. C. Ritchie & T. K. Bhatia (Eds.), *Handbook of second language acquisition* (pp. 49–81). San Diego, CA: Academic Press.

Haas, H. L., & Buzsaki, G. (Eds.). (1988). *Synaptic plasticity in the hippocampus.* Berlin, Germany: Springer.

Henry, K. R. (1983). Lifelong susceptibility to acoustic trauma: Changing patterns of cochlear damage over the life span of the mouse. *Audiology, 22,* 372–383.

Hubel, D. H., & Wiesel, T. N. (1965). Binocular interaction in the striate cortex of kittens reared with artificial squint. *Journal of Neurophysiology, 21,* 1041–1059.

Hurford, J. R. (1987). *Language and number: The emergence of a cognitive system.* Oxford, England: Basil Blackwell.

Hurford, J. R. (1991). The evolution of the critical period for language acquisition. *Cognition, 40,* 159–201.

Johnson, J. S. , & Newport, E. L. (1989). Critical period effects in second language learning: The influence of maturational state on the acquisition of English as a second language. *Cognitive Psychology, 21,* 60–99.

Johnson, J. S., & Newport, E. L. (1991). Critical period effects on universal properties of language: The status of subjacency in the acquisition of second languages. *Cognition, 30,* 215–258.

Johnson, J. S., Shenkman, K. D., Newport, E. L., & Medin, D. L. (1996). Indeterminacy in the grammar of adult language learners. *Journal of Memory and Language, 35,* 335–352.

Kalil, R. (1989). Synapse formation in the developing brain. *Scientific American, 261,* 76–85.

Kellerman, E. (1995). Age before beauty: Johnson and Newport revisited. In L. Eubank, L. Selinker, & M. Sharwood Smith (Eds.), *The current state of interlanguage* (pp. 219–231). Amsterdam: John Benjamins.

Kelley, D. B. (1992). Opening and closing a hormone-regulated period for the development of courtship song: A cellular and molecular analysis of vocal neuroeffectors. In G. Turkewitz (Ed.), *Developmental psychobiology* (pp. 178–188). New York: New York Academy of Sciences.

Krashen, S. D. (1975). The critical period for language and its possible bases. In D. Aaronson & R. W. Rieber (Eds.), *Developmental psycholinguistics and communication disorders* (pp. 211–224). New York: New York Academy of Sciences.

Larsen-Freeman, D., & Long, M. H. (1991). *An introduction to second language acquisition research.* London: Longman.

Long, M. H. (1990). Maturational constraints on language development. *Studies in Second Language Acquisition, 12,* 251–285.

Long, M. H. (1993). Second language acquisition as a function of age: Substantive findings and methodological issues. In K. Hyltenstam & A. Viberg (Eds.), *Progression and regression in language* (pp. 196–221). Cambridge, England: Cambridge University Press.

Marler, P. (1991). The instinct for vocal learning: Songbirds. In S. E. Brauth, W. S. Hall, & R. J. Dooling (Eds.), *Plasticity of development* (pp. 107–125). Cambridge, MA: MIT Press.

Martohardjono, G. & Gair, J. W. (1993). Apparent UG inaccessibility in second language acquisition: Misapplied principles or principled misapplications? In F. R. Eckman (Ed.), *Confluence: Linguistics, L2 acquisition, and speech pathology* (pp. 79–103). Amsterdam: John Benjamins.

Meisel, J. (1996). *Initial states of grammatical knowledge in second language acquisition.* Unpublished manuscript, University of Hamburg.

Moltz, H. (1973). Some implications of the critical period hypothesis. In E. Tobach, H. E. Adler, & L. L. Adler (Eds.), *Comparative psychology at issue* (pp. 144–146). New York: New York Academy of Sciences.

Morris, R. G. M., & Davis, M. (1994). The role of NMDA receptors in learning and memory. In G. L. Collingridge & J. C. Watkins (Eds.), *The NMDA receptor* (2nd ed., pp. 340–375). Oxford, England: Oxford University Press.

Mueller, N. (1996). *Subordinate clauses in second and first language acquisition: A case against parameters.* Unpublished manuscript, University of Hamburg.

Neville, H. (1995). Developmental specificity in neurocognitive development in humans. In M. S. Gazzaniga (Ed.), *The cognitive neurosciences* (pp. 219–231). Cambridge, MA: MIT Press.

Neville, H., Nicol, J., Barss, A., Forster, A., & Garrett, M. (1991). Syntactically based sentence processing classes: Evidence from event-related potentials. *Journal of Cognitive Neuroscience, 3,* 151–165.

Newport, E. L. (1990). Maturational constraints on language learning. *Cognitive Science, 4,* 11–28.

Pettet, M. W., & Gilbert, C. D. (1992). Dynamic changes in receptive-field size in the cat primary visual cortex. *Proceedings of the National Academy of Sciences, USA, 89,* 8366–8370.

Pinker, S. (1995). Language acquisition. In L. Gleitman & M. Liberman (Eds.), *Language: An invitation to cognitive science* (2nd ed., Vol. 1, pp. 135–182). Cambridge, MA: MIT Press.

Pollock, J.-Y. (1989). Verb movement, Universal Grammar, and the structure of IP. *Linguistic Inquiry, 20,* 365–424.

Rakic, P. (1991). Plasticity of cortical development. In S. E. Brauth, W. S. Hall, & R. J. Dooling (Eds.), *Plasticity of development* (pp. 127–161). Cambridge, MA: MIT Press.

Rice, M. (1991). Children with specific language impairment: Toward a model of teachability. In N. A. Krasnegor, D. M. Rumbaugh, R. L. Schiefelbusch, & M. Studdert-Kennedy (Eds.), *Biological and behavioral determinants of language development* (pp. 447–480). Hillsdale, NJ: Lawrence Erlbaum Associates.

Rice, M., Wexler, K., & Cleave, P. (1995). Specific language impairment as a period of extended optional infinitives. *Journal of Speech and Hearing Science, 38*, 850–863.

Ross, J. R. (1995). A first crosslinguistic look at paths: The difference between end-legs and medial ones. In L. Eubank, L. Selinker, & M. Sharwood Smith (Eds.), *The current state of interlanguage* (pp. 271–283). Amsterdam: John Benjamins.

Schachter, J. (1989). Testing a proposed universal. In S. Gass & J. Schachter (Eds.), *Linguistic perspectives on second language acquisition* (pp. 73–88). Cambridge, England: Cambridge University Press.

Schwartz, B. D. & Sprouse, R. (1994). Word order and nominative case assignment in non-native language acquisition: A longitudinal study of (L1 Turkish) German interlanguage. In T. Hoekstra & B. D. Schwartz (Eds.), *Language acquisition studies in generative grammar* (pp. 317–368). Amsterdam: John Benjamins.

Schwartz, B. D., & Sprouse, R. (1996). L2 cognitive states and the full transfer/full access model. *Second Language Research, 12*, 40–72.

Shao, J., & Neville, H. (1996, March/April). *ERPs elicited by semantic anomalies: Beyond the N400*. Poster presented at the annual meeting of the Cognitive Neuroscience Society, San Francisco.

Singer, W. (1995). Development and plasticity of cortical processing architectures. *Science, 270*, 758–764.

Thompson, R. F. (1993). *The brain: A neuroscience primer* (2nd ed.). New York: Freeman.

Tomaselli, A., & Schwartz, B. D. (1990). Analysing the acquisition stages of negation in L2 German: Support for UG in adult SLA. *Second Language Research, 6*, 1–38.

Vainikka, A., & Young-Scholten, M. (1994). Direct access to X'-theory: Evidence from Korean and Turkish adults learning German. In T. Hoekstra & B. Schwartz (Eds.), *Language acquisition studies in generative grammar* (pp. 265–316). Amsterdam: John Benjamins.

Vainikka, A., & Young-Scholten, M. (1996). Gradual development of L2 phrase structure. *Second Language Research, 12*, 7–39.

Valian, V. (1991). Syntactic subjects in the early speech of American and Italian children. *Cognition, 40*, 21–81.

Van der Lely, H. (1996). Empirical evidence for the modularity of language from grammatical SLI children. In A. Stringfellow, D. Cahana-Amitay, E. Hughes, & A. Zukowsky (Eds.), *Proceedings of the 20th annual Boston University Conference on Language Development* (pp. 792–803). Somerville, MA: Cascadilla Press.

Van der Lely, H., & Ullman, M. (1996). The computation and representation of past-tense morphology in specifically language impaired and normally developing children. In A. Stringfellow, D. Cahana-Amitay, E. Hughes, & A. Zukowsky (Eds.), *Proceedings of the 20th annual Boston University Conference on Language Development* (pp. 804–815). Somerville, MA: Cascadilla Press.

Waddington, C. H. (1975). *The evolution of an evolutionist.* Ithaca, NY: Cornell University Press.

Webelhuth, G. (1992). *Principles and parameters of syntactic saturation.* New York: Oxford University Press.

Webelhuth, G. (Ed.). (1995). *Government and binding theory and the minimalist program.* Oxford, England: Basil Blackwell.

Weber-Fox, C. M., & Neville, H. J. (1996). Maturational constraints on functional specializations for language processing: ERP and behavioral evidence in bilingual speakers. *Journal of Cognitive Neuroscience, 8,* 231–256.

Wexler, K. (1996, June). *What children don't know really tells us a lot about linguistic theory.* Lecture handout, University of Utrecht.

White, L. (1990/91). The verb movement parameter in second language acquisition. *Language Acquisition, 1,* 337–360.

White, L. (1992). Long and short verb movement in second language acquisition. *Canadian Journal of Linguistics, 37,* 273–286.

White, L., & Genesee, F. (1996). How native is near-native? The issue of ultimate attainment in adult second language acquisition. *Second Language Research, 12,* 233–265.

Whorf, B. L. (1941). Grammatical categories. *Language, 21,* 1-11. Reprinted in J.B. Carroll (Ed.). (1956). *Language, thought, and reality: Selected writings of Benjamin Lee Whorf* (pp. 87-101). Cambridge, MA: MIT Press.

Zelinski, E. M., & Hyde, J. C. (1996). Old words, new meanings: Aging and sense creation. *Journal of Memory and Language, 35,* 689–707.

Zohary, E., Celebrini, S.,Britten, K. H., & Newsome, W. T. (1994). Neuronal plasticity that underlies improvement in perceptual performance. *Science, 263,* 1289–1292.

CHAPTER FIVE

Age of Learning
and Second Language Speech

James E. Flege
University of Alabama, Birmingham

In this chapter, we consider the relation between the age at which the naturalistic acquisition of a second language (L2) begins, and the accuracy with which the L2 is pronounced. Quite clearly, earlier is better as far as L2 pronunciation is concerned. However, the widely accepted critical period hypothesis does not appear to provide the best explanation for this phenomenon.

INTRODUCTION

Although it is widely agreed that "earlier is better" as far as the pronunciation of an L2 is concerned, there is disagreement as to the exact nature of the relation between the age of L2 learning and degree of foreign accent, as well as the cause(s) of foreign accent (see Singleton, 1989, for a review). Long (1990) concluded from a review of previously published studies that an L2 is usually spoken without accent if learning begins by the age of 6, with a foreign accent if learning begins after the age of 12, and with variable success between the ages of 6 and 12. Patkowski (1990) concluded that the dramatic difference he noted in the foreign accents of participants who had first arrived in the United States before versus after the age of 15 was due to the passing of a critical period, which he defined as an "age-based constraint on the acquisition of full native fluency" in an L2. Indeed, Patkowski claimed that individuals who begin learning an L2 before versus after the critical period differ in a "fundamental, qualitative way" (p. 74).

101

The critical period hypothesis (CPH) is widely viewed as providing an explanation for why many individuals speak their L2 with a foreign accent. The end of a critical period for speech is usually associated with some sort of neurological change (e.g., lost plasticity, hemispheric specialization, or neurofunctional reorganization) that is thought to arise as the result of normal maturation (e.g., Lamendella 1977; Lenneberg, 1967; Patkowski, 1990; Penfield & Roberts, 1959; Scovel, 1969, 1988). Such a neurofunctional change(s), which might be expected to occur at roughly the same chronological age in many individuals, could conceivably affect the processing and storage in long-term memory of information pertinent to the L2 (e.g., Genesee et al., 1978). The CPH seems to imply that some aspect(s) of the capacity that permits children to learn to pronounce their L1 accurately is reduced or lost beyond the critical period.

Patkowski's (1990) conclusion that a critical period exists for speech learning was based on a pattern of empirical data that has not been replicated in two recent studies. Flege, Munro, and MacKay (1995) examined the production of English sentences by 240 native speakers of Italian who immigrated to Ottawa, Canada, between the ages of 2 and 23. Given Patkowski's (1990) admonition that the CPH can be properly evaluated only by considering participants who have reached their ultimate attainment in L2 pronunciation under optimal learning conditions, Flege et al. (1995) recruited participants who had been living in Canada for at least 15 years at the time they were tested. In fact, the native Italian participants had lived in Ottawa for 32 years on average; most of them indicated that they spoke English more than Italian.

The 240 native Italian participants' productions of five short English sentences (e.g., *The red book was good*), along with those of a control group of 24 native English participants, were digitized and then presented randomly to native speakers of English from Ontario. These listeners rated the sentences they heard for overall degree of perceived foreign accent using a continuous scale. Figure 5.1 shows the mean ratings obtained for the 264 participants. As expected, the native English participants received higher ratings than most native Italian participants, whose ratings decreased systematically as age of arrival (AOA) increased. Importantly, there was no discontinuity in the ratings at an AOA of 15 years, or at any other AOA. The straight line fit to the data obtained for the 240 native Italian participants accounted for 71.4% of the variance in the ratings accorded their sentences ($p < .01$). (Language use factors accounted for roughly 15% of additional variance; see Flege et al., 1995). A subsequent study by Yeni-Komshian, Flege, and Liu (1997) that employed a similar design also yielded a near-linear relation between AOA and degree of foreign

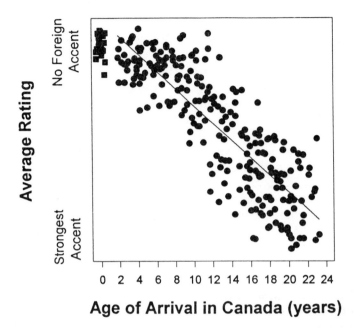

Age of Arrival in Canada (years)

FIG. 5.1. Average foreign accent ratings for 240 native speakers of Italian who arrived in English-speaking Canada between the ages of 2 and 23 (filled circles) and 24 native English controls (squares). Data are from Flege, Munro and MacKay (1995).

accent in a population of 240 Korean–English bilinguals living in the United States.

We can only speculate on the cause of the important difference in the results obtained by Flege et al. (1995) and Yeni-Komshian et al. (1997), on the one hand, and by Patkowski (1990), on the other hand. The difference was probably not due to differences in average length of residence in an English-speaking country of the participants who were studied—roughly 32 years for the Flege et al. (1995) participants, 20 years for the Patkowski (1990) participants, and 15 years for the Yeni-Komshian et al. (1997) participants. It is conceivable, however, that one or more of the following other factors contributed to the observed difference: heterogeneity of the nonnative groups that were studied (many different native languages (L1s) in the Patkowski, 1990, study, just one L1 in the other two studies); the size of the nonnative population (67 vs. 240); the scaling techniques employed (a 5-point scale by Patkowski, 1990, vs. continuous and 9-point scales in the other two studies); and judges who evaluated the speech materials (trained

English as a Second Language teachers in the Patkowski study vs. untrained).

I think it more likely, however, that the difference was an indirect consequence of the kind of speech materials that were examined. The participants examined by Flege et al. (1995) and by Yeni-Komshian et al. (1997) produced a standard set of sentences, whereas Patkowski (1990) examined 30-second excerpts of spontaneous speech samples that his participants had produced in interviews lasting from 15 to 30 minutes. It is therefore possible that Patkowski's trained judges were influenced by the nonnative participants' word choices and grammatical accuracy in addition to differences in pronunciation accuracy. If so, then the results obtained by Patkowski may be indicative of a sharp age-related discontinuity in performance in some linguistic domain other than the phonetic–phonological domain.

In my view, the lack of a nonlinearity in the function relating AOA to degree of foreign accent is inconsistent with the view that a critical period exists for speech learning (see also Bialystok & Hakuta, this volume). There was, however, one aspect of the data obtained by Flege et al. (1995) that was consistent with a CPH. None of the native Italian participants who began learning English after the age of 15 obtained a score that fell within two standard deviations (SDs) of the mean value obtained for the 24 native English control participants, and thus might be deemed to have learned to speak English without a detectable foreign accent. However, the data presented by Bongaerts, Planken, and Schils (1995; see also Bongaerts, Chap. 6, this volume) suggest that certain highly motivated individuals who begin learning their L2 beyond the age traditionally thought to mark the end of a critical period do manage to speak their L2 without foreign accent.

AN INTERACTIONIST PERSPECTIVE

The data just presented pose a problem for the CPH in that they did not reveal a sharp decline in pronunciation accuracy as a function of age. A more general problem with the CPH is that it does not specify the actual mechanism(s) that supposedly deteriorate, or are lost altogether, as the result of maturation. Several possibilities come to mind. For example, neurofunctional change(s) might reduce a person's ability to add or modify the sensorimotor programs used for producing the vowels and consonants of an L2 (McLaughlin, 1977). Or, change(s) might reduce the ability to establish perceptual representations for new vowels and consonants (Flege, 1995; Rochet, 1995).

Still another problem is that the CPH is not directly testable. This is because factors that might conceivably influence speech learning are inevitably confounded with chronological age, which is the usual surrogate for the state of neurofunctional maturation that is thought to precipitate a lost or slowed ability to learn speech (see Flege, 1987, for discussion). For example, participants' age of first exposure to an L2 in a predominantly L2-speaking environment may be related to their strength of emotional attachment to the L1-speaking community, their willingness to sound just like members of the L2-speaking culture, or both. To take another example, either length of residence in an L2-speaking environment or chronological age must be confounded in a research design meant to compare groups of participants differing in their AOA in an L2-speaking environment.

As I see it, the most serious problem is that, because of its widespread appeal, the CPH dampens researchers' enthusiasm for seeking and testing other potential explanations for the ubiquitous presence of foreign accents (as well as age-related declines in other aspects of L2 performance). Other general hypotheses can indeed be formulated. For example, according to what might be called the *exercise hypothesis*, one's ability to learn to produce and perceive speech remains intact across the life span, but only if one continues to learn speech uninterruptedly (see Bever, 1981; Hurford, 1991). On this view, foreign accents increase as a function of AOA because as AOA increases, fewer individuals can be found who have never stopped learning speech. However, although it is interesting, the exercise hypothesis may be difficult or impossible to test. It may not be possible to recruit matched groups of participants who have begun to learn some language, X, at the same age and under similar circumstances but who differ according to whether other languages were learned between L1 acquisition and the time of first exposure to language X.

According to an *unfolding hypothesis*, foreign accents are the indirect consequence of previous phonetic development, not the result of lost or attenuated speech learning abilities (Oyama, 1979; see also Elman, 1993, and Marchman, 1993, for a connectionist perspective). For example, the phonetic categories established for vowels and consonants in the L1 may become better defined with age (Flege, 1992a, 1992b) and so become ever more likely to "assimilate" phonetically different vowels and consonants in an L2 (Best, 1995). The unfolding hypothesis predicts that the more fully developed the L1 phonetic system is at the time L2 learning begins, the more foreign-accented the pronunciation of the L2 will be. A problem also exists for the unfolding hypothesis, however. The state of development of the L1 phonetic system is apt to covary with maturation and development (and, of course, chronological age). This means that differentiating the unfolding hypothesis from the CPH may be impossible.

Still another general hypothesis might be called the *interaction hypothesis*. Weinreich (1953) was apparently the first to suggest that a mutual influence of a bilingual's two languages on one another is inevitable. If so, it may be impossible for a bilingual to control two languages in exactly the same way as two monolinguals. Indeed, a number of investigators have suggested that it is not appropriate to assess bilinguals in the same way that one assesses monolinguals (Grosjean, 1982). For example, Cook (1995) observed that divergences from monolingual-defined norms for the L1 or the L2 should not be viewed as a failure, as suggested by Selinker (1972), but as the necessary consequence of "multicompetences" in two languages. Cook (1995) suggested that, in the aggregate, the multicompetences of a bilingual normally exceeds the competence of any one monolingual. Mack (1986) noted that although early bilinguals may be quite fluent in both of their languages, the way they process language may differ from that of monolinguals because of a "pattern of linguistic organization that is unlike that of a monolingual" (p. 464; see also Neville, Mills, & Lawson, 1992; Weber-Fox & Neville, 1992).

According to the interaction hypothesis, bilinguals are unable to fully separate the L1 and L2 phonetic systems, which necessarily interact with one another. The L1 and L2 systems may, of course, form constrained subsystems that can be activated and deactivated to varying degrees (Paradis, 1993). This is what permits different modes of pronunciation in the L1 and L2. However, according to the interaction hypothesis, the phonic elements of the L1 subsystem necessarily influence phonic elements in the L2 system, and vice versa. The nature, strength, and directionality of the influence may vary as a function of factors such as the number and nature of categories established for phonic elements of the L1 and L2, the amount and circumstances of L1 and L2 use, language dominance, and so on (see e.g., Anisfeld, Anisfeld, & Semogas 1969; Cutler, Mehler, Norris, & Segui, 1989; Flege, 1995; Ho, 1986; Macnamara, 1973). The interaction hypothesis leads to a prediction that is not generated by a CPH or any other hypothesis. It predicts that the loss of the L1, or its attenuation through disuse (Grosjean, 1982; Romaine, 1995), may reduce the degree of perceived foreign accent in an L2. In other words, the "less" L1 there is, the smaller will be its influence on the pronunciation of an L2 (Dunkel, 1948).

The interaction hypothesis was tested by Flege, Frieda, and Nozawa (1997) in a study that examined foreign accent in English sentences spoken by native speakers of English and two groups of native Italian participants. The participants in both native Italian groups had arrived in Canada from Italy at an average age of 5 but differed in self-reported use of Italian, 3% on average for the "LoUse" participants versus 33% for the "HiUse" participants. The sentences spoken by the native Italian participants and those spoken by the native English controls were randomly presented to native English-speaking listeners who labeled each sentence as "definitely English" (i.e., definitely spoken by a native speaker of English), "probably English," "probably

Italian" (i.e., probably spoken by a native speaker of Italian), or "definitely Italian."

The results of two analyses[1] yielded two findings that run counter to the CPH. First, sentences spoken by both the HiUse and LoUse participants were found to be foreign accented even though the participants in these groups had learned English as young children and had spoken English for more than 30 years, on the average. The CPH would lead one to expect that childhood learners of an L2 could evade being detected as foreign accented. Second, the HiUse participants were found to speak English with significantly stronger foreign accents than did the LoUse participants. Given that the CPH attributes foreign accent to the state of neurological maturation present *at the time L2 learning begins*, it would not lead one to expect a difference in L2 performance as a function of amount of L1 use.

The mutual influence of L1 and L2 on one another was also demonstrated in a study by Yeni-Komshian, et al., (1997). The participants for this study were 240 Korean–English bilinguals who had arrived in the United States between the ages of 2 and 23 and had lived in the United States for 15 years on the average (range: 8–30 years). Native English-speaking listeners used a 9-point scale to rate English sentences spoken by the bilingual participants and a control group of 24 English monolinguals for overall degree of foreign accent. In a parallel experiment, native Korean-speaking listeners used a comparable scale to rate Korean sentences spoken by the bilinguals and a control group of 24 Korean monolinguals. When plotted as a function of the bilinguals' AOA in the United States, the functions established for Korean foreign accent in English sentences and for English foreign accent in Korean sentences formed an "X" pattern. The later the Koreans had arrived in the United States, the less accurately they were judged to have pronounced the English sentences and the more accurately they were judged to have pronounced the Korean sentences.

The Yeni-Komshian et al. (1997) study provided evidence that few if any bilinguals pronounce both of their languages without a detectable foreign accent. Just 16 (7%) of the bilinguals received a rating for their production of English sentences that fell within +/- 2 SDs of the mean rating obtained for the 24 English monolinguals. Those who met the criterion had AOAs ranging from 1.5 to 8.5 years. A much larger number of the bilinguals, 111 (46%), received a rating for their

---

[1]In one analysis, the native English-speaking listeners' judgments were converted to a 4-point rating scale. In another analysis, the correct identifications of native Italian participants' sentences as Italian were counted as hits and incorrect identifications of native English participants' sentences as Italian were counted as false alarms. A-prime (A') scores representing an unbiased measure of the listener's sensitivity to foreign accent in the native Italian participants' sentences were then calculated from the proportion of hits and false alarms.

production of Korean sentences that fell within +/− 2 SDs of the mean obtained for the 24 Korean monolinguals. The bilinguals who met this criterion had AOAs ranging from 8.5 to 22.5 years. However, just one bilingual out of 240, a woman with an AOA of 8.5 years, met the criterion in both English and Korean.

In summary, there is evidence that the two languages spoken by a bilingual interact with one another. If it is true that one continues to learn and refine the phonetic–phonological system of the L1 through childhood and adolescence, then the interaction hypothesis might provide an account for age effects on L2 performance that differs from the one offered by the CPH. Moreover, the interaction hypothesis seems to be more consistent with the observed linear relation between AOA and degree of foreign accent than does the CPH, which leads one to expect a discontinuity.

PRODUCTION AND PERCEPTION

So far we have considered only the overall pronunciation of the L2, that is, degree of foreign accent in sentences. Of course, individuals who learn an L2 often produce particular L2 vowels and consonants inaccurately, which contributes to what is perceived as foreign accent. Some part of nonnatives' divergences from the segmental phonetic norms of the L2 in speech production may arise from an inability to master new forms of articulation. It would be interesting to know, for example, whether native speakers of English who are highly proficient speakers of a Southern Bantu language such as Xhosa are able to master the motorically complex clicks found in that language. If clicks can never be mastered by native English-speaking adults, it would suggest the existence of age constraints on articulatory motor learning.

However, many researchers (e.g., Flege, 1988b) believe that certain speech production errors arise from an incorrect *perceptual* representation of the properties that specify L2 vowels and consonants. For example, Rochet (1995) used a synthetic /i/-/y/-/u/ continuum of vowels to assess nonnatives' vowel perception. Native Portuguese participants tended to misidentify French /y/ as /i/, whereas native English participants tended to misidentify the same vowel stimuli as /u/. In a repetition task, native Portuguese participants produced /i/-quality vowels when they heard French /y/ tokens, whereas native English participants tended to produce /u/. This finding led Rochet to conclude that some vowel production errors are "the consequence of the target phones having been assigned to an L1 category" (p. 404).

The Speech Learning Model ([SLM], e.g., Flege, 1995) posits that the L1 and L2 influence one another, and that this interaction constrains performance accuracy in both languages. According to the SLM, a variety of factors such as an individual's age of L2 learning and the perceived dissimilarity of L2 sounds from the closest L1 sound(s) determines whether an L2 learner will discern the phonetic differences that may exist between an L2 sound and the closest (nonidentical) sound in the L1. Awareness that a cross-language difference exists, in turn, may precipitate the formation of a new L2 phonetic category. Flege hypothesized that "the production of an (L2) sound eventually corresponds to the properties present in its phonetic category representation" (p. 239). This implies that, for certain L2 learners, the perception of an L2 sound may be more accurate than its production.

The hypothesis that production accuracy is constrained by perceptual accuracy is by no means new. Researchers generally agree that speech perception becomes attuned to the contrastive sound units of a particular language very early in life and that, in time, children's production of speech corresponds to what they have heard. Kuhl and Meltzoff (1996) posited that skilled articulation arises out of language-specific perception. They observed that, for the mature native speaker, information specifying auditory-articulatory relations is "exquisitely detailed . . . as though adults have an internalized auditory-articulatory 'map' that specifies the relations between mouth movements and sound" (p. 2425). They also observed that the formation of memory representations "derives initially from perception of the ambient input and then acts as guides for motor output" (p. 2425). Pisoni (1995) noted that the phonetic contrasts that are produced by talkers are "precisely the same acoustic differences that are distinctive in perceptual analysis," making the relation that exists between speech production and perception 'unique' among category systems.[2] Pisoni noted further that although the relation between production and perception is apt to be "complex," it is a nonarbitrary relation that reflects the properties of a "unitary articulatory event" (pp. 22–23).

L1 acquisition research has yielded results that are consistent with the views expressed by researchers such as Kuhl and Pisoni. For example, Kuijper's (1996) work suggested that children's ability to produce and perceive L1 segmental contrasts develops slowly and in parallel through early childhood. However, it is not universally

---

[2]However, a close relation between motor control and perception may not be a characteristic that is unique to speech. A close relation between production and perception seems to reflect a general characteristic of brain functioning. Churchland (1986) observed that "evolution [has] solved the problem of sensory processing and motor control simultaneously," so that "theories [must] mimic evolution and aim for simultaneous solutions as well" (p. 473). According to Edelman's theory of neuronal group selection (e.g., Edelman, 1989), a "dynamic loop . . . continually matches gestures and posture to several kinds of sensory signals." In Edelman's view, perception "depends upon and leads to action." Motor activity is considered to be "an essential part of perceptual categorization" (54–56).

accepted that the same kind of parallelism between production and perception exists in L2 acquisition. In fact, Bever (1981) hypothesized that a critical period for learning speech exists because the development of production and perception will not be closely linked if speech learning occurs after the L1 is firmly established.

Bever (1981) postulated that, during L1 acquisition, a psychogrammar "equilibrates" (or aligns) production and perception. Bever rejected the view that the development of speech perception during L1 acquisition necessarily precedes corresponding developments in speech production, observing that advances in the two domains "leapfrog." He posited that psychogrammar representations reflect the "conjoint" operation of perception and production, and that it is only through the mediation of such representations that what the child has acquired perceptually can influence production, and vice versa.[3]

According to Bever (1981), as the L1 phonology is acquired, production and perception are brought into alignment. Use of the psychogrammar will cease once its primary role, which is to align production and perception, has been accomplished. At this point in speech development, Bever hypothesized that speech production and perception become "independent" and the critical period for speech learning ends. Although psychogrammar representations for the L1 might be accessed, the psychogrammar can no longer be used to align production and perception in an L2 learned after the critical period, that is to say, after the L1 phonology has been fully acquired. It is for this reason that L2 learners "often learn to discriminate sounds . . . they cannot distinctively produce" (Bever, 1981, p. 196).

Bever's version of the CPH is valuable because of its specificity. However, it is not compatible with the results obtained in recent studies that examined L2 segmental production and perception. These studies suggest that, as in L1 acquisition, the production and perception of L2 vowels and consonants may "align" with one another. However, before turning to these segmental studies, I first review a number of related studies dealing with sentence production and perception.

Sentence-Level Studies

By extension, Bever's (1981) psychogrammar hypothesis might lead one to expect that a nonnative's ability to produce and comprehend sentences in their L2 will be unrelated. However, two studies suggest otherwise.

---

[3]It is presumably the existence of psychogrammar representations that permits a child to know that /fɪs/ and /fɪʃ/ are two ways to say the same thing (one her own way and the other an adult's way).

Oyama (1973; see also Oyama, 1982a, 1982b) tested 60 Italian men living in New York City who had arrived in the United States between the ages of 6 to 20 and had lived there for 5 to 18 years. She assessed the participants' degree of perceived foreign accent by having English-speaking listeners rate paragraph-length speech samples. Sentence comprehension was assessed by having the participants repeat as many words as possible in a set of English sentences presented in noise. The foreign accent ratings and the scores from the comprehension test (i.e., the total number of words that could be repeated) for the individual participants were not available for reanalysis. However, when the mean values obtained for six subgroups of the participants (defined on the basis of length of residence and AOA in the United States) was examined, a significant correlation ($r = 0.818$) was obtained. This indicated that the better the native Italian participants pronounced English, the better they were at comprehending English sentences in noise.

The sentences examined by Oyama (1973) included some words that were predictable from context (e.g., *Shepherds seldom lose their sheep*). The scores Oyama obtained were therefore likely to have been influenced to some extent by the participants' higher order knowledge of English. Meador, Flege, and MacKay (1997) recently replicated and extended the Oyama study. To obtain scores that more closely reflected the bottom-up processing of vowels and consonants, semantically unpredictable English sentences (e.g., *The blond dentist ate the heavy bread*) having a single syntactic form (NP-V-NP) were examined. Figure 5.2 shows the results obtained for 54 native Italian participants with a mean age of 48. These participants had arrived in Canada between the ages of 3 and 23 and had lived there for an average of 34 years. The more accurately the participants pronounced English sentences (as rated by native English-speaking listeners), the larger the number of words they were able to repeat, $r = 0.646$, $df = 52$, $p < 0.001$.

The correlation just reported ($r = 0.646$) may actually have underestimated the relation between the participants' ability to produce and perceive the vowels and consonants in the sentences. Repeating the words of a sentence presented in noise requires that words, or parts of words, be held in memory while additional information is processed. Individual differences in phonological short-term memory (PSTM) might therefore be expected to influence performance on a sentences-in-noise task. The participants' PSTM was assessed by having them repeat nonwords formed by concatenating two to five Italian CV syllables. When the variation in the PSTM scores was partialled out, the correlation between the participants' degree of

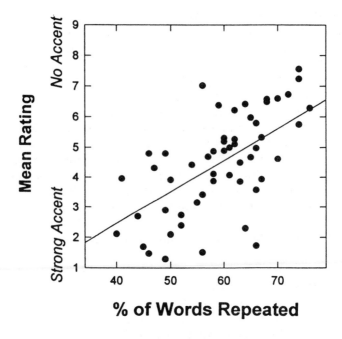

% of Words Repeated

FIG 5.2. The relation between 54 native Italian participants' ability to repeat words in semantically unpredictable English sentences and their overall degree of foreign accent. Data are from Meador, Flege, and MacKay (1997).

foreign accent and the number of words they were able to repeat in the sentences-in-noise test increased to $r = 0.734$.

As mentioned earlier, the SLM posits that the perception of L2 sounds may be more accurate than is their production, but that a divergence in the opposite direction is not expected. At the sentence level, this might lead one to expect that nonnatives who produce English sentences with an accent might nevertheless be able to accurately gauge degree of foreign accent in the same sentences. Flege (1988a) tested this prediction in an experiment with three groups of listeners: monolingual speakers of English, Chinese adults from Taiwan who had lived in the United States for an average of 1.5 years, and Chinese adults from Taiwan who had lived in the United States for 5.3 years on the average. The listeners used a continuous scale ranging from "strongest foreign accent" to "no foreign accent" to rate English sentences spoken by participants with widely varying degrees of foreign accent.

The foreign accent ratings obtained from both groups of Chinese listeners were correlated significantly with those obtained from the native English-speaking listeners ($p < 0.01$). However, the more experienced Chinese listeners showed a significantly stronger correlation, $r = 0.947$, $df = 45$, than did the less experienced Chinese listeners, $r = 0.884$, $df = 45$; $X^2 = 7.79$, $df = 1$, $p < 0.01$. When the foreign accents of the two Chinese listener groups were evaluated, it was found that they spoke English with equally strong foreign accents ($p > 0.10$). Thus, the participants who had lived in the United States for 5.3 years were more sensitive perceptually to the phonetic characteristics of English than were those who had lived in the United States the for just 1.5 years, whereas these two groups did not differ in the accuracy with which they pronounced English sentences. This finding is consistent with the hypothesis that perception "leads" production in L2 acquisition.

Segmental Studies

As mentioned earlier, Bever (1981) hypothesized that speech production and perception develop independently during L2 acquisition because the psychogrammar is no longer used to align production and perception after the end of a critical period. If this hypothesis is correct, then one would not expect to observe correlations between measures of post-critical period L2 learners' production and perception of L2 vowels and consonants. However, the results obtained in recent studies do show significant, albeit modest, correlations.

Vowels

A study by Flege, Bohn, and Jang (1997) provided evidence that a relation exists between late bilinguals' production and perception of L2 vowels. The participants were 20 native speakers each of English, German, Spanish, Korean, and Mandarin. The 80 nonnative participants were first exposed to English on a regular basis when they arrived in the United States as adults; they had lived in the United States for an average of 4.0 years (range: 0.2–23 years) at the time of testing. The participants read a list of consonant-vowel-consonant (CVC) English words containing the vowels /i/, /ɪ/, /ɛ/ and /æ/. Later, they identified the members of two continua containing the same vowels. The perceptual stimuli used in two-alternative forced-choice identification experiments consisted of synthetic vowels that ranged from *beat* to *bit* (/i/-/ɪ/) in one continuum, and from *bet* to *bat* (/ɛ/-/æ/) in the other continuum. In both continua, spectral quality (F1 and F2 frequency) was varied in 11 steps and vowel duration was varied orthogonally in three steps.

One method used to assess vowel production accuracy was to measure the size of the spectral (F1, F2) differences that the participants produced between /i/-/ɪ/ and /ɛ/-/æ/. The native English participants relied primarily on spectral (F1, F2) variation to identify vowels as /i/ versus /ɪ/ (or as /ɛ/ versus /æ/). Many nonnative participants, on the other hand, relied mostly or even entirely on vowel duration, perhaps because they did not have two separate, spectrally defined representations for the perceptual continuum endpoints. Thus, one way used to assess the participants' accuracy in perceiving English vowels was to determine the extent to which their identification responses changed from one response category to the other as a function of the 11-step spectral manipulation in each continuum.

Figure 5.3a shows the relation between the 80 nonnative participants' vowel production and perception accuracy for English /i/-/ɪ/. The percentage change in /i/ responses that occurred as a result of the spectral manipulation in the synthetic vowel stimuli is shown on the x-axis. The y-axis shows the magnitude of the spectral differences between /i/-/ɪ/ that the participants produced (i.e., the Euclidean distance between the values measured in two vowels when plotted in a 2-dimensional bark-difference space, B2–B2 vs. B1–B0.) The more the participants changed their identifications as formant frequencies were changed, the larger were the spectral differences between /i/ and /ɪ/ that they produced, $r = 0.529$, $p < 0.01$. Similarly, as shown in Fig. 5.3b for /ɛ/-/æ/, the greater the increase in /æ/ responses in the perception experiment, the larger the spectral difference that the participants produced between /ɛ/-/æ/, $r = 0.523$, $p < 0.01$.

Both production–perception correlations just reported were significant, but they were modest in size. This does not undermine the view that production accuracy is constrained by perception accuracy in L2 acquisition. Indeed, it is just what one expects if accuracy in perception is a prerequisite for accuracy in production but does not guarantee it. Inspection of the individual participant data in Fig. 5.3 reveals that the participants who showed a large (and thus English-like) shift in judgments as spectral quality varied showed a wide range in production accuracy. On the other hand, most of the participants who showed little perceptual effect of spectral quality also produced little spectral difference between the English vowels.

There were, of course, individual exceptions to the general pattern. Thus, the following analysis was carried out to determine if the participants with inaccurate perception also tended to produce vowels inaccurately. The nonnative participants were assigned to one of three subgroups based on their performance in the identification experiment. Those who showed more than an 80% decrease in /i/ as F1 values increased in the /i/-/ɪ/ stimuli ($n = 18$) were designated the "accurate" perceivers. Those who showed shifts of 10% to 79% ($n = 22$) were designated the "moderately accurate" perceivers; and those who showed shifts of less than 10% in the expected direction ($n = 40$) were

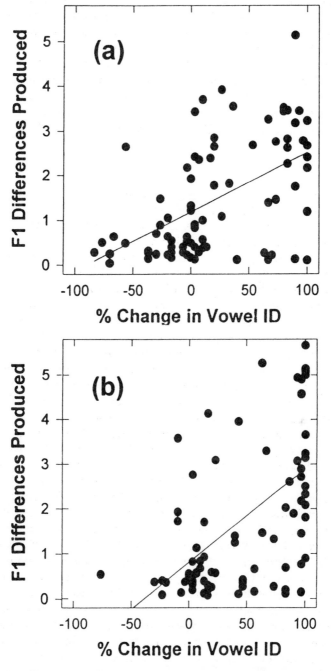

FIG 5.3 (a, b). The relation between producing and perceiving spectral quality differences between English vowels. Data are from Flege, Bohn, and Jang (1996).

designated the "inaccurate" perceivers. The accurate perceivers were found to have produced significantly larger spectral differences between /i/-/ɪ/ (M = 2.6 barks) than the moderately accurate perceivers (M = 1.7 barks), who in turn produced a significantly larger spectral contrast between /i/-/ɪ/ than the inaccurate perceivers (M = 0.8 barks; p < .05). Similarly, 30 accurate perceivers and 28 moderately accurate perceivers of the /ɛ/-/æ/ continua were found to have produced significantly larger spectral contrasts between these two vowels than the inaccurate perceivers (2.9 and 1.2 vs. 0.8 barks; p < .05).

Consonants

Flege (1993) examined Chinese participants' production and perception of /t/ and /d/ in the final position of English words. This phonetic contrast was of interest because Chinese words are not differentiated by word-final obstruents that differ in voicing. The study focused on vowel duration. Native speakers of English make vowels longer before /d/ than /t/ in words such as *bead* versus *beat*. If asked to identify an ambiguous word-final stop as /d/ or /t/, a relatively long vowel gives rise to the perception of /d/ by native speakers of English. Thirty of the Chinese participants who participated were "late" bilinguals who were first exposed to English on a regular basis as adults when they arrived in the United States; nine others were "early" bilinguals who had arrived in the United States prior to the age of 10. Both the late and early bilinguals made vowels significantly longer in English words ending in /d/ than /t/ (p < .01), but the size of the late bilinguals' contrasts were significantly smaller than those produced by the native English controls and the early Chinese–English bilinguals (p < .01).

A parallel perception experiment by Flege (1993) assessed the Chinese–English bilinguals' use of vowel duration as a cue to the voicing feature in stops. Both 17-member perceptual continua that were developed consisted of naturally produced English CVC words in which the original vowel durations were altered in such a way that native English controls heard a word ending in /d/ (for stimuli with the longest vowels) or words ending in /t/ (for stimuli with the shortest vowels). The method of adjustment was used. In one session making use of a *beat–bead* continuum, the participants were asked to choose the member of the continuum that represented the best example of *beat*. In a second session using the same continuum, they were asked to choose the best instance of *bead*. In two sessions using a *bat–bad* continuum, the participants were asked to choose the best examples of *bat* or *bad*.

Both groups of Chinese–English bilinguals examined by Flege (1993) chose stimuli with significantly longer vowels as the best instances of /d/-final compared to /t/-final English words. However, the magnitude of the perceptual effect was significantly smaller for the late bilinguals than for the native English controls or for the early bilinguals ($p < .01$). The bilinguals' perceptual and productive use of vowel duration thus seemed to parallel one another. Indeed, a significant correlation was obtained between the size of vowel duration differences that the bilinguals produced in /t/-final versus /d/-final words and the size of the vowel duration differences observed between the stimuli preferred as the best instances of /t/-final versus /d/-final words, $r = .535, p < .01$.

Recent studies examining the voice onset time (VOT) dimension in the production and perception of word-initial English stop consonants also suggest that production and perception are related at a segmental level during the acquisition of L2 speech. This work (Flege and Schmidt, 1995; Schmidt and Flege, 1995) examined 40 native speakers of Spanish who came to the United States as young adults. The participants judged the members of two synthetic continua. The stimuli in the continua were heard by native English control participants as /bi/, /pi/, or exaggerated /pi/ (i.e., a stop with too much aspiration) depending on VOT. One continuum consisted of short-duration CVs that simulated a fast speaking rate; the other consisted of long-duration CVs that simulated a slower rate of speech.

The participants rated randomly presented members of both continua for goodness as instances of the English /p/ category. As shown in Fig. 5.4, native English control participants gave low ratings to the stimuli that had VOT values that were shorter than is typical for English /p/. As VOT increased, so too did their goodness ratings; but as VOT values increased beyond values typical for English, the goodness ratings began to decrease systematically. The native English participants exhibited "internal category structure" in that, for them, some stimuli were better examples of /p/ than others.

The VOT value of the stimulus that received the highest rating, called the *preferred VOT value*, was determined for each participant. A significant correlation was found to exist between the VOT values that the native English participants produced and their perceptually preferred VOT values, $r = .536, p < .01$ (see Newman, 1996, for similar results). That is, the native English participants who produced /p/ with relatively long VOT values tended to prefer stimuli having relatively long VOT values.[4] This evidence of alignment does not contradict Bever's (1981) hypothesis, for the alignment could have been established during L1 acquisition, prior to the ending of a critical

[4]The finding just reported held true for the slow-rate continuum only. The results for two proficient participants whose preferred VOT values were dubious were excluded.

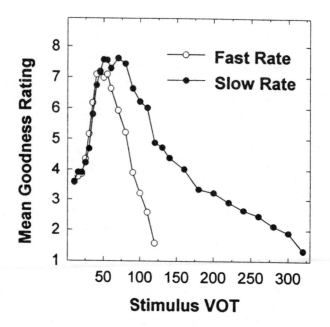

FIG 5.4. Mean goodness ratings obtained from native English participants for two voice onset time (VOT) continua, one simulating a fast speaking rate and one simulating a slower rate. Data are from Flege and Schmidt (1995).

period. The results obtained for native Spanish participants in other research do run counter to Bever's hypothesis, however.

In Spanish, /p/ is produced with short-lag VOT values rather than with the long-lag VOT values typical for English. Native speakers of Spanish who learn English in adulthood have been observed to produce voiceless English stops such as /p/ with VOT values ranging from Spanish-like short-lag VOT values to values that match or even exceed the long-lag VOT norm for English.

Flege and Schmidt (1995) determined the overall degree of foreign accent in English sentences spoken by 40 Spanish late bilinguals, assigning the 20 participants with the lowest ratings to a nonproficient group and the 20 with the highest ratings to a relatively proficient subgroup. The correlation between the VOT values produced by the proficient participants and their perceptually preferred VOT values was significant, $r = .489$, $p < .01$, whereas the correlation observed for the nonproficient native Spanish participants was nonsignificant, $r = -.004$, $p > .10$. This finding suggests that as nonnative adults gain proficiency in an L2, their production and perception align.

CATEGORY FORMATION

To summarize the evidence presented so far, it appears that adult learners' overall pronunciation of their L2 and their ability to comprehend it are related. However, the ability to perceptually gauge degree of accent in L2 sentences may develop more rapidly, or to a greater extent, than the ability to pronounce L2 sentences.

At the segmental level, modest correlations have been found to exist between production and perception accuracy. Segmental production and perception do not appear to develop independently as hypothesized by Bever (1981). One possible explanation for why the segmental production–perception correlations observed so far have been modest is that not all participants who adapt their perception to conform to the sound pattern of the target L2 make a comparable adaptation in production. If perception "leads" production in L2 acquisition, then the modest correlations that have been observed are just what one would expect. To use a term coined by Bever (1981), certain adult learners may not yet have *transported* what they learned about the perception to the domain of speech articulation.

Other explanations might also be advanced for the modest size of the correlations observed. For example, although segmental phonetic contrasts are based on multiple dimensions, most published studies have focused on a single dimension. It is possible that some dimension(s) other than the one examined in a study have undergone change as the result of learning in one or both domains. Or, a stronger underlying relation between production and perception may have been obscured by measurement error or some inadequacy in experimental design. For example, the speech production samples may have represented fast-rate speech, whereas the speech perception data may have represented careful speech produced at a slower rate.

Still another possible explanation for why the observed L2 production–perception correlations tend to be significant but weak is that the most meaningful perceptual variable has not yet been examined. According to the SLM (e.g., Flege, 1995), category formation exerts a powerful influence on L2 learners' accuracy in producing L2 vowels and consonants. The notion of category formation implies a discontinuity in performance. This being the case, it might prove more fruitful to compare the segmental level performance of participants who have versus have not formed a category than to compare, for example, groups of participants differing in overall L2 proficiency or AOA in an L2-speaking environment.

There is some preliminary evidence to support the hypothesis that production accuracy is related to category formation. Flege, MacKay, and Meador (1998) elicited the production of 11 English vowels in two ways. One of the two elicitation methods was thought likely to require the presence of English vowel categories. The participants examined were three groups of 18 native Italian speakers each who had arrived in Canada at average ages of 7, 13, and 19 respectively, plus a group of English controls.[5] These participants were all long-time residents of Ottawa, Canada, with a mean age of 48.   The native Italian participants had lived in Canada for an average of 34 years at the time of testing, and estimated speaking Italian 31% of the time, on average.

The participants in the Flege et al. (1998) study were given a list of the CVC words so that they could read as well as hear the vowels that were said. For each vowel of interest, the participants first repeated a sequence of four real words containing a single vowel (example: *read, deed, heed, bead*) after hearing the words via a loudspeaker. After hearing the same four-word sequence a second time, the participants inserted the vowel found in all four words (/i/, in the example given) into a /b_do/ frame. After a third and final presentation of the four-word sequence, they inserted the /bVdo/ nonword (where V = the vowel common to all four real words) into a carrier phrase (*I say__again and again*). After digitization, productions of each vowel were randomly presented in separate blocks (one for each vowel of interest) to native speakers of English from Ottawa for goodness ratings. The identity of the intended vowel in each block was always known beforehand to the listeners.

Figure 5.5a shows the goodness ratings obtained for four English vowels that have a phonetically different counterpart in Italian. Separate mean ratings are shown for the vowels that were produced in real words (i.e., the vowels in the last words of the four-word sequences)[6] and the vowels spoken in a /b_do/ frame (i.e., the nonwords inserted into the carrier phrase).   The native Italian participants' accuracy in producing /i ɛ o u/, all of which have a counterpart in Italian, decreased somewhat as a function of AOA. However, there was little difference in the accuracy with which the four groups of participants produced these vowels in words versus nonwords, so the Group x Vowel interaction in the ANOVA examining the goodness ratings for /i ɛ o u/ was nonsignificant, $F(3,68) = 2.4, p > .05$.

As shown in Fig. 5.5b, however, a different pattern of results was obtained for four English vowels that are unlike any vowel in the Italian inventory, namely /ɪ æ ʊ ɚ/. The native Italian participants with AOAs of 7 and 13 did not differ significantly from the native English controls when producing these vowels in real words ($p > .10$).

---

[5]Another group of native Italian participants with an AOA of 7 years was made up of individuals who seldom spoke Italian. As might be expected from the interaction hypothesis, they performed more like the native English controls than did participants matched for AOA who reported speaking Italian more often.

[6]The vowels in the real word condition shown in Fig. 5.5 were those in *bead, bid, bed, bad, bode, hood, booed, bird.*

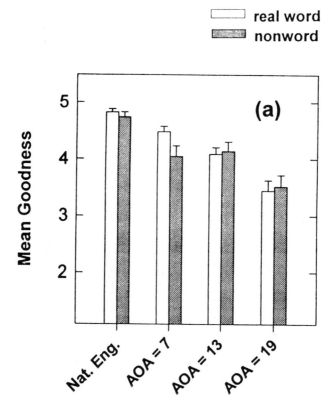

FIG 5.5a. Mean goodness ratings obtained for English vowels with a counterpart in Italian.

However, unlike the participants in the other two groups, they produced /ɪ æ ʊ ɚ/ significantly less accurately in nonwords than in real words, and significantly less accurately than the native English controls ($p < .01$). This led to a significant two-way interaction, $F(3,68) = 15.8, p < .001.$[7]

To produce the /ɪ æ ʊ ɚ/ accurately in nonwords, the native Italian participants had to identify the vowel heard in four real words, hold that vowel in working memory for an interval of time, and then produce the represented vowel in a /b_do/ context, thereby forming a nonword. It is unlikely that the difficulty experienced by the native Italian

[7]The lack of an effect of Condition for the native Italian participants with an average AOA of 19 years can be attributed to the fact that they produced /ɪ æ ʊ ɚ/ so inaccurately in real words that a further reduction in accuracy in the nonword condition was not realistically possible.

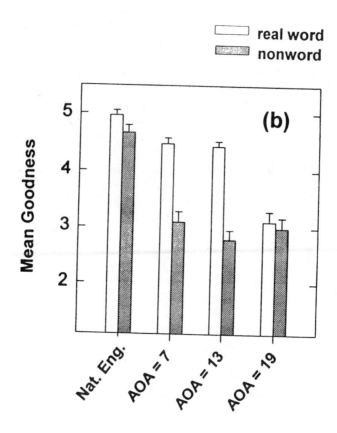

FIG 5.5b. Mean goodness ratings obtained for English vowels that do not have a counterpart in Italian.

participants with AOAs of 7 and 13 years in producing /ɪ æ ʊ ɚ/ was due to memory limitations. First, they did not produce English vowels that have a counterpart in Italian (namely, /i ɛ o u/) less accurately in nonwords than in words. Second, the participants' phonological STM was evaluated by having them repeat nonwords formed by concatenating two to five Italian CV syllables. The participants with AOAs of 7 and 13 years did not differ in their nonword repetition ability from any other group. The fact that these participants produced /ɪ æ ʊ ɚ/ as accurately as the native English participants in the real-word condition suggests that they were motorically able to articulate these vowels accurately. It is likely, therefore, that the native Italian participants' inaccurate production of /ɪ æ ʊ ɚ/ in the nonwords was due either to a lack of long-term memory representations for these vowels, or to representations that did not conform as closely to the /ɪ æ ʊ ɚ/ tokens as was the case for the native English controls.

Two other recent studies related to the issue of category formation examined the production and perception of English /p/ by 10 Spanish late bilinguals (Flege, Schmidt & Wharton, 1996; Schmidt & Flege, 1996). The participants rated the members of slow-rate and fast-rate VOT continua (see earlier sections) for goodness as instances of English /p/. As was shown previously in Fig. 5.4, the rating function obtained from native English controls differed as a function of the simulated speaking rate in the two sets of VOT stimuli. More specifically, the English controls gave different goodness ratings to stimuli having VOT values of 50 to 125 msec. For example, a stimulus with a VOT of 75 msec was judged to be a better instance of /p/ if it occurred in a slow-rate syllable than in a fast-rate syllable. This rate-dependent perceptual processing observed for the native English participants corresponds closely to the changes in VOT production one observes across rate changes in the speech production of English monolinguals.

Given that the short-lag /p/ of Spanish shows little variation in VOT as a function of speaking rate (Schmidt & Flege, 1995), a question of interest was whether the Spanish late bilinguals would also show evidence of rate-dependent processing. They might show evidence of internal category structure (the rise–fall of ratings seen in Fig, 5.4), simply by recognizing that English /p/ has longer VOT values than Spanish /p/, and that VOT values that extend beyond the norm for English (the "exaggerated" /p/ tokens) do not occur in human languages. However, it seemed unlikely that they would also show rate-dependent processing (i.e., a systematic shift in their goodness rating as a function of speaking rate) if they did not have a long-term memory representation for English /p/.

Figure 5.6a shows the mean goodness ratings that were obtained for the 4 Spanish late bilinguals (out of 10) who produced English /p/ with the Spanish-like short-lag VOT values ranging from 13 to 18 msec. These four participants showed little if any effect of the speaking rate manipulation when rating the stimuli for goodness as instances of English /p/.

As shown in Figure 5.6b, on the other hand, the four participants who produced English /p/ with English-like long-lag VOT values ranging from 41 to 68 msec[8] did show evidence of rate-dependent processing.

One might speculate that they were able to produce English /p/ accurately because they had established a phonetic category for it.

---

[8](The remaining two participants in the study, whose ratings are not shown, produced English /p/ with VOT values that were intermediate to the values typical for Spanish and English).

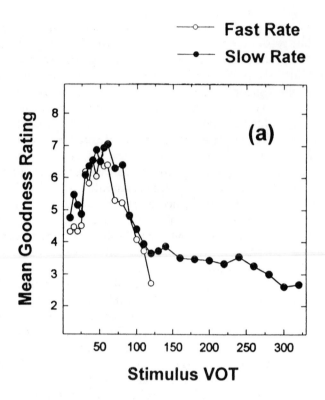

FIG 5.6a. Mean goodness ratings obtained for voice onset time (VOT) continua, one simulating a fast speaking rate and one simulating a slower rate, from four Spanish late bilinguals who each either produced English /p/ with Spanish-like short-lag VOT values. Data are from Flege and Schmidt (1995).

Additional research of a longitudinal nature will be needed to evaluate this interpretation before it can be accepted, of course. It would also be valuable to determine if teaching native Spanish participants to accurately produce long-lag stops in English would precipitate rate-dependent processing (see Bradlow, Pisoni, Yamada, & Tohkura, 1996). Were such a finding obtained, it would undermine the claim that perception accuracy precedes, and limits, L2 segmental production accuracy.

SUMMARY

In the first section, we presented the results of recent studies examining the relation between age of learning an L2 and degree of foreign accent in the L2. The finding that production accuracy declines linearly with

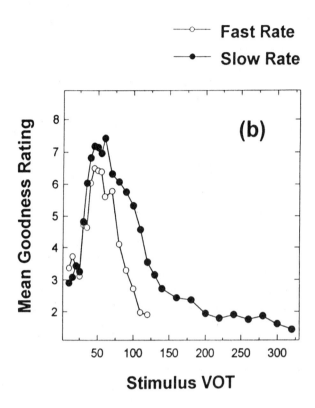

FIG 5.6b. Mean goodness ratings obtained for two voice onset time (VOT) continua, one simulating a fast speaking rate and one simulating a slower rate, from four Spanish late bilinguals who each either produced English /p/ with English-like long-lag VOT values. Data are from Flege and Schmidt (1995).

age is inconsistent with the view that foreign accents occur as the result of the passing of a maturationally defined critical period. Then we described alternate hypotheses that might be advanced to account for the fact that earlier is better in regard to the pronunciation of an L2. L2 pronunciation accuracy may decline, not because one has lost the ability to learn to pronounce, but because one has learned to pronounce the L1 so well. The results presented suggest that one's accuracy in pronouncing an L2 varies as a function of how well one pronounces the L1, and how often one speaks the L1.

We next considered a CPH presented by Bever (1981), one that was more specific (and thus testable) than most CPHs. Bever proposed that a critical period for speech learning ends when humans lose the capacity for adapting their production of sounds (vowels and consonants) to conform to their perceptual representations of the sounds. Empirical evidence was presented that disconfirmed this hypothesis. Other studies were cited showing that modest albeit significant correlations exist between the accuracy with which vowels and consonants are produced and perceived.

According to the SLM (Flege, 1995), the likelihood that L2 learners will establish new categories for L2 vowels and consonants decreases as the age of exposure to an L2 being learned naturalistically increases. It is also hypothesized that the likelihood of category formation for a particular L2 vowel or consonant is related directly to its degree of perceived phonetic dissimilarity to the closest L1 vowel or consonant. In the fourth section, we presented results that were consistent with these hypotheses and with the view (Flege, 1995) that L2 segmental production accuracy is limited by the accuracy of the perceptual representations that are developed for L2 vowels and consonants.

As mentioned earlier, one hypothesis that warrants additional testing is that late bilinguals sometimes establish phonetic category representations for English sounds not found in the L1. Those who do establish a phonetic category representation for an L2 sound may be more accurate in producing it than those who do not. If this hypothesis is correct, then future research examining the relation between production and perception should use discrete tests of category formation instead of (or in addition to) continuous tests of the perception of particular perceptual "cues" (e.g., vowel duration, VOT). Such a research strategy may yield greater insight into the perception–production relation than has yet been obtained in segmental studies.

One caveat should be offered before closing. We are not sure at present what precipitates category formation. It would be prudent, therefore, to remain open to the possibility that category formation is precipitated by the discovery of articulatory means for producing a novel L2 phonetic contrast, and that perceptual fine tuning is mediated by an implicit knowledge of how L2 sounds are produced. One serious obstacle we must face in pursuing these and other important questions is that, at present, an accepted method does not exist with which to test for the formation of new phonetic categories (but see Flege, 1998). To implement the research strategy proposed here, a reliable method must be developed.

Another promising avenue for future research is to study the effects of training. Work by Yamada and Bradlow (Bradlow et. al., 1996; Yamada, Tohkura, Bradlow & Pisoni, 1996) showed that training-induced improvements in perceiving a novel L2 phonetic contrast lead to more accurate production of the L2 contrast in the absence of speech production training. It would be valuable to replicate and extend these findings. Also, it would be worthwhile to determine if training nonnatives to produce new or difficult contrasts will lead to a concomitant improvement in their *perception* of the L2 contrasts in the absence of perceptual training.

ACKNOWLEDGMENTS

This research was supported by grants DC00257 and DC02892 from the National Institute for Deafness and Other Communicative Disorders. I thank the following individuals for their important contribution to work presented here: Elaina Frieda, Hua Liu, Diane Meador, Ian R. A. MacKay, Murray J. Munro, Takeshi Nozawa, and Grace Yeni-Komshian.

REFERENCES

Anisfeld, M., Anisfeld, E., & Semogas, R. (1969). Cross-influences between the phonological systems of Lithuanian-English bilinguals. *Journal of Verbal Learning and Verbal Behavior, 8,* 257–261.

Best, C. (1995). A direct realist view of cross-language speech perception. In W. Strange (Ed.), *Speech perception and linguistic experience: Theoretical and methodological issues* (pp. 171–206). Timonium, MD: York Press.

Bever, T. (1981). Normal acquisition processes explain the critical period for language learning. In K. Diller (Ed.), *Individual differences and universals in language learning aptitude* (pp. 176–198). Rowley, MA: Newbury House.

Bongaerts, T., Planken, B., & Schils, E. (1995). Can late learners attain a native accent in a foreign language? A test of the critical period hypothesis. In D. Singleton & Z. Lengyel (Eds.), *The age factor in second language acquisition* (pp. 30–50). Clevedon, England: Multilingual Matters.

Bradlow, A., Pisoni, D., Yamada, R., & Tohkura, Y. (1996). Training Japanese listeners to identify English /r/ and /l/: IV. Some effects of perceptual learning on speech production. *Journal of the Acoustical Society of America, 101,* 2299–2310.

Churchland, P. (1986). *Neurophilosophy.* Cambridge, MA: MIT Press.

Cook, V. (1995). Multicompetence and effects of age. In D. Singleton & Z. Lengyel (Eds.), *The age factor in second language acquisition* (pp. 51–66). Clevedon, England: Multilingual Matters.

Cutler, A., Mehler, J., Norris, D., & Segui, J. (1989). Limits on bilingualism. *Nature, 340,* 229–230.

Dunkel, H. (1948). *Second language learning.* Boston: Ginn & Company.

Edelman, G. (1989). *The remembered present: A biological theory of consciousness.* New York: Basic Books.

Elman, J. (1993). Learning and development in neural networks: The importance of starting small. *Cognition, 48,* 71–99.

Flege, J. E. (1987). A critical period for learning to pronounce foreign languages? *Applied Linguistics, 8,* 162–177.

Flege, J. E. (1988a). Factors affecting degree of perceived foreign accent in English sentences. *Journal of the Acoustical Society of America, 84,* 70–79.

Flege, J. E. (1988b). The production and perception of speech sounds in a foreign language. In H. Winitz (Ed.), *Human communication and its disorders, a review 1988* (pp. 224–401). Norwood, NJ: Ablex.

Flege, J. E. (1992a). The intelligibility of English vowels spoken by British and Dutch talkers. In R. Kent (Ed.), *Intelligibility in speech disorders: Theory, measurement, and management* (pp. 157–232). Amsterdam: John Benjamins.

Flege, J. E. (1992b). Speech learning in a second language. In C. Ferguson, L. Menn, & C. Stoel-Gammon (Eds.), *Phonological development, models, research, and applications* (pp. 565–604). Parkton, MD: York Press.

Flege, J. E. (1993). Production and perception of a novel, second-language phonetic contrast. *Journal of the Acoustical Society of America, 93,* 1589–1608.

Flege, J. E. (1995). Second-language speech learning: Findings, and problems. In W. Strange (Ed.), *Speech perception and linguistic experience: Theoretical and methodological issues* (pp. 233–273). Timonium, MD: York Press.

Flege, J. E. (1998). Assessing non-natives' perception of English vowels: A categorial discrimination test. *Applied Linguistics.*

Flege, J. E., Bohn, O.-S., & Jang, S. (1997). The production and perception of English vowels by native speakers of German, Korean, Mandarin, and Spanish. *Journal of Phonetics, 25,* 437–470.

Flege, J. E., & Fletcher, K. (1992). Talker and listener effects on the perception of degree of foreign accent. *Journal of the Acoustical Society of America, 91,* 370–389.

Flege, J. E., Frieda, A. M., & Nozawa, T. (1997). Amount of native-language (L1) use affects the pronunciation of an L2. *Journal of Phonetics, 25,* 169–186.

Flege, J. E., MacKay, I. A. R., & Meador, D. (1998). Effects of age and L1 use on non-native subjects' production and perception of English vowels. *Journal of the Acoustical Society of America.*

Flege, J. E., Munro, M. & MacKay, I. (1995). Factors affecting degree of perceived foreign accent in a second language. *Journal of the Acoustical Society of America, 97,* 3125–3134.

Flege, J. E. & Schmidt, A. M. (1995). Native speakers of Spanish show rate-dependent processing of English stop consonants. *Phonetica, 52,* 90–111.

Flege, J. E., Schmidt, A. M., & Wharton, G. (1996). Age affects rate-dependent processing of stops of stops in a second language. *Phonetica, 53,* 143–161.

Genesee, F., Hamers, J., Lambert, W., Mononen, L., Seitz, M., & Starck, R. (1978). Language processing in bilinguals. *Brain and Language, 5,* 1–12.

Grosjean, F. (1982). *Life with two languages: An introduction to bilingualism.* Cambridge, MA: Harvard University Press.

Ho, D. (1986). Two contrasting positions on second-language acquisition: A proposed solution. *International Review of Applied Linguistics, 24,* 35–47.

Hurford, J. (1991). The evolution of the critical period for language acquisition. *Cognition, 40,* 159–201.

Kuhl, P. & Meltzoff, A. (1996). Infant vocalizations in response to speech: Vocal imitation and developmental change. *Journal of the Acoustical Society of America, 100,* 2425–2438.

Kuijpers, C. T. L. (1996). Perception of the voicing contrast by Dutch children and adults. *Journal of Phonetics, 24,* 367–382.

Lamendella, J. (1977). General principles of neurofunctional organization and their manifestation in primary and non-primary language acquisition. *Language Learning, 27,* 155–196.

Lenneberg, E. (1967). *Biological foundations of language.* New York: Wiley.

Long, M. (1990). Maturational constraints on language development. *Studies in Second Language Acquisition, 12,* 251–285.

Mack, M. (1986). A study of semantic and syntactic processing in monolinguals and fluent early bilinguals. *Journal of Psycholinguistic Research, 15,* 463–488.

Macnamara, J. (1973). Nurseries, streets, and classrooms. *The Modern Language Journal, 57,* 250–254.

Marchman, V. A. (1993). Constraints on plasticity in a connectionist model of English past tense. *Journal of Cognitive Neuroscience, 5,* 215–234.

McLaughlin, B. (1977). Second-language learning in children. *Psychological Bulletin, 84,* 438–459.

Meador, D., Flege, J. E., & MacKay, I. R. A. (1997). Nonnatives' perception of English sentences presented in noise. *Journal of the Acoustical Society of America, 101(A),* 3129.

Neville, H., Mills, D., & Lawson, D. (1992). Fractionating language: Different neural subsystems with different sensitive periods. *Cerebral Cortex, 2,* 244–258.

Newman, R. (1996). Individual differences and the perception-production link. *Journal of the Acoustical Society of America, 99,* 2592.

Oyama, S. (1973). *A sensitive period for the acquisition of a second language.* Unpublished doctoral dissertation, Harvard University.

Oyama, S. (1979). The concept of the critical period in developmental studies. *Merrill-Palmer Quarterly, 25,* 83–103.

Oyama, S. (1982a). A sensitive period for the acquisition of a nonnative phonological system. In S. Krashen, R. Scarcella, & M. Long (Eds.), *Child-adult differences in second language acquisition* (pp. 20–38). Rowley, MA: Newbury House.

Oyama, S. (1982b). The sensitive period for the comprehension of speech. In S. Krashen, R. Scarcella, & M. Long (Eds.), *Child-adult differences in second language acquisition* (pp. 39–51). Rowley, MA: Newbury House.

Paradis, M. (1993). Linguistic, psycholinguistic, and neurolinguistic aspects of the "interference" in bilingual speakers: The activation threshold hypothesis. *International Journal of Psycholinguistics, 9,* 133–145.

Patkowski, M. (1990). Age and accent in a second language: A reply to James Emil Flege. *Applied Linguistics, 11,* 73–89.

Penfield, W., & Roberts, L. (1959). *Speech and brain mechanisms.* Princeton, NJ: Princeton University Press.

Pisoni, D. (1995). Some thoughts on "normalization" in speech perception. *Research on Spoken Language Processing, Progress Report No. 20,* 3–30. Speech Research Laboratory, Dept. of Psychology, Indiana University.

Rochet, B. (1995). Perception and production of L2 speech sounds by adults. In W. Strange (Ed.), *Speech perception and linguistic experience: Theoretical and methodological issues* (pp. 379–410). Timonium, MD: York Press.

Romaine, S. (1995). *Bilingualism.* Oxford, England: Blackwell.

Schmidt, A. M., & Flege, J. E. (1995). Effects of speaking rate changes on native and non-native production. *Phonetica, 52,* 41–54.

Schmidt, A. M., & Flege, J. E. (1996). Speaking rate effects on stops produced by Spanish and English monolinguals and Spanish/English bilinguals. *Phonetica, 53,* 162–179.

Scovel, T. (1969). Foreign accents, language acquisition, and cerebral dominance. *Language Learning, 19,* 245–253.

Scovel, T. (1988). *A tme to speak: A psycholinguistic inquiry into the critical period for human speech.* New York: Newbury House/Harper & Row.

Selinker, L. (1972). Interlanguage. *International Review of Applied Linguistics, 10,* 209–231.

Singleton, D. (1989). *Language acquisition: The age factor.* Clevedon, England: Multilingual Matters.

Weber-Fox, C., & Neville, H. (1992).   Maturational constraints on cerebral specialization for language processing: ERP and behavioral evidence in bilingual speakers. *Neuroscience Abstracts, 18,* 335.

Weinreich, U. (1953). *Languages in contact.* New York: Linguistic Circle of New York.

Yamada, R., Tohkura, Y., Bradlow, A., & Pisoni, D. (1996).   Does training in speech perception modify speech production? *Proceedings of the ICSLP-96.*

Yeni-Komshian, G., Flege, J. E., & Liu, H. (1997).   Pronunciation proficiency in L1 and L2 among Korean-English bilinguals: The effect of age of arrival in the US. *Journal of the Acoustical Society of America, 102(A),* 3138.

CHAPTER SIX

Ultimate Attainment in L2 Pronunciation: The Case of Very Advanced Late L2 Learners

Theo Bongaerts
University of Nijmegen, The Netherlands

It is now more than three decades ago that Lenneberg (1967) advanced the hypothesis that there is a critical period, roughly between age 2 and puberty, for the acquisition of language. He argued that, due to a loss of neural plasticity, languages could no longer be completely successfully acquired after the close of that period. Whereas Lenneberg's claims were not restricted to the acquisition of accent, Scovel (1969, 1988) singled out pronunciation as the one area of language performance that was subject to the constraints of a critical period. His arguments were that pronunciation is "the only aspect of language that has a neuromuscular basis," requires "neuromotor involvement," and has a "physical reality" (Scovel 1988, p. 101). He predicted that learners who start to learn a second language (L2) later than around age 12 will never be able "to pass themselves off as native speakers" and will "end up easily identified as nonnative speakers of that language" (p. 185). Clearly, such arguments and predictions hinge on the assumption that basic neurologically based abilities are irreversibly lost around the onset of puberty.[1]

---

[1]It should be noted, however, that Scovel (1988) allowed for the possibility that there may be some "superexceptional" L2 learners, about 1 out of 1,000 in any population of adult learners, who are not bound by the biological constraints of the critical period. Indeed, a number of studies published between 1988 and 1995

Besides the neurological one, various other explanations have been advanced to account for age-related differences in accentedness of L2 speech. Flege (1992a, 1992b, 1995), for example, suggested that foreign accents may be largely perceptually based. In his argumentation, the distinction between two modes of speech perception—the continuous mode and the categorical mode (see Wode, 1993, 1994, 1995)—plays a central role. The continuous mode relates to the perception of minute differences between speech sounds, for example, between the realizations of a given phonetic category by different speakers and in different phonetic contexts. The categorical mode, on the other hand, implies that attention is paid to only those sound cues that signal contrasts between different categories of sounds, for example, /b/ and /d/. Although very young children learning their native language (L1) initially rely heavily on the continuous mode, they soon begin to tune their perception to those sound cues that signal phonetic contrasts, and by the time they are 7 and have formed stable L1 phonetic categories, their perception is strongly guided by those categories (Flege 1992a, 1992b, 1995).

As pointed out before, the idea of a critical period for the acquisition of pronunciation is based on the assumption that some basic abilities that are available to young children are no longer available to adult learners. The question, then, that needs to be addressed at this point is whether there is evidence that the foreign accents that are typical of the speech of late L2 learners are, in fact, due to loss of original perceptual abilities, or whether these accents occur because access to these abilities merely becomes more difficult after a certain age (Wode, 1993). There is now abundant empirical evidence (e.g., Best, McRoberts & Sithole, 1988; Klein, 1995; Neufeld, 1977, 1978; Rochet, 1995; Werker, 1994, 1995; Werker & Logan, 1985; Werker & Tees, 1983) that the first possibility must be ruled out. Flege (1992a, 1992b, 1995)

---

by Schneiderman and Desmarais (1988), Novoa, Fein, and Obler (1988), Ioup, Boustagui, El Tigi and Moselle (1994), and Ioup (1995) documented individual cases of superexceptional talent for L2 learning. We refrain from discussing these cases here and only observe that the authors of the case studies just mentioned provide evidence that their participants owe their phenomenal language learning success to two factors that distinguish them from the "normal" population of language learners: an exceptional brain organization for language and a high incidence of features (e.g., lefthandedness, twinning, autoimmune disorders, homosexuality), which according to Geschwind and Galaburda (1985) are associated with talent. In this respect, they seem to be clearly different from the very successful learners reported on in this chapter (for a review of such cases and discussion, see Bongaerts, 1997). We further note that it is not always the case that research in exceptional L2 acquisition targets learners who attain nativelike proficiency, as opposed to learners who make extraordinarily fast progress. It may be that the components of talent are not the same for these two types of success.

offered arguments in support of the second possibility. His own research led him to conclude that one of the main causes of foreign accents is the tendency of L2 learners, once they have firmly established the categories of their L1, to perceive L2 sounds in terms of those categories, particularly in the case of those L2 sounds that are close to L1 sounds. It should be pointed out, however, that Flege's position does not rule out the possibility that some learners will eventually work out the phonetic categories for the L2. Those that do will be the ones that are somehow able to reactivate the continuous mode of perception.

A related question is whether or not foreign accents can be attributed to loss of original motoric abilities needed for authentic pronunciation. In a recent article, Klein (1995) observed that although it is well known that the complex and finely tuned motor control, without which an authentic accent in an L2 is unattainable, becomes increasingly difficult with age, there is no evidence of any drastic changes in this biological component of what he termed the *language processor* before well into adulthood. In other words, Klein argued that there are no absolute barriers to the accurate production of a new system of speech sounds by late learners. Support for Klein's observation is found in a study by Neufeld (1977, 1978), who, in a laboratory experiment with young adults, showed that they had not lost the ability to successfully mimic short phrases in a language totally unknown to them.

Still others have linked the success of younger vis-à-vis older learners to experiential and sociopsychological factors (e.g., Schumann, 1975, 1978). Younger learners, it is argued, generally receive more and more varied input from native speakers than adult learners do and are intrinsically motivated to acquire the L2 at a native-like level. Klein (1995), however, pointed out that it is not always the case that adults receive less adequate input and are less motivated language learners. He suggested, in fact, that if a learner has continued access to massive L2 input from native speakers and if it is of vital importance to him to sound like a native speaker, there is a possibility that he will attain a native-like accent, in spite of a late start.

The Evidence

Let us now consider the empirical evidence for Scovel's (1988) prediction that an authentic pronunciation of an L2 is unattainable after a certain age has been passed. In their literature reviews, Long (1990, 1993) and Patkowski (1994) concluded that this prediction is supported by the collective research evidence. This is how Long (1990) summarized his findings: "A native-like accent is impossible unless

first exposure is quite early, probably before 6 in many individuals and
by about age 12 in the remainder" (p. 206). Interestingly, while
supporting Scovel's (1988) claim, Long's (1990) conclusion also suggests
(a) that there is no sharp cut-off point at the close of the purported
critical period and (b) that even within the boundaries of this period,
there is a high degree of variability in the degree to which L2 learners
at the same age of learning succeed in attaining native-like mastery.[2]
Such findings could be interpreted to suggest that the biological factor
of age is only one of the determinants, although arguably an important
one, of success in achieving an authentic pronunciation of an L2.

Although the studies reviewed by Long (1990, 1993) and Patkowski
(1994) all provide support for Scovel's claim, it should be pointed out
that such results might at least partly be due to participant selection
factors, a possibility also hinted at by Long (1990, 1993). Practically
none of the studies surveyed, although addressing the question of age-
related differences in L2 acquisition, had been specifically designed to
establish whether or not it is possible for—at least some—late learners
to ultimately attain a nativelike accent in an L2. In order to come to
conclusive findings with respect to this issue, it is imperative, as Long
(1990, 1993) suggested, for ultimate attainment studies to include
highly successful, very advanced late learners in their designs.

Aims of the Present Chapter

In this chapter I report on three studies, two with Dutch learners of
English and one with Dutch learners of French. The aim of the studies,
which were all conducted at the University of Nijmegen, was to find
out whether or not some learners could be identified who, in spite of a
late start, had attained such a good pronunciation of an L2 that native
listeners would judge them to be native speakers of the language. The
studies were inspired, as were similar studies on ultimate attainment in
the domain of grammatical competence by Birdsong (1992), Van Wuijtswinkel (1994), and White and Genesee (1996), by Long's suggestion that
future ultimate attainment studies should focus on very advanced
learners. The studies I review in this chapter, therefore, all included a
group of carefully screened, highly successful learners in their designs.
For reasons of space I cannot give full accounts of any of the three

---

[2]That even a (very) early start is no guarantee for nativelike attainment is
shown by a recent study by Flege, Munro, and MacKay (1995) that examined
foreign accentedness in the English spoken by Italians who had lived in Canada
for an average of 32 years and reported using English more than Italian on a daily
basis. The authors reported that of the participants who had started to acquire
English before the age of 4, no less than 22% had failed to achieve an authentic
English accent.

studies. Rather, I briefly summarize the design and main findings of the first study and give more detailed information on what I consider the central aspects of the second and third studies.

THE FIRST STUDY[3]

There were three groups of participants in this study: a control group with 5 native speakers of British English and two groups of learners. One group consisted of 10 Dutch learners of English who had been brought to our attention by English as a Foreign Language (EFL) experts, who described them as highly successful learners with an excellent command of British English. The English learners in this group were the key participants in our study. The other experimental group was composed of 12 learners of English at various levels of proficiency. None of the learners had received instruction in English before the age of 12. All participants provided four English speech samples: They talked briefly about recent holiday experiences and they read aloud a brief text, 10 sentences and a list of 25 words. Four linguistically inexperienced native speakers of British English rated the four speech samples for accent, using a 5-point scale, which ranged from 1 (*very strong accent: definitely non-native*) to 5 (*no foreign accent at all: definitely native*). The most important result of the study was that the judges appeared to be unable to make a distinction between the group of highly successful learners and the native speaker control group. In addition, there were some results that we had clearly not expected: (a) the average score assigned to the group of native speakers was rather low (3.94) and (b) half of the participants in the group of highly successful learners received higher ratings than any of the native speakers. We hypothesized that an explanation for these unexpected results might perhaps be found in the composition of the group of native speakers and the group of judges. The participants in the former group were from the south of England or from the Midlands, and their pronunciation contained some regional features. The participants from the group of very successful learners had all been intensively trained to speak the supraregional variety of British English known as Received Pronunciation (RP). The judges all lived in York, in the north of England. We speculated that there may have been an inclination on the part of the judges to assign higher scores to participants who spoke the supraregional variety than to those who spoke English with a regional accent with which they may not have been very familiar. As these are mere speculations, however, we decided to conduct a follow-

---

[3]For a full report on this study, see Bongaerts, Planken, and Schils (1995).

up experiment in which we took care to match native speaker controls and judges more closely in terms of the variety of English that they spoke.

THE SECOND STUDY[4]

Participants

As in the first experiment, there were three groups of participants:
• Group 1 was composed of 10 native speakers of standard English (mean age 27). They all spoke British English with a "neutral," supraregional accent, which is the target of instruction in most Dutch schools. They were selected from a larger pool of candidates who were originally recruited for the experiment. Only those candidates were invited to participate who had indicated on a questionnaire that they did not speak English with a regional accent and whom we had judged to have no regional accent after listening to four different speech samples they had provided.
• Group 2 consisted of 11 native speakers of Dutch (mean age 42), 9 of whom had also participated in the first study. They were selected for the experiment because university-based EFL experts had designated them as highly successful, very advanced learners with an exceptionally good command of British English. The participants reported to have been not more than incidentally exposed to English input, through the Dutch media, before entering high school at or around the age of 12. While at high school, they received 2 hours of instruction in English per week from native speakers of Dutch, who most of the time did not use English as the medium of instruction. After graduating from high school, they all studied English at a university, where they were for the first time exposed to a large amount of English input. During their first year at the university, they also received intensive instruction in the pronunciation of the supraregional variety of British English known as RP. During the last stage of their study, most participants spent a year abroad at a British university. At the time of the experiment, all but 2 of the 11 participants taught English at a Dutch university or a Dutch teacher-training institute. All participants reported in a questionnaire that it was very important for them to have very good pronunciation in English.
• Group 3 consisted of 20 native speakers of Dutch (mean age 30) at widely different levels of proficiency in English. This group was

---

[4]For more details, in particular on the preparation of speech samples and on procedures, as well as for extended discussion, see Bongaerts, Van Summeren, Planken, and Schils (1997).

composed of students of English, Dutch, and history, and of professors from various departments.

Speech Samples

All participants read aloud the following six sentences a total of three times:

(1) Arthur will finish his thesis within three weeks.
(2) My sister Paula prefers coffee to tea.
(3) The lad was mad about his dad's new fad.
(4) Mat's flat is absolutely fantastic.
(5) It's a pity we didn't go to the city.
(6) You'd better look it up in a cookbook.

The sentences were picked such that they contained phones ranging from very similar to to very different from Dutch phones. Only the participants' last two renderings were used for the experiment (henceforth called first and second versions, respectively), except when they contained irregularities such as slips of the tongue.

Judges and Procedure

The speech samples were judged by 13 native speakers of British English (mean age 44), who were selected from a larger pool of candidates using the following criteria: Their level of education should be comparable to that of the Dutch participants in the study, they had to be residents of Great Britain, and most important, they had to speak standard British English without a regional accent. Spontaneous speech samples the prospective judges had provided enabled us to ascertain whether the latter criterion had been met. Thirteen judges met all criteria; 6 of them were or had been EFL teachers or phoneticians (the experienced judges), and 7 had not received any formal training in languages or linguistics after high school (the inexperienced judges).

For each judge, a unique tape was prepared that contained 12 sets of speech samples, each set consisting of one sentence pronounced by all 41 participants. Within each set, the order of the participants was randomized. The 12 sets were administered to the judges in the following order: The first six sets, which contained the first versions of the sentences, were presented in the order 1, 2, 3, 4, 5, 6; and the second six sets, with the second versions, in the order 5, 3, 1, 6, 4, 2. The judges rated all ($2 \times 6 \times 41 = 492$) speech samples for accent on the same 5-point scale that was used in the first study. They were told that they would hear sentences pronounced by an unspecified proportion of native and nonnative speakers of British English.

Results

First, we calculated the scores assigned to each participant and averaged them across 12 samples (two renderings of six sentences) and 13 judges. These scores are displayed in Table 6.1.

Inspection of Table 6.1 reveals that the native speakers of English received very high scores: Individual means range from 4.67 to 4.94, with a group mean of 4.84, which is much higher than the average score of 3.94 assigned to the native speakers in the first study. The table also shows that the highly successful learners, too, were given high scores: Their means ranged from 4.18 to 4.93, with a group mean of 4.61.

Before further analyzing the differences between the scores assigned to the participants in each of the three groups, we first wanted to determine whether or not it would be justified to ignore the distinction between experienced and inexperienced judges in this analysis. In doing this, we used the following procedure. First we calculated the euclidian

TABLE 6.1
Mean Participant Scores Averaged Across Samples and Judges

Group 1[a]		Group 2[b]		Group 3[c]			
Parti-cipant	M	Parti-cipant	M	Parti-cipant	M	Parti-cipant	M
1	4.75	11	4.75	22	2.88	32	1.46
2	4.93	12	4.32	23	3.04	33	3.10
3	4.94	13	4.47	24	1.88	34	3.76
4	4.67	14	4.65	25	1.53	35	3.26
5	4.86	15	4.18	26	1.79	36	2.43
6	4.93	16	4.93	27	1.92	37	4.14
7	4.93	17	4.71	28	3.92	38	1.74
8	4.90	18	4.32	29	3.18	39	3.57
9	4.72	19	4.83	30	1.60	40	2.47
10	4.74	20	4.72	31	1.90	41	2.29
		21	4.83				

[a]$M = 4.84$.   [b]$M = 4.61$.   [c]$M = 2.59$.

distances between the rating patterns of the 13 judges. Each pattern contained 492 ratings, 1 for each participant–sample combination. Next, we constructed an artificial pattern, which we termed *strict*. This pattern was arrived at by first calculating, for each of the 492 participant–sample combinations, the mean and standard deviation across all 13 judges and then defining the pattern *strict* as representing an imaginary judge whose ratings are 1.5 standard deviations below the mean. Finally, we analyzed the differences between the rating patterns of the experienced judges and those of the inexperienced judges in terms of their distances from the pattern *strict*. This analysis revealed that the average distance of the inexperienced judges' score patterns from the pattern *strict* was 2.82 ($SD = 1.02$) as opposed to 2.26 ($SD = 1.04$) for the experienced judges. Application of the Mann-Whitney test resulted in a z of 0.57 ($p = 0.57$, two-tailed). On the basis of this result, we decided to ignore the distinction between experienced and inexperienced judges when further analyzing the data.

To examine the differences between the three groups of participants, we followed a similar procedure. This time we calculated the euclidian distances between the score patterns of the 41 participants. Each pattern contained 156 ratings, 1 for each judge–sample combination. We also defined an artificial pattern, which we termed *max* and which represents an imaginary participant who has only been given ratings of 5 by all 13 judges on all 12 samples. An analysis of the score patterns of the three groups of participants in terms of their distances from the pattern *max* revealed that the distances were smallest for the native speakers (0.17 on average; $SD = 0.09$), somewhat greater for the participants from Group 2 (0.41 on average; $SD = 0.41$), and much greater for the participants from Group 3 (2.61 on average; $SD = 0.99$). The difference between group 3 and the other two groups is obvious even without testing. The difference between the native speaker group and the group of highly successful learners also turned out to be significant: Application of the Mann-Whitney test resulted in a z of 2.82 ($p = 0.004$, two-tailed).

However, the main aim of the study was to find out whether or not at least some learners could be identified whose scores were comparable to those assigned to the native speakers. Our next analyses, therefore, focused on individual learners. In these analyses, we adopted the criterion of nativelikeness that Flege et al. (1995) used in their study of the strength of perceived foreign accent in the English spoken by Italian immigrants in Canada. They considered participants who received a mean rating for the sentences they had been asked to pronounce that fell within 2 standard deviations of the mean rating assigned to the native speakers of English in their study to have spoken the sentences with an authentic, nativelike accent. The results of the analyses of the ratings assigned to individual participants, adopting Flege et al.'s "z < 2" criterion, are displayed in Table 6.2.

As Table 6.2 shows, there are 5 participants in group 2 marked with an asterisk in the table (11: $z = 0.98$; 16: $z = 0.28$; 19: $z = 0.14$; 20: $z = 1.12$; 21: $z = 0.66$), who meet this criterion. In other words, this analysis, which was based on scores averaged across sentences, led to the conclusion that the pronunciation of five highly successful learners could be characterized as authentic. What if we apply the sameprocedure to the ratings obtained for each of the six sentences separately? The results of this analysis are given in Table 6.3.

In this table, the standard scores for nativelikeness are presented per sentence for each of the learners from Group 2. Ratings falling within the native speaker range as defined by the $z < 2$ criterion are marked with an asterisk. The table shows that 5 highly successful learners meet the criterion of nativelikeness on Sentences 1, 2, 3, 4, and 6 and that 3 of these participants reach the criterion on Sentence 5 as well. In comparison, the native speakers, whose scores are not displayed in Table 6.3, meet the criterion on all six sentences. The conclusion we can draw, then, is that, using very strict criteria, we have been able to identify a number of learners who, in the present study,

TABLE 6.2
Standard Scores for "Native(-like)ness" for All Participants

Group 1[a]		Group 2[b]		Group 3[c]			
Participant	z	Participant	z	Participant	z	Participant	z
1	1.70*	11	0.98*	22	25.06	32	40.41
2	-1.10*	12	5.73	23	22.92	33	22.17
3	-1.16*	13	3.53	24	37.26	34	13.77
4	0.34*	14	2.41	25	40.86	35	20.07
5	-0.10*	15	6.69	26	37.26	36	29.77
6	-1.26*	16	0.28*	27	35.67	37	5.59
7	0.33*	17	2.64	28	8.57	38	37.62
8	-0.44*	18	4.80	29	19.75	39	13.88
9	0.64*	19	0.14*	30	40.17	40	27.99
10	1.06*	20	1.12*	31	35.62	41	30.77
		21	0.66*				

[a]$M = 0.00$.   [b]$M = 2.63$.   [c]$M = 27.26$.
Note. * = native(-like).

Table 6.3
Standard Scores for "Native(-like)ness"
for the Highly Successful Learners per Sentence

Parti-cipant	Sent. #2	Sent. #3	Sent. #1	Sent. #4	Sent. #6	Sent. #5	M
16	−.96*	−.48*	.80*	−.51*	−.42*	1.89*	.05
19	−.82*	−.84*	.81*	.17*	1.48*	.31*	.19
21	−.52*	−.71*	.60*	.94*	1.81*	1.99*	.69
20	−.84*	1.27*	.96*	.87*	.15*	3.87	1.05
11	−.95*	−.06*	.37*	.38*	−.12*	9.53	1.52
14	.61*	.09*	2.88	.54*	2.50	2.99	1.60
17	−.22*	−.38*	.66*	3.22	3.19	13.95	3.40
13	.69*	.75*	−.03*	4.00	4.02	13.05	3.75
18	.68*	2.62	−.26*	6.50	3.16	11.69	4.07
15	1.74*	3.75	5.58	5.96	4.68	11.05	5.46
12	3.25	.89*	2.77	4.01	10.85	11.14	5.49
M	0.24	0.63	1.38	2.37	2.85	7.41	

Note. * = native(-like).

have consistently managed to convince native English judges that they are native speakers of British English.

It could be objected that the results of the experiments might not be generalizable to L1–L2 pairings other than the one in the present study or to other learning contexts, in view of the prominent position that English has in the Dutch media in comparison with other foreign languages. Such considerations led us to set up a third experiment.

THE THIRD STUDY[5]

The aim of this study was to find out whether the results of the second study could be replicated in an experiment involving a pairing of an L1 and an L2 that are typologically less related than Dutch and English, which are both Germanic languages. The learners in this study were Dutch learners of French, a Romance language. An additional reason for choosing French as the L2 in this experiment is that the chances of

[5]The first part of the experiment described next was also reported on in Palmen, Bongaerts, and Schils (1997). In this chapter, the results of the second part of the experiment are presented for the first time.

learners being exposed to French input via the Dutch media are minimal. The design of this study was very similar to the design of the second study.

Participants

Again, there were three groups of participants:
• Group 1 consisted of 9 native speakers of standard French (mean age 36), who all spoke French with a "neutral" supraregional accent. They were selected from a larger pool of candidates who had originally been recruited for the experiment. We excluded from participation all candidates who had indicated on a questionnaire that they spoke French with a regional accent, as well as those whom university-based French as a Foreign Language (FFL) experts judged to have a regional accent, after listening to spontaneous, recorded speech samples they had provided.
• Group 2 was composed of 9 native speakers of Dutch (mean age 40) who had been brought to our attention by university-based FFL experts as exceptionally successful learners of French. None of these learners had received instruction in French before the age of 12. From about age 12 to 18, they had received 2 to 3 hours of instruction in French per week at high school, where the French lessons were, at least initially, mainly conducted in Dutch, not in French. Outside school, exposure to French was minimal, except during holidays in France, in the case of some participants. At the time of the study, the participants were either senior university students of French or teachers or professors of French employed by Dutch institutions of secondary or tertiary education. In that capacity, most of them had spent periods of up to one academic year in France. All participants reported in a questionnaire that they considered it important to have very good French pronunciation.
• Group 3 consisted of 18 native speakers of Dutch (mean age 33) at widely different levels of proficiency in French.

Speech Samples

Two sets of speech samples were obtained from all participants:
(A) The first set consisted of 10 sentences that were read aloud three times:

(1) Jacques est bien arrivé chez mes anciens amis anglais.
(2) Jules César alla chercher ses javelots chez les Germains.
(3) Il va falloir que tu te fasses valoir.

(4) Geneviève songe que la vie est longue mais très vide.
(5) Avec ce brouillard horrible j'allumerais mes phares.
(6) C'est une drôle d'idée de tirer les rideaux.
(7) Dans le garage Gaston fait des exercices de prononciation.
(8) Il parle du livre formidable sur la table ovale.
(9) Le huit juillet j'arriverai en Suisse.
(10) Nous cachions l'assiette que nous avions cassée.

These sentences are seeded with problems for native speakers of Dutch. We only used each participant's last attempt at reading a given sentence for the experiment, unless it contained an irregularity, such as a slip of the tongue.

(B) The second set consisted of 27 phrases, each of which started with *Je dis*, followed by a CV slot in which the C position was filled with one of three consonants, to provide three different phonetic contexts for nine different vowels that occupied the V position. It was decided to pay some special attention to vowels, as Dutch learners are known to find it very hard to acquire an authentic pronunciation of French vowels, particularly when they occur in open syllables. The procedure just sketched resulted in the following 27 combinations (henceforth called *frames*), which were read aloud three times:

Je dis . . .

i	pis	ti*	lit
e	pé*	thé	lé
a	pas	ta	la
y	pu	tu	lu
ø	peu	teu*	leu*
u	pou	tout	loup
o	peau	taux	lot
õ	pont	ton	long
ã	pan	tant	lan*

Five of the 27 CV slots, marked by an asterisk, were not filled with existing French words but with orthographic sequences that were consistent with counterpart items; thus *ti* was used instead of *t'y*, and *lan* instead of *lent*. Before reading the frames, participants were told that some of the CV combinations following *Je dis* . . . had been made up by us and did not constitute real French words. We generally used the third attempts at reading the frames for the experiment. However, some participants tended to adopt a different intonation pattern on their last attempt than on their first two attempts. In those cases, the second realization was used for the experiment.

Judges and Procedure

The speech samples were judged by 10 native speakers of French (mean age 34). They were selected from a larger pool of candidates using a procedure and criteria that were very similar to the ones adopted in the second study. Of the 10 judges that were eventually selected, 5 were professors or advanced university students of French as a foreign language, phonetics, or linguistics (the experienced judges) and 5 had not received any formal training in French, foreign languages, or linguistics after high school (the inexperienced judges).

For each judge, a unique tape was prepared that contained five sets of sentences, five sets of frames, five sets of sentences, and four sets of frames in the order indicated. In each set of sentences, which consisted of one sentence pronounced by all 36 participants, the order of participants was randomized. The order in which the sets were presented was different for each judge. It was considered too tiresome a task for the judges to have to rate all 27 frames (containing nine vowels in three different phonetic contexts, i.e., preceded by /p/, /t/, or /l/) pronounced by all 36 participants. It was therefore decided to construct nine sets of frames, one frame per target vowel, such that each frame would contain (a) only one rendering of a vowel per participant and (b) four renderings of a vowel by different participants in each of the three different phonetic contexts. Moreover, as with the sentences, in each set of frames the order of participants was randomized, and the order in which the sets were presented was different for each judge.

The judges were asked to rate all (10 x 36 = 360) sentences using a French translation of the 5-point scale used in the two previous studies. With respect to the (9 x 36 = 324) frames, the judges only had to indicate for each frame whether they thought that it had been spoken by a native speaker of French or by a nonnative speaker of the language. The judges were told that they would hear speech samples that had been provided by an unspecified proportion of native and nonnative speakers of French.

Results: Sentences

In analyzing the results for the sentences, we adopted the same procedure we had used in the second study. Table 6.4 displays the ratings assigned to each participant averaged across 10 sentences and 10 judges.

Table 6.4 shows that the scores assigned to the native speakers ranged from 4.36 to 4.86, with a group mean of 4.66, and that those assigned to the highly successful learners ranged from 3.15 to 4.88, with a group mean of 4.18.

To determine whether it would be justified to pool the data from the two groups of judges, we first calculated the euclidian distances between the rating patterns of the 10 judges. Each pattern contained 360 ratings, one for each participant–sentence combination. Next, we constructed an artificial pattern, termed *strict*, according to the procedure delineated earlier. Finally, we analyzed the differences between the rating patterns of the experienced judges and those of the inexperienced ones in terms of their distances from the artificial pattern *strict*. It appeared that the average distance of the score patterns of the inexperienced judges from the pattern *strict* was 2.56 (SD = 0.98), compared with 2.77 (SD = 1.04) for the experienced judges. Application of the Mann-Whitney test resulted in a z of 0.52 (p = 0.60, two-tailed). Therefore, we decided to pool the ratings assigned by the two groups of judges for our subsequent analyses.

To examine the differences between the three groups of participants, we again calculated euclidian distances, this time between the score patterns of the 36 participants, each pattern comprising 100 ratings, one for each judge–sentence combination. Again, as in the second study, we defined an artificial pattern, termed *max*. An analysis of the distances

TABLE 6.4
Mean Participant Scores Averaged Across Sentences and Judges

Group 1[a]		Group 2[b]			Group 3[c]		
Parti-cipant	M	Parti-cipant	M	Parti-cipant	M	Parti-cipant	M
1	4.57	10	3.99	19	3.07	28	1.61
2	4.86	11	3.15	20	1.29	29	3.17
3	4.82	12	4.58	21	2.10	30	2.95
4	4.80	13	4.12	22	2.23	31	2.33
5	4.63	14	3.94	23	1.53	32	1.57
6	4.84	15	4.88	24	2.09	33	2.54
7	4.60	16	4.31	25	3.01	34	2.27
8	4.50	17	4.48	26	1.63	35	2.19
9	4.36	18	4.20	27	1.81	36	2.74

[a]M = 4.66.   [b]M = 4.18.   [c]M = 2.23.

of the score patterns of the three groups of participants from the
"ideal" pattern *max* brought to light that the distances from *max* were
on average 0.35 (*SD* = 0.19) for the native speakers, 0.88 (*SD* = 0.54) for
the highly successful learners, and 3.07 (*SD* = 0.64) for the participants
in Group 3. The difference between Group 3 and the two other groups is
immediately obvious. The groupwise difference between the native
speakers and the highly successful learners was also significant:
Application of the Mann-Whitney test resulted in a z of 2.43 (p = 0.015,
two-tailed).

However, if we adopt Flege et al.'s (1995) criterion of nativelikeness
and apply it to individual learners, we see that there are some learners
who meet this criterion, as shown in Table 6.5.

In Table 6.5, participants who were assigned scores that fall within
the native speaker range as defined by the $z < 2$ criterion are marked
with an asterisk. As it turns out, there are four participants from Group
2 with nativelike scores (12: z = 0.54; 15: z = –1.13; 16: z = 1.81; 17: z =
1.18). In a subsequent analysis, we applied the same procedure to the
ratings for each of the 10 sentences separately. The results of this
analysis are displayed in Table 6.6. Table 6.6 gives the standard scores
for nativelikeness per sentence for the native speakers and the learners

TABLE 6.5
Standard Scores for "Native(-like)ness" for All Participants

Group 1[a]		Group 2[b]		Group 3[c]			
Parti-cipant	z	Parti-cipant	z	Parti-cipant	z	Parti-cipant	z
1	1.06*	10	3.76	19	9.70	28	17.97
2	–1.10*	11	9.02	20	19.77	29	8.72
3	–0.87*	12	0.54*	21	15.22	30	10.05
4	–0.86*	13	3.10	22	14.46	31	14.07
5	0.14*	14	4.16	23	18.50	32	18.26
6	–1.02*	15	–1.13*	24	15.34	33	12.55
7	0.27*	16	1.81*	25	10.02	34	14.05
8	0.85*	17	1.18*	26	17.92	35	14.57
9	1.53*	18	3.02	27	17.05	36	21.31

[a]M = 0.00.   [b]M = 2.83.   [c]M = 14.97.
Note. * = native(-like).

TABLE 6.6
Standard Scores for "Native(-like)ness" for the Native Speakers
and the Highly Successful Learners per Sentence

	1	2	3	4	Sentences 5	6	7	8	9	10	M
Group 1											
1	−0.03	0.53	−0.04	0.32	−0.31	0.04	−0.33	−0.67	2.46**	0.80	0.28
2	−1.00	−0.70	−0.68	−0.90	−0.93	−1.42	−0.33	0.82	−0.57	−1.00	−0.67
3	−1.95	−0.74	−0.30	0.37	0.14	−0.73	−0.83	−1.22	−0.21	0.24	−0.52
4	0.85	−0.71	−0.86	−0.90	−0.41	0.47	−0.83	−0.93	−0.57	−1.00	−0.49
5	0.39	0.60	0.16	−0.90	−0.67	0.78	1.39	1.54	−0.75	−1.00	0.15
6	0.25	−1.52	−0.06	−0.90	−0.31	−0.82	−0.82	0.26	−0.57	−0.08	−0.46
7	0.50	−0.01	−0.04	0.54	−0.46	0.20	0.31	−0.61	−0.18	2.00**	0.22
8	−0.38	0.92	−0.68	0.32	0.53	1.93	1.88	−0.41	−0.16	0.40	0.44
9	1.36	1.63	2.49**	2.03**	2.41**	−0.45	−0.44	1.23	0.55	−0.36	1.04
Group 2											
10	2.94	3.25	1.61*	1.85*	2.08	2.11	6.20	0.36*	−0.10*	2.22	2.03
11	5.59	5.22	7.11	8.59	2.84	3.15	5.24	6.09	1.30*	6.76	5.19
12	−1.00*	2.85	1.54*	0.71*	−0.10*	−0.72*	−0.44*	−0.36*	−0.57*	2.76	0.47
13	4.14	1.12*	2.06	1.99*	0.96*	0.29*	3.53	1.14*	0.72*	3.70	1.96
14	11.06	−0.70*	1.43*	5.28	1.98*	0.66*	1.99*	1.95*	1.08*	1.83*	2.66
15	−1.49*	−0.29*	−1.19*	−0.89*	−0.82*	−0.88*	−0.83*	−1.23*	−0.48*	−0.13*	−0.82
16	4.25	2.43	4.59	3.49	−0.18*	1.21*	−0.03*	0.04*	0.06*	0.83*	1.67
17	0.24*	−1.51*	3.60	0.33*	1.92*	0.02*	2.25	1.20*	−0.57*	0.54*	0.80
18	1.28*	3.29	2.50	0.43*	0.86*	−0.75*	−0.44*	0.80*	3.58	2.14	1.37
M	3.00	1.74*	2.58	2.42	1.06*	0.56*	1.94*	1.11*	0.56*	2.29	

Note. * = learners with $z < 2$ (native-like). ** = native speakers with $z > 2$.

from Group 2. Scores assigned to participants from the latter group who met the criterion of nativelikeness are marked with an asterisk. Scores assigned to native speakers who did not meet this criterion are marked with a double asterisk in the table. If we look at the scores of individual participants, we can see that of the 4 participants who met the criterion in our overall analysis, 1 (15) reached it on all sentences, 2 (12 and 17) on eight sentences, and 1 (16) on only six sentences. In comparison, there were three native speakers of French who did not meet the criterion on all ten sentences: 1 participant (9) did not meet it on three sentences, one participant (1) failed to meet it on one sentence,

and there was one participant (7) who marginally missed it on one
sentence. The combined results of these analyses allow us to conclude
that, in the sentence-reading part of the experiment, three learners
could be identified who performed at a native-speaker level.

Results: Frames

In this part of the experiment, judges had to decide whether a given
sample had been pronounced by a native speaker of French or by a
nonnative speaker of the language. In our first global analysis, we
calculated how often each participant was judged to be a native
speaker of French. The results of these calculations are found in Table
6.7, in which the number of times a participant was judged to be a
native speaker is expressed in percentages, averaged across nine frames
and 10 judges.

As Table 6.7 shows, the number of times the native speakers of
French were judged to be native speakers ranged from 61.1% to 95.6%
(group $M = 85.6\%$). The corresponding percentages for the learners from
Group 2 ranged from 25.6% to 93.3% (group $M = 60\%$) and those for the
learners from group 3 from 0% to 60% (group $M = 16.6\%$).

As before, we wanted to know whether or not it would be justified to
ignore the distinction between experienced and inexperienced judges in
our subsequent, more detailed analyses of the data. We therefore
again calculated the euclidian distances between the rating patterns of

TABLE 6.7
Identifications as Native Speaker for All Participants
Averaged Across Frames and Judges (in Percentages)

Group 1[a]		Group 2[b]		Group 3[c]			
Parti-cipant	%	Parti-cipant	%	Parti-cipant	%	Parti-cipant	%
1	61.1	10	55.6	19	38.9	28	1.1
2	94.4	11	36.7	20	1.1	29	28.9
3	83.3	12	80.0	21	8.9	30	6.7
4	92.2	13	66.7	22	22.2	31	24.4
5	86.7	14	35.6	23	1.1	32	13.3
6	86.7	15	93.3	24	14.4	33	27.8
7	84.4	16	65.6	25	60.0	34	0.0
8	85.6	17	81.1	26	3.3	35	4.4
9	95.6	18	25.6	27	4.4	36	37.8

[a]$M = 85.6$.   [b]$M = 60.0$.   [c]$M = 16.6$.

the judges. For these calculations to be made, we assigned a score of 1 to all frames that were judged to have been spoken by a native speaker and a score of 0 to those that were judged to have been pronounced by a nonnative speaker. Each rating pattern comprised 324 ratings, one for each participant–frame combination. We also defined an artificial pattern, termed *strict*, which should be interpreted as representing an imaginary judge who assigned scores of 0 to all speech samples. Next, the differences between the rating patterns of the experienced judges and those of the inexperienced judges were analyzed in terms of their distances from the pattern *strict*. The average distance from this pattern of the inexperienced judges' score patterns was 2.25 ($SD = 1.13$) as against 2.72 ($SD = 0.79$) for the experienced judges. Application of the Mann-Whitney test resulted in a z of 0.73 ($p = 0.465$, two-tailed). Therefore, in our subsequent analyses, we ignore the distinction between experienced and inexperienced judges.

Next, differences between participant groups were examined, using euclidian distances that were calculated between the score patterns of the 36 participants, each pattern comprising 90 ratings, one for each judge–frame combination. As before, an artificial pattern *max* was also created. This pattern represents an imaginary participant whose pronunciation was judged to be "native" on all frames. Next, the distances of the participants' score patterns from the ideal pattern *max* were calculated. This analysis showed that the average distance from that pattern was 0.45 ($SD = 0.39$) for the native speakers, 1.48 ($SD = 0.97$) for the learners from Group 2, and 3.16 ($SD = 0.56$) for the learners from Group 3. As in the first part of the experiment, the difference between the group of native speakers and the group of highly successful learners turned out to be significant (Mann-Whitney: $z = 2.60$; $p = 0.009$).

The conclusion, then, is that the highly successful learners were as a group outperformed by the native speakers. But does this conclusion also apply to all learners individually? To answer this question, we again applied Flege et al.'s (1995) criterion of native-likeness to individual learners. The results are displayed in Table 6.8.

Table 6.8 shows that the same 4 participants who met the above criterion on the sentences also met it on the frames (12: $z = 0.36$; 15: $z = -0.74$; 16: $z = 1.91$; 17: $z = 0.46$). Among the native speakers there was 1 individual (1: $z = 2.50$) who failed to meet the criterion. The results of an application of the same procedure to each of the nine frames separately are presented in Table 6.9.

TABLE 6.8
Standard Scores for "Native(-like)ness" for All Participants

Group 1[a]		Group 2[b]		Group 3[c]			
Parti- cipant	z	Parti- cipant	z	Parti- cipant	z	Parti- cipant	z
1	2.50	10	2.97	19	5.27	28	8.20
2	−0.80*	11	5.35	20	8.19	39	5.87
3	0.04*	12	0.36*	22	7.77	30	7.78
4	−0.52*	13	2.08	22	6.65	31	6.51
5	−0.16*	14	5.53	23	8.15	32	7.23
6	−0.01*	15	−0.74*	24	7.33	33	6.53
7	−0.25*	16	1.91*	25	2.72	34	8.20
8	0.04*	17	0.46*	26	8.02	35	7.90
9	−0.87*	18	6.29	37	7.97	36	5.54

[a]$M = 0.00$.   [b]$M = 2.67$.   [c]$M = 6.99$.
Note. * = native(-like).

In Table 6.9, which gives the standard scores for nativelikeness for the native speakers and the learners from Group 2 per frame, scores assigned to learners who met the criterion are marked with an asterisk and scores assigned to native speakers who failed to meet the criterion are marked with a double asterisk. As the table shows, of the 4 participants who met the criterion in the overall analysis, there were three (12, 15, and 17) who met it on eight out of nine frames. One of the 4 participants (16), and another participant (13) who just failed to meet the criterion in the overall analysis (13: $z = 2.08$, see Table 6.8), had standard scores lower than 2 on six frames. In comparison, among the native speakers there was 1 individual (1) who failed to meet the criterion on two frames, and another (2) who did not meet it on one frame. The conclusion that we can draw from this study is that we have identified three highly successful learners who have managed to attain an authentic, nativelike French accent.

CONCLUSIONS AND DISCUSSION

According to those who support the notion of a critical period for accent, it would be impossible to achieve a nativelike pronunciation in an L2 after a specified, biological period of time. The three studies ummarized in this chapter were, unlike most previous studies on age-related differences in ultimate attainment, specifically designed to test

TABLE 6.9
Standard Scores for "Native(-like)ness" for the Native Speakers
and the Highly Successful Learners per Frame

					Frames					
	1	2	3	4	5	6	7	8	9	M
Group 1										
1	2.42**	1.78	1.91	1.93	0.88	1.48	2.24**	1.80	1.52	1.77
2	−0.78	−0.12	−1.00	−0.84	−0.95	−2.03**	−0.55	−1.04	0.51	−0.76
3	0.09	−0.31	−1.00	0.80	1.31	−0.52	0.69	−1.04	0.15	0.02
4	−0.78	−0.97	−0.11	−0.17	−0.64	0.38	−1.01	0.36	−1.18	−0.46
5	−0.20	0.84	−1.00	0.90	−0.95	−0.74	0.18	0.50	−0.75	−0.14
6	−0.38	−0.31	−0.26	−0.83	1.47	0.10	−0.02	−0.37	−0.57	−0.13
7	−0.78	−0.50	0.85	−0.13	0.24	0.73	−0.26	0.99	1.32	0.27
8	0.37	0.94	0.73	−0.83	−0.41	0.39	−0.26	−0.15	0.16	0.10
9	0.04	−1.36	−0.11	−0.83	−0.95	0.22	−1.01	−1.04	−1.16	−0.69
Group 2										
10	2.66	2.96	4.72	1.18*	−0.95*	1.74*	4.51	−1.04*	1.38*	1.91
11	0.75*	3.38	6.06	2.41	1.87*	−0.90*	2.79	7.09	5.55	3.22
12	0.18*	−0.97*	−0.11*	0.99*	0.13*	4.18	−0.28*	0.76*	1.58*	0.72
13	1.60*	−0.47*	3.46	1.37*	0.68*	5.24	1.78*	2.51	1.11*	1.92
14	2.84	2.04	5.00	2.00	1.88*	4.04	5.03	5.81	3.66	3.59
15	−0.78*	−0.51*	−0.11*	−0.33*	−0.21*	−2.03	−1.02*	−1.04*	0.26*	−0.64
16	0.94*	−0.47*	3.75	1.18*	1.85*	−0.53*	2.20	0.39*	3.37	1.41
17	0.67*	−0.97*	−0.12*	−0.20*	−0.96*	−0.90*	3.17	0.39*	0.50*	0.18
18	2.75	3.01	3.25	2.80	1.83*	9.04	5.37	6.50	4.95	4.39
M	1.29	0.89	2.88	1.27*	0.68*	2.21	2.62	2.37	2.48	

Note. * = learners with z < 2 (native-like). ** = native speakers with z > 2.

this claim. Each of the studies included a carefully selected group of very advanced, highly successful late learners in its design. These learners—learners of English or French with a Dutch L1 background—had, at least initially, primarily learned the L2 in an instructional context, in high school. They had not been massively exposed to input from native speakers of the target language until they were about 18 years of age, when they went to the university to study English or French. The main conclusion to be drawn from the combined results of the three studies is that the pronunciation of some of these learners was consistently judged to be native-like, or authentic, by listeners who were native speakers of the language. We argue that such results may be interpreted as evidence suggesting that claims concerning an absolute biological barrier to the attainment of a nativelike accent in a foreign language are too strong.

Having said this, it should also be pointed out that nativelike attainment in the domain of pronunciation seems to be a fairly exceptional phenomenon. The question that needs to be addressed is what is it that makes the exceptional learners identified in our experiments so different from the general population of less successful learners? We are far from being able to give a conclusive answer to this question, as we did not make a detailed study of the specific characteristics of these learners. We do not know, therefore, to what extent these learners differ from less successful learners in terms of cognitive variables such as language aptitude, cognitive style, or the use of learning strategies, or affective variables such as anxiety, empathy, or what Guiora (e.g., 1990, 1991) termed *ego permeability*.

Yet, on the basis of what we know about the learning histories of the highly successful learners in our studies, we would like to suggest that a combination of the following learner and context factors may have contributed importantly to their success. In the introduction, we referred to Klein's (1995) suggestion that a nativelike accent may be attainable for late L2 learners, provided that it is of vital importance to them to sound like native speakers and provided they have continued access to massive, authentic L2 input. As the description of the participants in our studies showed, both factors were clearly operative in the case of the very successful learners. They were all highly motivated individuals who reported that it was very important to them to be able to speak English or French without a Dutch accent, and they all received a large amount of input from native speakers from the time they entered the university around the age of 18. Another important learning-context factor may have been what we have elsewhere (Bongaerts, Van Summeren, Planken & Schils, 1997) called *input enhancement through instruction*, using a term adapted from Ioup (1995). In the introduction, we cited evidence that the original perceptual and motoric abilities that enable children to master the pronunciation of their L1 are not lost over time and can still be accessed by adults. We also cited evidence that late L2 learners tend to (over)rely on the categorical mode of perception and thus to perceive L2 sounds in terms of firmly established L1 phonetic categories. In this connection, we remind the reader that, in the course of their studies at the university, the highly successful learners in our experiments had all received intensive perceptual training that focused their attention on subtle phonetic contrasts between the speech sounds of the target language and those of their L1. We suggest that this may have helped them to rely less on the categorical mode and more on the continuous mode of perception, as they did when they acquired their L1, and thus to gradually work out what the relevant sound cues in the L2 are (Martohardjono & Flynn, 1995; see also Hammond, 1995) and to establish correct perceptual targets (Flege, 1995) for the L2 speech sounds. In addition, the very advanced learners had all received intensive training in the production of L2 speech sounds aimed at developing the finely tuned motor control required for accurate pronunciation. In sum, what we suggest is that the success of the exceptional adult learners we identified may have been at least partly due to the combination of three factors: high motivation, continued access to massive L2 input, and intensive training in the perception and production of L2 speech sounds. Clearly, much more work in this area is called for, and subsequent studies of ultimate attainment should put more effort into identifying the psychological and contextual correlates of exceptionally successful L2 learning.

So far, our studies have focused on the pronunciation of British English and French by adult learners with a Dutch L1 background. It is an empirical question whether the findings we reported in this chapter can be generalized to pairings of L1s and L2s that are typologically more distant than the L1–L2 pairings in our experiments. We intend to explore this issue in future studies with very advanced learners of Dutch who have Turkish, Moroccan Arabic, or Berber L1 backgrounds.

To conclude, although the speech of adult L2 learners is typically accented, it seems that we have identified at least some individuals who have beaten the predictions of the critical period hypothesis for accent by attaining a native-like pronunciation of an L2. A major challenge for the future would be to identify which (combinations of) learner, context, and language variables (L1–L2 pairings) are instrumental in making nativelike attainment possible.

ACKNOWLEDGMENTS

I gratefully acknowledge the contributions by Marie-José Palmen, Brigitte Planken, Chantal van Summeren, and Erik Schils to the research reported on in this chapter. I also thank David Birdsong, Kees de Bot, James Emil Flege, Daan Hermans, Margriet Jagtman, Annemieke Jansen-van Dieten, and Eric Kellerman for their valuable discussions and comments.

REFERENCES

Best, C., McRoberts, G., & Sithole, N. (1988). Examination of perceptual reorganization for nonnative speech contrasts: Zulu click discrimination by English-speaking adults and infants. *Journal of Experimental Psychology: Human Perception and Performance, 14*, 345–360.

Birdsong, D. (1992). Ultimate attainment in second language acquisition. *Language, 68*, 706–755.

Bongaerts, T. (1997). Exceptional learners and ultimate attainment in second language acquisition. In J. Aarts, I. de Mönnink, & H. Wekker (Eds.), *Studies in English language and teaching* (pp. 169–183). Amsterdam/Atlanta: Rodopi.

Bongaerts, T., Planken, B., & Schils, E. (1995). Can late learners attain a native accent in a foreign language? A test of the critical period hypothesis. In D. Singleton & Z. Lengyel (Eds.), *The age factor in second language acquisition* (pp. 30–50). Clevedon, England: Multilingual Matters.

Bongaerts, T., Van Summeren, C., Planken, B., & Schils, E. (1997). Age and ultimate attainment in the pronunciation of a foreign language. *Studies in Second Language Acquisition, 19* , 447–465.

Flege, J. (1992a). The intelligibility of English vowels spoken by British and Dutch talkers. In R. Kent (Ed.), *Intelligibility in speech disorders* (pp. 157–232). Amsterdam: John Benjamins.

Flege, J. (1992b). Speech learning in a second language. In C. Ferguson, L. Menn, & C. Stoel-Gammon (Eds.), *Phonological development: Models, research, implications* (pp. 565–604). Timonium, MD: York Press.

Flege, J. (1995). Second language speech learning. Theory, findings, and problems. In W. Strange (Ed.), *Speech perception and linguistic experience: Issues in cross-language research* (pp. 233–277). Timonium, MD: York Press.

Flege, J., Munro, M., & MacKay, I. (1995). Factors affecting strength of perceived foreign accent in a second language. *Journal of the Acoustical Society of America, 97*, 3125–3134.

Geschwind, N., & Galaburda, A. (1985). Cerebral lateralization: Biological mechanisms, associations and pathology: A hypothesis and a program for research. *Archives of Neurology, 42*, 428–459, 521–552, 634–654.

Guiora, A. (1990). A psychological theory of second language production. *Toegepaste Taalwetenschap in Artikelen, 37*, 15–23.

Guiora, A. (1991). The two faces of language ego. *Toegepaste Taalwetenschap in Artikelen, 41*, 5–14.

Hammond, R. (1995). Foreign accent and phonetic interference: The application of linguistic research to the teaching of second language pronunciation. In F. Eckman, D. Highland, P. Lee, J. Mileham, & R. Rutkowski Weber (Eds.), *Second language acquisition theory and pedagogy* (pp. 293–303). Mahwah, NJ: Lawrence Erlbaum Associates.

Ioup, G. (1995). Evaluating the need for input enhancement in post-critical period language acquisition. In D. Singleton & Z. Lengyel (Eds.), *The age factor in second language acquisition* (pp. 95–123). Clevedon, England: Multilingual Matters.

Ioup, G., Boustagui, E., El Tigi, M., & Moselle, M. (1994). Reexamining the critical period hypothesis: A case study in a naturalistic environment. *Studies in Second Language Acquisition, 16,* 73–98.

Klein, W. (1995). Language acquisition at different ages. In D. Magnusson (Ed.), *The lifespan development of individuals: Behavioral, neurobiological, and psychosocial perspectives. A synthesis* (pp. 244–264). Cambridge, England: Cambridge University Press.

Lenneberg, E. (1967). *Biological foundations of language.* New York: Wiley.

Long, M. (1990). Maturational constraints on language development. *Studies in Second Language Acquisition, 12,* 251–285.

Long, M. (1993). Second language acquisition as a function of age: Research findings and methodological issues. In K. Hyltenstam & A. Viberg (Eds.), *Progression and regression in language: Sociocultural, neuropsychological and linguistic perspectives* (pp. 196–221). Cambridge, England: Cambridge University Press.

Martohardjono, G., & Flynn, S. (1995). Is there an age factor for universal grammar? In D. Singleton & Z. Lengyel (Eds.), *The age factor in second language acquisition* (pp. 135–153). Clevedon, England: Multilingual Matters.

Neufeld, G. (1977). Language learning ability in adults: A study on the acquisition of prosodic and articulatory features. *Working Papers on Bilingualism, 12,* 46–60.

Neufeld, G. (1978). On the acquisition of prosodic and articulatory features in adult language learning. *The Canadian Modern Language Review, 34,* 163–174.

Novoa, L., Fein, D., & Obler, L. (1988). Talent in foreign languages: A case study. In L. Obler & D. Fein (Eds.), *The exceptional brain: Neuropsychology of talent and special abilities* (pp. 294–302). New York: Guilford.

Palmen, M.-J., Bongaerts, T., & Schils, E. (1997). L'authenticité de la prononciation dans l'acquisition d'une langue étrangère au-delà de la période critique: Des apprenants néerlandais parvenus à un niveau très avancé en français. [Authenticity of pronunciation in foreign language learning beyond the critical period: Dutch learners at an advanced level of French]. *Acquisition et Interaction en Langue Etrangère, 9,* 173–191.

Patkowski, M. (1994). The critical age hypothesis and interlanguage phonology. In M. Yavas (Ed.), *First and second language phonology* (pp. 205–221). San Diego: Singular.

Rochet, B. (1995). Perception and production of second-language speech sounds by adults. In W. Strange (Ed.), *Speech perception and linguistic experience: Issues in cross-language research* (pp. 379–410). Timonium, MD: York Press.

Schneiderman, E., & Desmarais, C. (1988). The talented language learner. Some preliminary findings. *Second Language Research, 4,* 91–109.

Schumann, J. (1975). Affective factors and the problem of age in second language acquisition. *Language Learning, 25,* 209–225.

Schumann, J. (1978). *The pidginization process: A model for second language acquisition.* Rowley, MA: Newbury House.

Scovel, T. (1969). Foreign accents, language acquisition, and cerebral dominance. *Language Learning, 19,* 245–253.

Scovel, T. (1988). *A time to speak. A psycholinguistic inquiry into the critical period for human speech.* Rowley, MA: Newbury House.

Van Wuijtswinkel, K. (1994). *Critical period effects on the acquisition of grammatical competence in a second language.* Unpublished B.A. thesis, Department of Applied Linguistics, University of Nijmegen.

Werker, J. (1994). Cross-language speech perception: Development change does not involve loss. In J. Goodman & H. Nusbaum (Eds.), *The development of speech perception: The transition from speech sounds to spoken words* (pp. 93–120). Cambridge, MA: MIT Press.

Werker, J. (1995), Exploring developmental changes in cross-language speech perception. In L. Gleitman & M. Liberman (Eds.), *An invitation to cognitive science. Vol.1: Language* (2nd ed., pp. 87–106). Cambridge, MA: MIT Press.

Werker, J., & Logan, J. (1985). Cross-language evidence for three factors in speech perception. *Perception and Psychophysics, 37,* 35–44.

Werker, J., & Tees, R. (1983). Developmental changes across childhood in the perception of non-native speech sounds. *Canadian Journal of Psychology, 37,* 278–286.

White, L., & Genesee, F. (1996). How native is near-native? The issue of ultimate attainment in adult second language acquisition. *Second Language Research, 12,* 233–265.

Wode, H. (1993).   The development of phonological abilities.   In K. Hyltenstam & A. Viberg (Eds.), *Progression and regression in language: Sociocultural, neuropsychological and linguistic perspectives* (pp. 415–438).   Cambridge, England: Cambridge University Press.

Wode, H. (1994).   Nature, nurture, and age in language acquisition: The case of speech perception. *Studies in Second Language Acquisition, 16,* 325–345.

Wode, H. (1995).   Speech perception, language acquisition, and linguistics: Some mutual implications.   In W. Strange (Ed.), *Speech perception and linguistic experience.   Issues in cross-language research* (pp. 321–347). Timonium, MD: York Press.

CHAPTER SEVEN

Confounded Age:
Linguistic and Cognitive Factors
in Age Differences
for Second Language Acquisition

Ellen Bialystok
York University
Kenji Hakuta
Stanford University

THE NATURE OF THE PROBLEM

In spite of what we all learned in our first statistics course, we just cannot resist attributing causality to correlation. We have to remind ourselves every time we see two events contiguously linked in time and space that the most natural explanation for their co-occurrence, namely, that one causes the other, might simply be false. The assumption of causality is one of the basic tenets of commonsense logic: Spring rains lead to flowers, knocking over the juice container results in spilled liquid, and clicking the power button on a small handheld instrument causes pictures to appear on the television screen. We all know, too, that it is counterexamples that compel caution in assuming the interpretation of causality: Superstition notwithstanding, carrying or not carrying an umbrella has no causal consequence for local meteorological conditions.

How are we to discover the correct logical relation between two events that share patterns of occurrence? The simplest explanation, that one event causes the other, is often taken at the expense of details that do not fit easily into the interpretation but are overlooked, set aside, or discounted. Indeed, it was the final effort to deal with the inconsistencies in the Ptolemeic description of planetary motion that led to the overthrow of that explanation, but it took 14 centuries and countless attempts to patch up the theory before the basic logic was rejected. No doubt one of the reasons that Ptolemy's description endured as long as it did was that prima facie it seemed to be correct. To an observer, it does indeed appear as though the earth is the center of the planetary system. Discovering the correct logical model requires stepping outside of the domain of the immediately perceptual data and imagining alternative explanations that are more subtle, more inaccessible, more indirect.

The problem of discovering the correct explanation for events that appear to have a simple observable relation with each other permeates the inquiry into the relation between age and the ability to learn a second language. Observationally, there is a co-occurrence between two events: The age at which a person starts learning a second language corresponds in some way to the ultimate success that the person will attain after years of having used that language. But are these two events—age and ultimate success—linked causally? Explanations of causality require stronger evidence than co-occurrence.

The critical period hypothesis is a causal explanation for the differential success in acquisition of a second language by younger and older learners. The explanation is causal because the bulk of the variance in achievement as a function of age is attributed to maturational changes in the brain that alter the possibility of successful acquisition. The controversy in the debate over the status of a critical period for second language acquisition has less to do with the documentation of observations than with the interpretation of those data. Are younger learners generally more successful than older ones when ultimate proficiency in a second language is assessed? Yes. Do younger and older learners approach the learning problem differently? Presumably. Are there neurological differences in the brains of younger and older learners? Probably. None of these statements, however, compels the conclusion that there is a critical period for second language acquisition. Similarly, neither the Ptolemeans nor the Copernicans disputed the observation that the sun rose in the east and set in the west; it was their interpretations of those events that were different. To use the terminology of the statistical test, there may well be a correlation between age of initial learning and ultimate achievement, but it does not necessarily follow that age is a causal factor in that relation. It may turn out that it is, but the data would need to show convincing evidence for causality.

Our approach to evaluating the argument for a critical period is to show that age intervenes in the effect that linguistic and cognitive factors have on success in second language acquisition. Therefore, correlations between age and success are spurious because the relation is actually reflecting the effects of these linguistic and cognitive factors. Statistically, this argument could be demonstrated by partialling age out of the equation and then studying the relation between these linguistic and cognitive factors in the absence of age. If our explanation is correct, then the partial correlations between linguistic and cognitive sources of variance and proficiency should remain significant when age is not included in the equation. Alternatively, if it could be shown that linguistic or cognitive factors (or social, although we do not discuss these) were capable of producing patterns of results that are sometimes attributed to age differences, then the role of age in explaining these effects would need to be reconsidered. Our approach, however, is to offer data that challenge the interpretation that the effects are caused by age by identifying areas in which empirical results contradict predictions from the critical period hypothesis.

The debate over the critical period hypothesis embodies some of the most basic questions about second language acquisition, and indeed, language acquisition in general. These questions permeate the foundations of several disciplines, such as linguistics, cognitive psychology, and neurolinguistics. Is language learning governed by environmental conditions or by an internal bioprogram? Do languages reside in independently constructed mental representations or are they mutually available in processing? Is transfer a legitimate process in language learning or an unwanted symptom of the improper separation of distinct languages? To some extent, the answers to these and other fundamental questions in human language learning rest partly in the role that age plays in acquiring languages. If there is a critical period for second language acquisition, then logically there is also one for first language acquisition, and the answers to questions about language processing take a clear direction. One must be prudent, therefore, in accepting the hypothesis for a critical period in second language acquisition. Methodologically, one must begin with the null hypothesis that no such limitation exists and produce reasons why this hypothesis should be rejected.

CHARACTERIZING CRITICAL PERIODS

What would constitute evidence for a critical period? Consider the following three definitions that have been offered:

> During select times in the life cycle many structures and functions become especially susceptible to specific experiences (or to the absence of those experiences) in a way that alters some future instantiation of that (or a related) structure or function. (Bornstein, 1989, p. 179)

> Certain environmental events must happen at certain times in the development of an organism in order for normal development to

occur. (Gazzaniga, 1992, p. 56)

Any phenomenon in which there is a maturational change in the
ability to learn, with a peak in learning at some maturationally
definable period ... and a decline in the ability to learn, given
the same experiential exposure, outside of this period.
(Newport, 1991, p. 112)

In addition, Colombo (1982) and Bornstein (1989) both identified
criteria that need to be specified in learning that is considered to be
constrained by a critical period. These criteria include onset and offset
times for the period, as well as other factors that characterize the
nature of the learning during the critical period. Two points recur
throughout all these definitions. First, learning during a critical
period is assured, similar across individuals, normatively described,
and probably governed primarily by endogenous factors. Exogenous
factors, therefore, should have minimal impact on this learning.
Second, learning outside of the critical period is different in both form
and success, especially in that it would be less certain and more erratic
in its outcomes. Therefore, there should be a clear discontinuity
between these two types of learning, and the time of that discontinuity
should reflect the close of the critical period.

  Some researchers have tried to take a moderate position by positing
a weakened version of the critical period hypothesis. These positions
are often signaled by terminological choices, notably, the use of
sensitive period instead of *critical period*. Colombo (1982) discusses the
reasons why this distinction has failed to clarify the issues, primarily
because of the difficulty of classifying phenomena as being one or the
other and the lack of evidence that the two phenomena were different
from each other. Similarly, some attempts have been made to weaken
the conditions that make critical periods distinct learning situations.
If a critical period is considered to be simply a period of heightened
sensitivity that can be overcome outside the period, as some accounts
posit, then there is almost no doubt that there is a critical period for
language acquisition, but by these standards, there would be a critical
period for virtually everything we learn (baseball, music, and calculus
being examples).

BUT COMPARED TO WHAT?

Our discussion proceeds by examining the role that some linguistic and
cognitive factors play in second language acquisition and considering
how age might interact with these factors. But first, we need to know
what the rules are. What is it we are trying to explain? What do we
mean by proficiency in a second language?

Pinker (1994) recounted the story of Dizzy Dean, a 1950s baseball announcer, who routinely described such plays as, "He slood into second base." Mr. Dean was a native speaker of English, but in his home state of Arkansas, dialectal peculiarities such as these were the standard. What is native speaker proficiency? Although this case may seem extreme, it is only a progression on a continuum of variation in language use.

There is an assumption in all research into second language acquisition that the learner is striving toward some stateable goal, a standard and perfect version of the language that is embodied in the mind of every native speaker. Chomsky (1957) formally acknowledged this idealization as linguistic competence and quickly discounted the likelihood that it would ever be produced by real speakers (Chomsky himself notwithstanding) because of the sobering reality of performance that prevents mortal humans from achieving that level of perfection. For that reason, most linguistic research is based on speaker judgments and not speaker performance because, the argument goes, judgments can be made solely from competence whereas performance cannot. But how would Mr. Dean judge his own sentence describing the runner's arrival at second base? Indeed, native speakers do not perform judgment tasks with 100% accuracy. What do we mean, then, when we speak vaguely of second language learners achieving native-like proficiency? This problem of designating a standard linguistic form is evident at all levels of analysis, but phonology is perhaps the most salient.

In addition to the problem of determining a standard for correctness is the problem of scope and generalizability. On the basis of some local assessment, conclusions are made about general competence, or language proficiency. What kind of assessment legitimately supports such claims? It depends in large measure on the nature of the hypothesis being tested. A theory about the process of second language acquisition, for example, should lead to specific predictions about acquisition that could be tested by detailed analysis of linguistic structures. Such theories, therefore, can be supported through a few discrete linguistic features. A theory about a critical period, however, may require more broadly based evidence covering many aspects of language proficiency. There is an inherent tension between the need to choose measures that are narrowly focused on the theoretical dimension of interest on the one hand, and the need to use measures that are global and ecologically more valid on the other.

Research into the critical period for second language acquisition has made use of a range of outcomes. The most sharply specified are the variables defined by Universal Grammar (UG), the putatively abstract and unlearnable elements of human language, such as subjacency and the complex noun phrase constraint (e.g., Johnson & Newport, 1991 Juffs &

Harrington, 1995; Martohardjono & Flynn, 1995). The idea is that these principles are part of the biological language program that constrain the hypotheses learners are able to construct about grammar. If learners lose access to this bioprogram, then presumably they lose access as well to the specific grammatical hypotheses that follow from these constraints of UG, making it difficult or even impossible to discover such rules naturally. UG, then, is endowed with a level of reality that virtually moves it into the realm of concrete rules rather than abstract constraints. It should be particularly troubling to such theories, then, when a recantation of those constraints is proclaimed, as Chomsky (1995) recently did.

Another kind of outcome is defined by grammatical rules that do not necessarily require formal grammatical theory for explanation. Johnson and Newport (1989), for example, examined 12 rule types, including past tense, plurals, and third-person singular verb. Violations of these grammatical rules were created by omitting the required morpheme, replacing the required morpheme with an inappropriate morpheme, making an irregular item regular, or by attaching a regular marking to an already irregularly marked item. These rules could be abstract in the sense that they are part of a general theory of abstract grammar, but they can also be explained through nonlinguistic models rooted in cognitive analysis. Thus, outcomes defined by these rules are ambiguous with respect to the language specificity of the phenomenon.

A third kind of outcome is global assessment of some aspect of proficiency. For example, Patkowski (1980) asked trained judges to rate the overall syntactic proficiency of transcripts of tape-recorded narratives by second language learners. Oyama (1976) also recruited raters who listened to tape-recorded narratives and gave judgments of fluency. More recently, Bongaerts, Planken, and Schils (1995) elicited raters' judgments of learners' degree of foreign accent. In such studies, it is the overall proficiency that is being judged and as such, probably comes closest to a commonsense definition of language proficiency. Although the reliability of ratings and the criteria used to generate them can be questioned for their scientific authority, the evaluations are high in ecological validity.

The choice between precise specification of learning outcomes and the ecological validity of second language acquisition (L2A) offers an important methodological lesson for researchers. To the extent that a theory has explanatory precision, it is best served by testing for specific structures. For example, if the theory is that UG governs second language acquisition until puberty and then becomes unavailable, then UG-based structures are the prized items to be examined. Discovering age-related effects of non-UG structures may be problematic for a theory of UG but may fuel the development of various alternative theories. The nature of the linguistic data is critical in setting out the possible interpretations that may follow from those data, regardless of how the results turn out.

LINGUISTIC CONSIDERATIONS

If language is represented as innate abstract principles and there is a critical period for language acquisition, then L2A during the critical period should resemble first language acquisition (L1A) because both processes are governed by the learner's access to those principles. Therefore, L2A during the critical period should show little or no effect of transfer from the first language because direct access to UG should override cognitive intervention in the process of constructing the system of rules for the second language. Learning after the critical period, however, would reflect elements of the first language because general cognitive resources would be recruited to construct the linguistic system, and they would naturally begin with the linguistic structures already in place. Demonstrating different types of language transfer before and after the close of the critical period, therefore, would support the argument for a critical period in L2A.

Historically, evidence for language transfer has been one means of explaining the uniqueness of L2A and was used as the empirical method in early research on this problem to define that difference (Hakuta & Cancino, 1977). If L2A were the same as L1A, it was argued, then the process was largely a linguistic development. Whatever was responsible for the child's assured access into the arcane world of abstract rules and representations would equally guide the second language learner into proficiency. Furthermore, the prevailing linguistic theory that posited universal structures that were wired into the child made neurological factors an essential aspect of first language acquisition. However, if the course and outcomes of L2A were considered to be importantly different from those of L1A, then other kinds of factors, notably cognitive and social ones, needed to be invoked. Empirical evidence attempting to pronounce on this matter turned out to be largely equivocal: L2A was exactly like L1A in some ways and completely unlike it in others. Accordingly, both linguistic-neurological and cognitive-social explanations were going to be needed. The critical period debate entails a return to some of these arguments. If transfer from the first language is discovered to characterize learning even for the youngest learners, then some of the responsibility for second language learning would need to be reassigned to these other factors.

Although it is true that transfer distinguishes L2A from L1A in some respects, it is not clear that the process itself is unique to L2A. A major aspect of children's development consists of their connecting linguistic competence with conceptual knowledge. In this sense, children's L1A also involves something like transfer from cognitive structures to linguistic ones. Transfer, that is, can be considered to be a much broader process than just the extension of linguistic structures from one language system to another. It also involves the generalization or use of knowledge from one domain into another. To what extent does this cognitive interpretation of transfer in language acquisition apply to the kinds of transfer observed in second language acquisition?

Consider first the kinds of transfer that can be observed in L2A. Transfer has been reported at different levels of linguistic analysis, described earlier as either comprising part of the abstract rules of UG (e.g., subjacency constraint), or surface structure similarity between two languages (e.g., negation, determiners). Transfer has also been detected in semantic interpretations of individual words (e.g., Ijaz, 1986; Kellerman, 1986). These examples fall along a continuum from abstract linguistic structure to cognitive conceptualization. In the first case, the learner is drawing on prewired constraints of UG that characterize the structure of the first language to formulate utterances; in the second, the learner is using knowledge of a structure and applying it to the L2 on the hypothesis that the two will be similar. These processes are different from each other in many respects: They are based on different kinds of mental representations, they involve different degrees of intentionality by the learner, and they are differentially susceptible to variation in the specific language pairs. Nonetheless, they all occur during the construction of an L2. Is transfer, therefore, a linguistic process or a cognitive process?

The important evidence from transfer for the critical period hypothesis, however, comes from the interaction between the type of transfer observed and the maturational stage of the learner. If there is a language learning faculty that undergoes change as a function of maturation, neurological development, or atrophy, then over time the transferred structures would presumably shift away from abstract linguistic principles toward more surface features or cognitively determined structures. This would reflect the move away from the control over language acquisition residing in a specific language center that is both formally (i.e., neurologically) and functionally (i.e., language acquistion device) defined to more general cognitive processes. Consequently, as access to UG becomes weaker, L2 learners' intuitions about the new language will rely less on the constraints of UG that were set for the L1, decreasing transfer of these abstract principles into the L2. This may be compensated by an increasing reliance on transfer effects based on language-specific features. Empirically, the important observation would be a qualitative shift in the extent or nature of transfer from the L1 at different maturational stages of second language acquisition.

The evidence on this point suggests that it is not the case. For example, Juffs and Harrington (1995) found as much transfer of subjacency from older and younger Chinese learners of English. Both groups performed well on a judgment task assessing their mastery of English subjacency, but all the learners took significantly longer to make these judgments than did native speakers. On aspects of linguistic structure that were less constrained by UG, that is, more along the dimension toward surface rules or cognitive regularities, Bialystok and Miller (1998) found no change as a function of the transfer of six structures from Chinese to English. As shown in Fig. 7.1, both younger and older learners made more errors in a sentence judgment task on items containing grammatical features that were different between Chinese and English than on items containing grammatical features that were

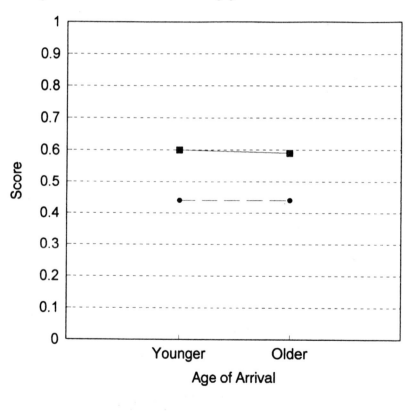

FIG. 7.1. Mean score for Chinese bilinguals by age of arrival.

similar in the two languages. Similarly, older and younger Spanish-speaking learners of English had more difficulty in judging sentences containing an error in a structure that was different between the languages than in judging sentences with errors that were common. The younger learners performed at a higher level than older ones, but the pattern was exactly the same. In other words, even though the amount of first language interference was different for younger and older learners, the nature of the interference was the same. These data are plotted in Figure 7.2. The results of the study by Johnson and Newport (1989) also support the position that older learners transfer <u>more</u> than younger ones in absolute terms. However, accepting the experimental hypothesis for a critical period requires evidence of a discontinuity in the quality of rules that are transferred within and outside of that

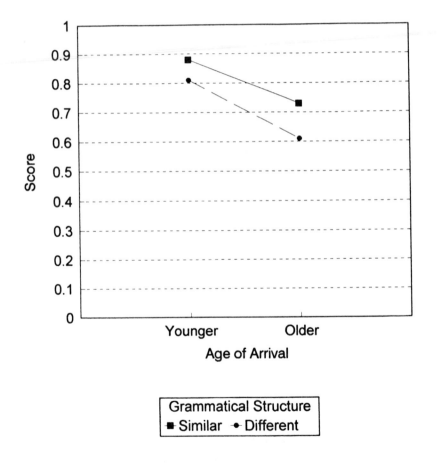

FIG. 7.2. Mean score for Spanish bilinguals by age of arrival.

period. No such discontinuity has been found (Bialystok & Hakuta, 1994).

COGNITIVE CONSIDERATIONS

Even for those theorists who view language as an independently functioning module, governed by domain-specific principles and acquired through dedicated mechanisms, it overflows at every turn into the realm of cognition. Indeed, it was Chomsky (1957) who made the study of language a cognitive problem and unleashed a shift in psychological theorizing that has come to be known as the "cognitive revolution." But how is cognition implicated in the debate over the existence of a critical period for second language acquisition?

In spite of the degree to which language acquisition may be governed by innate principles, aspects of language learning and use are clearly beyond the reach of such dedicated modules. The acquisition of literacy, for example, inflicts permanent change on children's conceptions of language. We know that children who learn to read in alphabetic scripts develop more sophisticated conceptions of phonological structure, and all children, irrespective of the language they read, advance rapidly in their metalinguistic concepts as literacy is established (review in Adams, 1990). To the extent that literacy is a factor in second language acquisition, that aspect of the process must be considered to be controlled by cognitive and not purely linguistic mechanisms. Although there is little research into the role that literacy plays in second language acquisition, some inferences are possible. For example, certain forms of instruction are possible with literate, that is older, learners that are unavailable to preliterate or younger learners. Different instructional forms could lead to differences in proficiency. The literacy factor might also influence the outcomes of language acquisition in situations of immigration, a common population for critical period studies, where such differences as literacy of the learners, availability of written texts, opportunity for instruction, and other such factors influence the proficiency of the learners. In general, younger immigrants would likely attend schools in the host language and learn the literate grammatical forms through texts as part of their curriculum. Some older learners, especially those without strong cultures of literacy, may not have access to these standard written forms. It would not be surprising if the eventual attainment of those immigrants who had attended schools in the target language surpassed in large measure that of their parents. However, these factors are rarely discussed in the literature, and so demonstrations of simple age-related differences in ultimate proficiency do not determine the cause of those differences.

Another example of the cognitive influences on assessments of second language proficiency, if not the process of acquisition itself, can be seen through differences in performance that are attributable to testing methods. In a replication of the study by and Newport (1989), Johnson (1992) gave the same sentences to the same participants but used written presentation instead of the original oral format. Not only did participants perform at a higher level overall, but there were fewer structures for which differences in age were relevant. In other words, evidence for age-related differences in learning depended not only on which structures were being examined but also on the testing modality. This difference in modality, in which written presentation elicits higher levels of performance than oral ones, was also found in the studies by Bialystok and Miller (1998). Why would this be the case? It is possible that here, too, some effects of literacy emerge in the results. Again, for age to be a main effect and be credited with the explanatory power in these results, the role of testing method needs to be clarified.

If second language acquisition is under the control of cognitive processes that are not unique to a language learning module, then the age-related changes in ultimate proficiency must be explained to some extent by changes in these general cognitive mechanisms. Because ultimate proficiency declines with age of initial acquisition, these general cognitive mechanisms must also deteriorate in their efficiency or effectiveness to serve as part of the explanation for changes in proficiency. There is evidence from studies in lifespan cognition that exactly this sort of deterioration takes place (Schaie & Willis, 1991). In a paired-associate task (like vocabulary acquisition), older learners were more sensitive to timing factors in the presentation of the material and required longer intervals than younger learners to recall the same pairs (Craik, 1986). Older learners were also more cautious and unlikely to venture a response if they were unsure of its correctness (Birkhill & Schaie, 1975). The encoding stage of establishing long-term memory also took longer for older learners, and they required more trials to learn the list (Rabinowitz & Craik, 1986). There is also a decline across the lifespan in the ability to recall details, and as learners aged they increasingly remembered only the gist (Hultsch & Dixon, 1990). These are examples of declining cognitive functions that take place across the lifespan. All of these abilities are involved in learning and using language, so their decline would adversely affect the ability to learn a new language. However, the decline of these functions is gradual and constant. No one has ever suggested that there is a critical period for memory and cognition. Therefore, if age-related changes in ultimate language proficiency are to be attributable to these cognitive changes and not to a specific language module that is constrained by a maturational schedule, then the decline in ultimate proficiency in a second language should also be gradual and constant. Conversely, if the age-related changes in ultimate proficiency are reflections of a critical period for second language acquisition, proficiency should show a discontinuity at a certain point in time, probably around puberty. Such a discontinuity is the minimal essential evidence needed to reject the null hypothesis of no critical period.

The empirical issues that reflect these concerns are the shape of the function that relates proficiency to age of language learning and the role that other factors play in this relation. If there is a critical period, then the relation between age of learning and proficiency will be nonlinear because of a sharp break at the critical period; if there is no critical period, the relation will be linear. Regarding other factors, if there is a critical period, then age will be the exclusive or primary factor accounting for proficiency; if there is no critical period, then other factors will be significant.

We conducted a preliminary analysis of data from the 1990 U.S. population census (U.S. Department of Commerce, 1995) to test these two hypotheses. The data set includes information on a large number of population characteristics, such as home language background, age of immigration to the United States, level of formal education, and English ability. Population data of this sort have both advantages and disadvantages. The advantages are (a) the sample is close to the universe of the population and relatively free from bias; (b) the numbers are large enough that parameter estimates are highly reliable; and (c) the data have already been collected, and the empirical properties of many of the demographic variables are well understood. The major weakness is that the measure of English proficiency is obtained through self-report, which is susceptible to various forms of corruption. However, a number of studies have compared self-report on English proficiency with behaviorally measured proficiency and report reasonable positive relationships between these two measures (Hakuta & D'Andrea, 1992). Kominski, 1989, cited in McArthur, 1993; McArthur & Siegel, 1983;

The present analysis is based on data from New York State, which, along with California, Florida, Illinois, and Texas, has among the largest language minority numbers in the United States. From the New York population, individuals were selected whose home language was either Spanish or Chinese. The following variables were estimated:

1. Length of Residence in the United States (based on year of entry)
2. Current Age (as of 1990)
3. Age of Arrival (subtraction of Length of Residence from Current Age)
4. Years of Formal Education
5. English Proficiency ("Not at all", "Not well", "Well", "Very Well", "Speak only English").

Because census data are categorical, models are best tested through log-linear analysis. However, one of our goals is to ask whether the data are linear, so the categorical data were converted into individual scores through interpolation, and some assumptions had to be made to make the data interpretable through linear analysis.

Because we are interested in asymptotic effects that reveal ultimate proficiency rather than the learning curve, we assumed that length of residence of 10 years would be ample time for most individuals to reach stable proficiency in English. Therefore, we eliminated participants who had length of residence of 10 years or less. This left us with a sample that included 24,903 speakers of Chinese and 38,787 speakers of Spanish. The initial analysis plots English proficiency as a function of Age of Arrival. The question of linearity can be answered by fitting a locally weighted, nonlinear function to the data using the LOWESS procedure available through SYSTAT (Wilkinson, 1996). The linear trend in these data is shown in Fig. 7.3 for Chinese ($r = -.52$) and Fig. 7.4 for Spanish ($r = -.44$). Superimposing the two curves

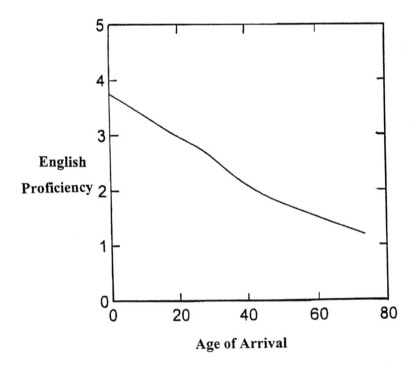

FIG. 7.3. Proficiency by age of arrival for Chinese speakers.

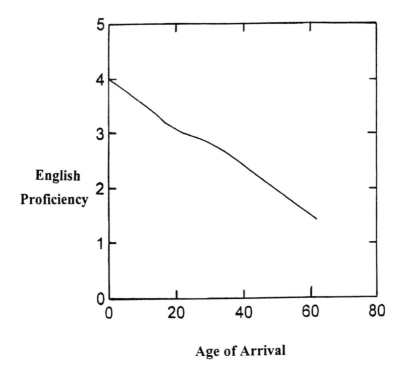

Age of Arrival

FIG. 7.4. Proficiency by age of arrival for Spanish speakers.

on each other shows how similar the slopes are, although there is a slightly higher mean score for Spanish than for Chinese. Most important, there appears to be nothing special about the age range before puberty. The decline in proficiency remains constant across the ages and is similar for both Spanish and Chinese.

To separate out the effects of cognition, the data were disaggregated by the educational level of the participants. Three categories were created: (a) less than 9 years of formal education; (b) between 9 and 13 years of formal education; and (c) more than 13 years of formal education. The graphs are shown in Fig. 7.5 for Chinese and Fig. 7.6 for Spanish. Schooling was positively related to proficiency, independently of age of arrival or language. These data should be interpreted carefully with respect to cause and effect: for those participants who immigrated as children, increased English proficiency could just as easily lead to more formal education as the other way around.

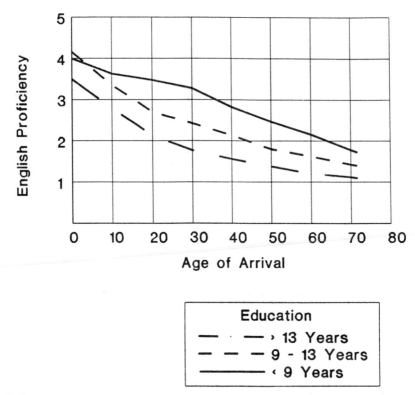

FIG. 7.5. Effect of education level for Chinese speakers.

We will conduct further analyses to separate out those individuals who were educated in the United States from those who were educated prior to immigration. Nevertheless, the graphs reveal systematic effects for educational level for both groups of participants.

CONCLUSION

It is tempting to believe that children are better second language learners than adults because their brains are specially organized to learn language, whereas those of adults are not. This is the explanation of the critical period hypothesis. The evidence for it comes from several sources. Informal observation irrefutably shows children to be more successful than adults in mastering a second language. Empirical studies confirm this pattern by demonstrating performance differences between children and adult learners on various tasks and measures. Yet both informal observation and empirical testing also yield exceptions to this rule. Late learners are sometimes

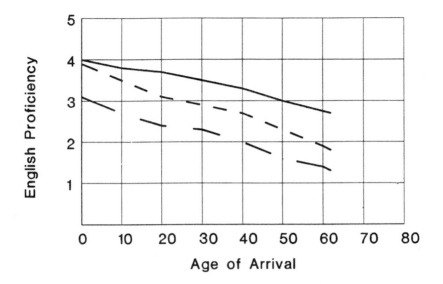

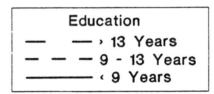

FIG. 7.6. Effect of education level for Spanish speakers.

able to achieve native-like perfection in a second language (e.g., Ioup, Boustagui, El Tigi, & Moselle, 1994) and experimental results sometimes show late learners performing just as well as early learners, even though the older group on average performs worse (e.g., Birdsong, 1992). Biological restrictions such as brain maturation should not be so easily overturned.

Neurological evidence has also been amassed to support claims for a critical period in second language acquisition. Neville (1995; Neville & Weber-Fox, 1994; see also Weber-Fox & Neville, chap. 2, this volume), for example, demonstrated event-related brain potential differences that show that neural organization is different for early and late language learners. Again, however, correlation is not causality. Researchers remind us that neural organization can reflect different kinds of experiences without being abnormal or supporting inferior performance (Elbert, Pantev, Wienbruch, Rockstroh, & Taub, 1995; Locke, 1993; Merzenich et al., 1984). Special experiences, in other words, may influence neural organization without affecting performance. As Gazzaniga (1992) pointed out, neural configurations are just as likely to be altered by cognitive processes as cognitive processes are to be determined by neurological structures. It is not surprising that the experience and knowledge we accumulate as we grow changes the way in which new information, including new languages, will be represented and that these differences can be detected as different patterns of neural organization in the brain. Indeed, brain patterns vary in the population: In some people, language is lateralized to the right hemisphere instead of the left, but they can still write, draw, and throw a baseball. The only issue is whether or not learning is impaired by these differences and whether the critical variable in determining the difference is age of first exposure. Here, only behavioral evidence is relevant, and the behavioral evidence does not make a sufficiently compelling case.

A more unusual argument for a critical period in language acquisition (but not specifically second language acquisition) was offered by Hurford (1991; see also Hurford & Kirby, chap. 3, this volume). Using computer modelling to simulate population growth and evolution, he demonstrated how a critical period for language acquisition is an adaptive feature in population terms. His explanation was that there is no selective pressure to keep the capacity for language learning available after puberty, so it turns off. The argument is interesting, but the amount of conjecture in the discussion is staggering.

Our discussion described some linguistic and cognitive factors involved in the language learning process that both contradict specific claims from the critical period hypothesis and offer an alternative means of explaining the advantage younger learners normally enjoy in second language acquisition. In addition, social factors conspire to ease the effort for young children by providing a nurturing environment, simplified input, educational opportunities, cooperative peers, and other supporting aspects of a social context that facilitate the acquisition of any language. Armed with these problems in the experimental studies designed to support a critical period, unconvinced that performance differences for younger and older learners reflect more than simple correlation, and given alternative explanations for the patterns of data that do occur, we see no reason to reject the null hypothesis that there is no critical period for second language acquisition.

REFERENCES

Adams, M. J. (1990). *Beginning to read: Thinking and learning about print.* Cambridge, MA: MIT Press.

Bialystok, E., & Hakuta, K. (1994). *In other words: The science and psychology of second-language acquisition.* New York: Basic Books.

Bialystok, E., & Miller, B. (1998). *The problem of age in second language acquisition: Influences from language, task, and structure.* Unpublsihed manuscript, York University.

Birdsong, D. (1992). Ultimate attainment in second language acquisition. *Language, 68,* 706–755.

Birkhill, W. R., & Schaie, K. W. (1975). The effect of differential reinforcement of cautiousness in the intellectual performance of the elderly. *Journal of Gerontology, 30,* 578–583.

Bongaerts, T., Planken, B., & Schils, E. (1995). Can late learners attain a native accent in a foreign language? A test of the critical period hypothesis. In D. Singleton & Z. Lengyel (Eds.), *The age factor in second language acquisition* (pp. 30–50). Clevedon, England: Multilingual Matters.

Bornstein, M. H. (1989). Sensitive periods in development: Structural characteristics and causal interpretations. *Psychological Bulletin, 105,* 179–197.

Chomsky, N. (1957). *Syntactic structures.* The Hague: Mouton.

Chomsky, N. (1995). *The minimalist program.* Cambridge, MA: MIT Press.

Colombo, J. (1982). The critical period concept: Research, methodology, and theoretical issues. *Psychological Bulletin, 91,* 260–275.

Craik, F. I. M. (1986). A functional account of age differences in memory. In F. Klix & H. Hagendorf (Eds.), *Human memory and cognitive capabilities* (pp. 409–422). Amsterdam: Elsevier.

Elbert, T., Pantev, C., Wienbruch, C., Rockstroh, B., & Taub, E. (1995). Increased cortical representation of the fingers of the left hand in string players. *Science, 270,* 305–306.

Gazzaniga, M. S. (1992). *Nature's mind: The biological roots of thinking, emotions, sexuality, language, and intelligence.* New York: Basic Books.

Hakuta, K., & Cancino, H. (1977). Trends in second language acquisition research. *Harvard Educational Review, 47,* 294–316.

Hakuta, K., & D'Andrea, D. (1992). Some properties of bilingual maintenance and loss in Mexican background high-school students. *Applied Linguistics, 13,* 72–99.

Hultsch, D., & Dixon, R. (1990). Learning and memory and aging. In J. E. Birren & K. W. Schaie (Eds.), *Handbook of the psychology of aging* (3rd edition, pp. 258–274). New York: Academic Press.

Hurford, J. R. (1991). The evolution of the critical period for language acquisition. *Cognition, 40,* 159–201.

Ijaz, H. (1986). Linguistic and cognitive determinants of lexical acquisition in a second language. *Language Learning, 36,* 401–451.

Ioup, G., Boustagui, E., El Tigi, M., & Moselle, M. (1994). Reexamining the critical period hypothesis: A case study of successful adult SLA in a naturalistic environment. *Studies in Second Language Acquisition, 16,* 73–98.

Johnson, J. S. (1992).   Critical period effects in second language
    acquisition: The effect of written versus auditory materials on the
    assessment of grammatical competence. *Language Learning, 42,* 217–
    248.
Johnson, J. S., & Newport, E. L. (1989). Critical period effects in second
    language learning: The influence of maturational state on the
    acquisition of English as a second language. *Cognitive Psychology,
    21,* 60–99.
Johnson, J. S., & Newport, E. L. (1991). Critical period effects on
    universal properties of language: The status of subjacency in the
    acquisition of a second language. *Cognition, 39,* 215–258.
Juffs, A., & Harrington, M. (1995).   Parsing effects in L2 sentence
    processing: Subject and object asymmetries in Wh-extraction.
    Studies in Second Language Acquisition, 17, 483–516.
Kellerman, E. (1986). An eye for an eye: Crosslinguistic constraints on
    the development of the L2 lexicon. In E. Kellerman & M. Sharwood
    Smith (Eds.), *Crosslinguistic influence in second language acquisition*
    (pp. 35–48). New York: Pergamon.
Locke, J. L. (1993). *The child's path to spoken language.* Cambridge,
    MA: Harvard University Press.
Martohardjono, G., & Flynn, S. (1995).   Is there an age-factor for
    universal grammar? In D. Singleton & Z. Lengyel, (Eds.), *The age
    factor in second language acquisition* (pp. 135–153).   Clevedon,
    England: Multilingual Matters.
McArthur, E. (1993). *Language characteristics and schooling in the
    United States: A changing picture, 1979 and 1989* (NCES 93–699).
    U.S. Department of Education: National Center for Education
    Statistics.
McArthur, E., & Siegel, P. (1983). *Developments in the measurement of
    English language proficiency.* American Statistical Association,
    Proceedings of the Social Statistics Section (pp. 373–378).
Merzenich, M. M., Nelson, R. J., Stryker, M. P., Cynader, M. S.,
    Schoppmann, A., & Zook, J. M. (1984). Somatosensory cortical map
    changes following digit amputation in adult monkeys. *Journal of
    Comparative Neurology, 224,* 591–605.
Neville, H. J. (1995).   Developmental specificity in neurocognitive
    development in humans. In M. S. Gazzaniga (Ed.), *The cognitive
    neurosciences* (pp. 219–231). Cambridge, MA: MIT Press.
Neville, H. J., & Weber-Fox, C. M. (1994). Cerebral subsystems within
    language. In B. Albowitz, K. Albus, U. Kuhnt, H.-Ch. Norhdurft, &
    P. Wahle (Eds.), *Structural and functional organization of the
    neocortex* (pp. 424–438). Berlin: Springer-Verlag.
Newport, E. (1991). Contrasting conceptions of the critical period for
    language. In S. Carey & R. Gelman (Eds.), *The epigenesis of mind:
    Essays on biology and cognition* (pp. 111–130). Hillsdale, NJ:

Lawrence Erlbaum Associates.

Oyama, S. (1976). A sensitive period for the acquisition of a nonnative phonological system. *Journal of Psycholinguistic Research, 5,* 261–285.

Patkowski, M. (1980). The sensitive period for the acquisition of syntax in a second language. *Language Learning, 30,* 449–472.

Pinker, S. (1994). *The language instinct.* New York: Morrow.

Rabinowitz, J. C., & Craik, F. I. M. (1986). Prior retrieval effects in young and old adults. *Journal of Gerontology, 41,* 368–375.

Schaie, K. W., & Willis, S. L. (1991). *Adult development and aging* (3rd ed.). New York: Harper Collins.

U. S. Department of Commerce (1995). *Census of Population and Housing: Detailed Cross-tabulations of Selected Language Groups for States: 1990.* CD-ROM, Bureau of the Census, Population Division, Decennial Programs Coordination Branch.

Wilkinson, L. (1996). *Systat 6.0 for Windows: Graphics.* Chicago: SPSS Inc.

AUTHOR INDEX

A

Adams, M. J., 171, *178*
Ahrens, K., 30,*36*
Anderson, B., 89, *93*
Andriew, A., 68, *93*
Anisfeld, E., 106, *127*
Anisfeld, M., 106, *127*
Artola, A., 72, *93*

B

Baldwin, J. M., 46, *62*
Baron-Cohen, S., 90, *93*
Barss, A., 27, 30, *37*, 73, *97*
Bates, E. A., 7, 8, *19, 20*
Beck, M.-L., 87, *93*
Best, C., 105, *127, 134, 156*
Bever, T. G., 6, 7, 17, *18*, 84, *93*, 105, 110, 113, 117, 119, 125, *127*
Bialystok, E., 11, *19*, 169, 171, 172, *178*
Birdsong, D., 5, 9, 11, 12, 13, 14, *19*, 81, *93*, 136, *156*, 177, *179*
Birkhill, W. R., 172, *179*
Bley-Vroman, R., 4, 5, 12, *19*, 84, *93*
Bloom, P., 91, *93*
Bodmer, W. F., 40, *62*
Bogen, J., 76, *94*

Bohn, O.-S., 113, 115, *128*
Bongaerts, T., 104, *127*, 134, 137, 138, 143, 154, *156, 158*, 166, *179*
Borer, H., 85, *94*
Bornstein, M. H., 71, 72, 73, 75, 77, 79, *94*, 163, 164, *179*
Boustagui, E., 14, *20*, 134, *157*, 177, *179*
Boyd, R., 39, *62*
Bradlow, A., 124, 126, *127, 131*
Brauth, S. E., 67, *94*
Britten, K. H., 78, *99*
Buzsaki, G., 69, *96*

C

Cancino, H., 167, *179*
Canseco, E., 30, *36*
Cappa, S. F., 35, *37*
Cavalli-Sforza, L. L., 40, *62*
Celebrini, S., 78, *99*
Chen, C.-M., 71, *95*
Chomsky, C., 91, *94*
Chomsky, N., 79, 84, 85, *94*, 165, 166, 171, *179*
Christiansen, M. H., 42, *63*
Churchland, P., 109, *127*
Clahsen, H., 74, 79, 80, *94*
Cleave, P., 86, *98*
Coffey, S. A., 34, *37*

Cohen, G., 89, *94*
Cohen, L., 35, *37*
Collingridge, G. L., 69, *94*
Colombo, J., 69, 73, 79, 82, 88, *94,*
    164, *179*
Cook, V. J., 79, *94,* 106, *127*
Coppieters, R., *19,* 81, *94*
Coppola, M., 12, *21*
Corkin, S., 12, *21*
Craik, F. I. M., 172, *179, 181*
Crair, M. C., 70, *94*
Cranshaw, A., 13, *19*
Crawford, M., 23, *36*
Curtiss, S. R., 1, 8, *19,* 74, *94*
Cutler, A., 106, *127*
Cynader, M. S., 177, *180*

D

D'Andrea, D., 173, *179*
Davis, M., 70, *97*
Dawkins, R., 39, *63*
Deacon, T. W., 39, *63*
Dehaene, S., 35, *37*
Desmarais, C., 134, *158*
Dixon, R., 172, *179*
Dooling, 67, *94*
Duncan, G., 23, *36*
Dunkel, H., 106, *127*
duPlessis, J., 80, *94*
Dupoux, E., 35, *37*

E

Edelman, G., 109, *127*
Eichen, E. B., 24, *36*
Elbert, T., 177, *179*
Ellis, R., 67, *94*
Elman, J. L., 4, 7, 8, *19,* 43, 44,
    63, 105, *128*
El Tigi, M., 14, *20,* 134, *157,* 177,
    179

Epstein, S., 79, *95*
Eubank, L., 66, 80, 83, 84, 87, *95*

F

Fazio, F., 35, *37*
Fein, D., 134, 136, *157*
Felix, S., 5, *19,* 80, *95*
Finer, D. L., 86, *95*
Flege, J. E., 9, 12, 14, *19, 20,* 102,
    103, 104, 105, 106, 108, 111,
    112, 113, 115, 116, 117, 118,
    119, 120, 123, 124, 125, 126,
    128, 129, 130, 131, 134, 141,
    148, 151, *156*
Flynn, S., 4, *20,* 79, 80, *95,* 155,
    157, 166, *180*
Forster, A., 73, *97*
Forster, K. I., 27, 30, *37*
Fox, K., 68, 71, *95*
Fox, M. W., 68, *95*
Freeman, R. D., 23, *36*
Frieda, A. M., 9, *20,* 106, *128*

G

Gair, J. W., 80, *97*
Galaburda, A., 134, *156*
Garrett, M. F., 27, 30, 73, *37, 97*
Gazzaniga, M. S., 164, 177, *179*
Genesee, F., 13, *22,* 80, 81, 82, 83,
    88, *99,* 102, *129,* 136, *159*
Geschwind, N., 134, *156*
Gilbert, C. D., 78, 79, *95, 97*
Glazewski, S., 71, *95*
Gleitman, L., 74, 75, *95*
Goldowsky, B. N., 4, *20*
Gopnik, M., 74, 86, *95*
Grace, S., 87, *95*
Grassi, F., 35, *37*
Gregg, K. R., 66, 84, *95, 96*
Grosjean, F., 106, *129*

Growdon, J. H., 12, *21*
Guiora, A., 154, *157*

H

Haas, H. L., 69, *96*
Hakuta, K., 11, 19, 167, 171, 173, *178, 179*
Hall, W. S., 67, *94*
Hamers, J., 102, *129*
Hammond, R., 155, *157*
Harrington, M., 14, *20,* 166, 169, *180*
Harwerth, R., 23, *36*
Hawkins, R., 4, *21*
Henry, K. R., 68, *96*
Hickok, G., 12, *21*
Hinton, G., 46, *63*
Hirsch, J., 24, *36*
Ho, D., 106, *129*
Holcomb, P. J., 30, 34, *37*
Hubel, D. H., 23, *38,* 71, *96*
Hultsch, D., 172, *179*
Hurford, J. R., 6, *20,* 41, 42, 43, 44, 45, 46, 48, 51, 60, 61, *63,* 66, 68, 72, 77, *96,* 105, *129,* 178, *179*
Hyde, J. C., 89, *99*

I

Ijaz, H., 168, *179*
Ioup, G., 14, *20,* 134, 154, *157,* 177, *179*

J

Jacobs, B., 3, *20*
Jang, S., 113, 115, *128*

Johnson, J. S., 10, 11, 13, 14, *20,* 24, 27, *36,* 79, 80, *96,* 165, 166, 170, 172, *180*
Johnson, M. H., 7, *19*
Juffs, A., 14, *20,* 22, 165, 169, *180*

K

Kaas, J. H., 23, *36*
Kalil, R., 70, 71, *96*
Karmiloff-Smith, A., 7, *19*
Kellerman, E., 80, *96,* 168, *180*
Kelley, D. B., 71, 72, 90, *96*
Killackey, H. P., 23, *36*
Kim, K. H. S., 24, 35, *36*
Kirby, S., 44, 45, 46, 48, 51, 60, *63*
Klein, W., 9, *20,* 134, 135, 154, *157*
Knight, C., 41, *63*
Knudsen, E., 23, *36*
Koroshets, W. J., 12, *21*
Krashen, S. D., 68, *96*
Krebs, J. R., 39, *63*
Kuhl, P., 109, *129*
Kuijpers, C. T. L., 109, *129*

L

Lambert, W., 102, *129*
Lamendella, J., 102, *129*
Larsen-Freeman, D., 67, *96*
Lawson, D. S., 33, *37,* 106, *129*
Lee, K-M., 24, *36*
Lenneberg, E. H., 3, *20,* 24, 36, *36,* 102, *129,* 133, *157*
Li, P., 8, *20*
Liu, H., 8, 12, *20,* 102, *131*
Locke, J. L., 177, *180*
Logan, J., 134, *158*

Long, M. H., 2, 3, 11, 12, 15, 17, 20, 36, 41, 63, 67, 79, 96, 97, 101, 129, 135, 136, 157
Love, T., 30, 36
Lumsden, C. J., 39, 63

M

Mack, M., 106, 129
MacKay, I., 14, 20, 102, 103, 111, 112, 119, 120, 128, 129, 136, 156
Macnamara, J., 106, 129
MacWhinney, B., 8, 21
Malenka, R. C., 70, 94
Manuel, S., 79, 95
Marchman, V. A., 8, 21, 105, 129
Marler, P., 67, 97
Martohardjono, G., 4, 20, 79, 80, 95, 97, 155, 157, 166, 180,
Mayberry, R. I., 13, 21, 24, 36
McArthur, E., 173, 180
McLaughlin, B., 104, 129
McRoberts, G., 134, 156
Meador, D., 111, 112, 119, 128, 129
Medin, D. L., 80, 96
Mehler, J., 35, 37, 106, 127
Meier, R. P., 5, 21
Meisel, J., 80, 97
Meltzoff, A., 109, 129
Merzenich, M. M., 23, 36, 177, 180
Miller, B., 169, 172, 178
Miller, J., 62, 63
Mills, D. L., 33, 37, 106, 129
Molis, M., 11, 12, 14, 19
Moltz, H., 68, 97
Mononen, L., 102, 129
Morris, R. G. M., 70, 97
Moselle, M., 14, 20, 134, 157, 177, 179

Mueller, N., 83, 97
Munro, M. J., 14, 20, 102, 103, 128, 136, 156
Muysken, P., 79, 80, 94

N

Nelson, R. J., 177, 180
Neufeld, G., 134, 135, 157
Neville, H. J., 24, 25, 26, 27, 28, 29, 30, 33, 34, 36, 37, 66, 71, 73, 76, 77, 88, 90, 97, 98, 99, 129, 131, 106, 177, 180
Newman, R., 117, 129
Newport, E. L., 4, 5, 10, 11, 13, 14, 20, 21, 24, 27, 36, 37, 74, 75, 76, 77, 79, 80, 95, 96, 97, 164, 165, 166, 170, 172, 180
Newsome, W. T., 78, 99
Newson, M., 79, 94
Nicol, J. L., 27, 30, 37, 73, 97
Norris, D., 106, 127
Novoa, L., 134, 157
Nowlan, S., 46, 63
Nozawa, T., 9, 20, 106, 128

O

O'Neil, W., 4, 20
Obler, L., 134, 157
Osterhout, L., 30, 37
Oyama, S., 11, 21, 24, 37, 105, 111, 130, 166, 181

P

Palmen, M.-J., 143, 158
Pantev, C., 177, 179
Paradis, M., 106, 130
Parisi, D., 7, 19

Patkowski, M., 3, 10, 12, 17, *21*, 23, *37*, 101, 102, 103, 104, *130*, 135, 136, *158*, 166, *181*
Penfield, W., 3, *21*, 102, 120, *130*
Perani, D., 35, *37*
Pettet, M. W., 78, *97*
Pinker, S., 5, 6, 12, *21*, 91, *97*, 165, *181*
Pisoni, D., 109, 124, 126, *127*, *130*, *131*
Planken, B., 104, *127*, 137, 138, 154, *156*, 166, *179*
Plunkett, K., 7, *19*
Pollock, J.-Y., 85, *97*
Pulvermüller, F., 3, 11, *21*

R

Rabinowitz, J. C., 172, *181*
Rakic, P., 67, *97*
Relkin, N. R., 24, *36*
Rice, M., 74, 86, *98*
Richerson, P. J., 39, *62*
Roberts, L., 3, *21*, 102, *130*
Rochet, B., 104, 108, *130*, *158*
Rockstroh, B., 177, *179*
Romaine, S., 106, *130*
Rosansky, E., 5, *21*
Ross, J. R., 92, *98*
Rutledge, V., 89, *93*

S

Schachter, J., 79, *98*
Schaie, K. W., 172, *179*, *181*
Schils, E., 104, *127*, 137, 138, 143, 154, *156*, *158*, 166, *179*
Schmidt, A. M., 117, 118, 123, 124, 125, *128*, *129*, *130*
Schneiderman, E., 134, *158*
Schoppmann, A., 177, *180*

Schumann, J. H., 3, 11, *21*, 135, *158*
Schwartz, B. D., 80, 83, 89, *98*
Scovel, T., 3, 17, *21*, 102, *130*, 133, 135, 136, *158*
Segui, J., 106, *127*
Seitz, M., 102, *129*
Seliger, H. W., 16, *21*
Selinker, L., 12, *21*, 106, *130*
Semogas, R., 106, *127*
Shao, J., 73, *98*
Shenkman, K. D., 80, *96*
Siegel, P., 173, *180*
Silva, A., 71, *95*
Singer, W., 69, 72, 89, *93*, *98*
Singleton, D., 101, *130*
Sithole, N., 134, *156*
Smith, E., 23, *36*
Solin, D., 80, *94*
Sprouse, R., 80, 89, *98*
Starck, R., 102, *129*
Stryker, M. P., 177, *180*
Swinney, D., 30, *36*

T

Tallal, P., 34, *37*
Taub, E., 177, *179*
Tees, R., 134, *158*
Thibos, L. N., 23, *36*
Thompson, R. F., 69, 72, *98*
Tohkura, Y., 124, 126, *127*, *131*
Tomaselli, A., 83, *98*
Towell, R., 4, *21*
Travis, L., 80, *94*

U

Ullman, M. T., 12, *21*, 74, 87, *99*

V

Vainikka, A., 80, 83, 89, *98*
Valian, V., 91, *98*
Van der Lely, H., 74, 87, *98, 99*
Van Summeren, C., 138, 154, *156*
Van Wuijtswinkel, K., 13, *22,*
  136, *158*
von Noorden, G., 23, *36*

W

Waddington, C. H., 67, 68, *99*
Walenski, M., 30, *36*
Watkins, J. C., 69, *94*
Webelhuth, G., 74, 86, *99*
Weber-Fox, C. M., 24, 25, 26, 27,
  28, 29, 30, 33, 34, *37,* 88, *99,*
  106, *131,* 177, *180*
Weinert, R., 62, *63*
Weinreich, U., 105, *131*
Werker, J., 134, *158*
Wexler, K., 86, 91, *98, 99*
Wharton, G., 123, *129*
White, L., 13, 14, *22,* 80, 81, 82,
  83, 88, *94, 99,* 136, *159*
Whorf, B. L., 92, *99*
Wienbruch, C., 177, *179*
Wiesel, T. N., 23, *38,* 71, 78, 79,
  95, 96
Wilkinson, L., 174, *181*
Willis, S. L., 172, *181*
Wilson, E. O., 39, *63*
Wode, H., 134, *159*
Woodward, J., 76, *94*

Y

Yamada, R., 124, 126, *127, 131*
Yeni-Komshian, G., 12, *20,* 102,
  103, 104, 107, *131*

Young-Scholten, M., 80, 83, 89,
  98

Z

Zelinski, E. M., 89, *99*
Zohary, E., 78, 89, *99*
Zook, J. M., 177, *180*

SUBJECT INDEX

A–D

age function, 2, 10–12, 101–104, 167–176
age of arrival (age of immersion), 9–12, 24–38, 102ff, 111, 167–178
ASL (American Sign Language), 13, 75, 88
behavioral evidence for Critical Period, 23–38, 178
canalization, 67–68
causality, 161–178
census data, 173–176
central nervous system, 67, 71, 90
Chelsea, 74–75, 77–79, 88, 91
Chinese, 10, 13–14, 24ff, 112–113
closed-class words (vs. open-class words), 16, 34ff
cognition, 18, 171–178
    domain-general, 5
Competition Model
    Felix, 5
    MacWhinney, 8
connectionism, 7–8, 43–44
consonants, 116–119
discontinuity (non-linearity in age function), 18, 103ff, 164, 172–176
dissociations, 12, 15–16, 27ff, 34ff, 168–171

domain-specificity, 79
Dutch, 17–18, 136ff

E–G

earlier is better, 101–104, 162ff
ego permeability, 154
end state, 9–15, 18, 164ff *see also* ultimate attainment
English, 17–18, 24ff, 84, 91, 111–118, 119–124, 137
ERP (Event-Related Brain Potential), 15–16, 27ff, 76–77
evolution, 2, 5–6, 16, 39–63, 109, 178
    gene-culture co-evolution, 39ff
    gene-language co-evolution, 39–63
exceptional brain organization, 134
exercise hypothesis, 105
exogenous factors in L2A, 14–15
failure in L2A, 1, 12–15
falsification of Critical Period Hypothesis, 11, 12–15, 17–18, 105, 165
first language acquisition, 73–77, 79, 80, 89
fMRI (Functional Magnetic Resonance Imaging), 24ff

foreign accent, 101–127, 133–155
    see also speech; pronunciation
formulations of Critical Period
    Hypothesis, 2–8, 67–73, 104–
    108, 163–164
French, 7, 13–14, 18, 91, 143ff
GB (Government and Binding),
    84
genetic factors in L2A, 6, 39–63
Genie, 43, 74–75, 77–79, 88, 91
German, 113–116

H–L

hardwiring, 66, 69, 91
inhibition, 7–8
innateness, 5
innovation (linguistic), 50
input, 15, 154
interactive hypothesis, 106–108
Italian, 102, 111, 120–123
Japanese, 92
Korean, 10, 113–116
language complexity, 47–48, 61
language size, 16, 40–62
lateralization, 3, 67
length of residence, 103ff, 111
less is more, 5
literacy, 171
long-term potentiation
    /depression, 69–70, 78

M–O

Mandarin, 113–116
maturational effects, 4–5, 9–12,
    23–38, 88–89 see also post-
    maturational effects
metabolism, 6–7
minimalist program, 84
modality of testing, 172

modularity, 65–67
motoric ability, 135
multiple critical periods, 16, 77
nativelike attainment, 9, 12–15,
    81–83, 137–155
neural evidence for critical
    period, 23–38, 177–178
neural imaging, 16
neural subsystems (in
    bilingualism), 3, 7, 23–28, 133
neural plasticity, 3
neurological processes, 68–70,
    76, 77
neurophysiology of maturation,
    12
onset/offset of Critical Period,
    79, 136

P–S

parameter (re)setting, 4, 83–89,
    91–92
perception, 108–124, 134
perceptual categories, 118–124,
    135
periphery, 66
PET (Positron Emission
    Tomography), 35
Piagetian development, 5
plasticity, 3, 16, 23–24, 36, 67, 69,
    71, 91–92, 133
post-maturational age effects, 9–
    12, 120–124, 174–178
pragmatic competence, 66
pronunciation, 17–18, 101–131,
    133–159 see also foreign
    accent; speech
psychogrammar (Bever), 6–7,
    110–111, 113
puberty, 11, 13, 36, 41–62, 133
senescence, 6
sensitive period, 2, 68, 72, 90,
    164

Spanish, 113–116, 123–125
speech *see also* pronunciation;
 foreign accent
 accuracy, 139ff
 production and perception,
 108–110
Speech Learning Model, 109,
 119ff, 126
speed of acquisition, 49–62
SPS (syntactic positive shift), 30–
 34
success in L2A, 12–15
Swahili, 84
starting small, 4–5, 16, 43–45, 60
Subset Principle, 4
syntactic versus semantic
 deficits, 27ff

T–Z

target language use, 9, 102, 106–
 107, 171
training (in pronunciation), 126–
 127, 137–155
transfer (cross-linguistic
 influence), 8, 104–126, 167–
 171
UG (Universal Grammar), 3, 4,
 5, 7, 16–17, 18, 79–89, 91–92,
 165–171
ultimate attainment, 10, 136–155
 see also end state
unfolding hypothesis, 105
use it or lose it, 6–7
use it then lose it, 5–6
VOT (Voice Onset Time), 117–
 119, 126
vowels, 113–116
working memory, 43–45